KANT'S *GROUNDWORK OF THE METAPHYSICS OF MORALS*

In his *Groundwork of the Metaphysics of Morals*, Immanuel Kant portrays the supreme moral principle as an unconditional imperative that applies to all of us because we freely choose to impose upon ourselves a law of pure practical reason. Morality is revealed to be a matter of autonomy. Today, this approach to ethical theory is as perplexing, controversial and inspiring as it was in 1785, when the *Groundwork* was first published. The essays in this volume, by international Kant scholars and moral philosophers, discuss Kant's philosophical development and his rejection of earlier moral theories, the role of happiness and inclination in the *Groundwork*, Kant's moral metaphysics and theory of value, and his attempt to justify the categorical imperative as a principle of freedom. They reflect the approach of several schools of interpretation and illustrate the lively diversity of Kantian ethics today.

JENS TIMMERMANN is Senior Lecturer in Moral Philosophy at the University of St Andrews. He is the author of *Kant's 'Groundwork of the Metaphysics of Morals': A Commentary* (Cambridge, 2007) and *Sittengesetz und Freiheit* (2003) as well as the editor of *Immanuel Kant, Kritik der Reinen Vernunft* (1998) and *Immanuel Kant, Grundlegung zur Metaphysik der Sitten* (2004).

CAMBRIDGE CRITICAL GUIDES

Titles published in this series:

Hegel's *Phenomenology of Spirit: A Critical Guide*
EDITED BY DEAN MOYAR AND MICHAEL QUANTE

Mill's *On Liberty: A Critical Guide*
EDITED BY C. L. TEN

Kant's *Idea for A Universal History with a Cosmopolitan Aim:*
A Critical Guide
EDITED BY AMÉLIE OKSENBERG RORTY AND JAMES SCHMIDT

Kant's *Groundwork of the Metaphysics of Morals: A Critical Guide*
EDITED BY JENS TIMMERMANN

KANT'S
Groundwork of the Metaphysics of Morals
A Critical Guide

EDITED BY

JENS TIMMERMANN
University of St Andrews

CAMBRIDGE
UNIVERSITY PRESS

CAMBRIDGE UNIVERSITY PRESS
Cambridge, New York, Melbourne, Madrid, Cape Town,
Singapore, São Paulo, Delhi, Mexico City

Cambridge University Press
The Edinburgh Building, Cambridge CB2 8RU, UK

Published in the United States of America by Cambridge University Press, New York

www.cambridge.org
Information on this title: www.cambridge.org/9781107641143

First published 2009
First paperback edition 2013

A catalogue record for this publication is available from the British Library

ISBN 978-0-521-87801-2 Hardback
ISBN 978-1-107-64114-3 Paperback

Contents

List of contributors   *page* vii
List of translations and abbreviations   x

Introduction
Jens Timmermann   1

1   Ethics and anthropology in the development of Kant's moral philosophy
    Manfred Kuehn   7

2   Happiness in the *Groundwork*
    Alison Hills   29

3   Acting from duty: inclination, reason and moral worth
    Jens Timmermann   45

4   Making the law visible: the role of examples in Kant's ethics
    Robert B. Louden   63

5   The moral law as causal law
    Robert N. Johnson   82

6   Dignity and the formula of humanity
    Oliver Sensen   102

7   Kant's kingdom of ends: metaphysical, not political
    Katrin Flikschuh   119

8   Kant against the 'spurious principles of morality'
    J. B. Schneewind   140

9   Autonomy and impartiality: *Groundwork* III
    John Skorupski   159

10   Problems with freedom: Kant's argument in *Groundwork* III
     and its subsequent emendations
     Paul Guyer   176

11   Freedom and reason in *Groundwork* III
     Frederick Rauscher   203

Bibliography   224
Index   232

Contributors

PAUL GUYER is Professor of Philosophy and Florence R. C. Murray Professor in the Humanities at the University of Pennsylvania. He is the author of nine books chiefly on Kant, most recently *Knowledge, Reason, and Taste: Kant's Response to Hume* (2008). He is General Co-Editor of the *Cambridge Edition of the Works of Immanuel Kant in English Translation*, for which he has edited and translated the *Critique of Pure Reason* (with Allen Wood), the *Critique of the Power of Judgment* (with Eric Matthews), and *Notes and Fragments* (with Curtis Bowman and Frederick Rauscher). He has also edited six anthologies, including the *Cambridge Companion to Kant* and the *Cambridge Companion to Kant and Modern Philosophy*; he is currently editing the *Cambridge Companion to the Critique of Modern Philosophy*. He is also writing a history of modern aesthetics.

ALISON HILLS is CUF Lecturer in Philosophy at St John's College, Oxford. She has written on many areas of moral philosophy and is currently completing a book, *The Beloved Self*.

ROBERT N. JOHNSON is Associate Professor of Philosophy at the University of Missouri. He is the author of many papers on ethical theory and Kant's ethics journals such as *Ethics*, *Philosophical Quarterly*, *Philosophical Studies* and *Pacific Philosophical Quarterly*. He is also the author of the entry 'Kant's Moral Philosophy' in the *Stanford Encyclopedia of Philosophy*.

MANFRED KUEHN is Professor of Philosophy at Boston University. He has written many papers on David Hume, Immanuel Kant, Thomas Reid, and the Scottish, French and German Enlightenment. His books include *Scottish Common Sense in Germany* (1987), and *Kant: A Biography* (2001). He is currently writing a biography of Johann Gottlieb Fichte.

ROBERT B. LOUDEN is Professor of Philosophy at the University of Southern Maine. He is the author of *The World We Want: How and*

Why the Ideals of the Enlightenment Still Elude Us (2007), *Kant's Impure Ethics: From Rational Beings to Human Beings* (2000), and *Morality and Moral Theory: A Reappraisal and Reaffirmation* (1992); co-editor and translator of Kant's *Anthropology, History, and Education* (2007); editor and translator of Kant's *Anthropology from a Pragmatic Point of View* (2006); editor of Schleiermacher's *Lectures on the Philosophical Ethics* (2002); and co-editor of *The Greeks and Us* (1996).

KATRIN FLIKSCHUH is Reader in Political Theory in the Government Department of the London School of Economics. She specializes in Kant's political philosophy, with a particular interest in the reception of Kant's thought in current liberal philosophy. Aside from numerous articles in journals and edited volumes, she is author of *Kant and Modern Political Philosophy* (2000), and *Freedom: Contemporary Liberal Perspectives* (2007).

FREDERICK RAUSCHER is Associate Professor of Philosophy at Michigan State University. He is author of many articles that focus on Kant's metaethics, particularly in relation to realism, naturalism and evolution. He has also translated Kant's *Nachlaß* on ethics for *Notes and Fragments* (2005), and is translating and editing Kant's *Lectures and Drafts on Political Philosophy*, both for the Cambridge Edition of the Works of Immanuel Kant.

J. B. SCHNEEWIND is Professor Emeritus, Department of Philosophy, Johns Hopkins University. He is the author of *Backgrounds of Victorian Literature* (1970), *Sidgwick's Ethics and Victorian Moral Philosophy* (1977), and *The Invention of Autonomy* (1998). He has edited *Moral Philosophy from Montaigne to Kant* (1990) as well as numerous other volumes. A collection of his essays on the history of moral philosophy is due to be published by Oxford University Press in 2009.

OLIVER SENSEN is Assistant Professor of Philosophy at Tulane University. His articles include 'Kant's Conception of Human Dignity', in *Kant-Studien* (forthcoming). He is co-editor of a commentary on Kant's *Tugendlehre* (forthcoming), and is currently completing a book manuscript on Kant's conception of human dignity.

JOHN SKORUPSKI is Professor of Moral Philosophy in the University of St Andrews. His interests are in epistemology, ethics and the history of philosophy in the nineteenth and twentieth centuries. His books include *Ethical Explorations* (1999).

JENS TIMMERMANN is Senior Lecturer in Moral Philosophy at the University of St Andrews, and is the author of *Sittengesetz und Freiheit* (2003), and *Kant's 'Groundwork of the Metaphysics of Morals': A Commentary* (2007). He has edited, in German, the *Critique of Pure Reason*, the *Groundwork of the Metaphysics of Morals* and, for the Berlin-Brandenburg Academy, the *Critique of Practical Reason*. Cambridge University Press will be publishing his facing-page edition of Kant's *Groundwork* in 2010.

Translations and abbreviations

Citations of Kant's works refer to the volume and page number in the Academy Edition of Immanuel Kant, *Gesammelte Schriften* (Berlin: Walter de Gruyter and predecessors, 1900–); the exception are references to the *Critique of Pure Reason*, which cite the page numbers of the first (A) and second (B) editions. Quotations have been adapted from the following translations:

G	*Groundwork of the Metaphysics of Morals*, Mary J. Gregor (trans.), in Immanuel Kant, *Practical Philosophy* (New York: Cambridge University Press, 1996)
CpV	*Critique of Practical Reason*, Mary J. Gregor (trans.), in Immanuel Kant, *Practical Philosophy* (New York: Cambridge University Press, 1996)
CrV	*Critique of Pure Reason*, Paul Guyer and Allen W. Wood (trans.) (New York: Cambridge University Press, 1998)
CU	*Critique of Judgment*, Paul Guyer and Eric Matthews (trans.) (New York: Cambridge University Press, 2000)
MdS	*The Metaphysics of Morals*, Mary J. Gregor (trans.), in Immanuel Kant, *Practical Philosophy* (New York: Cambridge University Press, 1996)
Collins	*Moral Philosophy: Collins*, Peter Heath (trans.), in Immanuel Kant, *Lectures on Ethics* (Peter Heath and J. B. Schneewind (eds.), New York: Cambridge University Press, 1997)
Religion	*Religion Within the Boundaries of Mere Reason*, George di Giovanni (trans.), in Immanuel Kant, *Religion and Rational Theology* (Allen Wood and George di Giovanni (eds.), New York: Cambridge University Press, 1996)
VRL	'On a Supposed Right to Lie from Philanthropy', Mary J. Gregor (trans.), in Immanuel Kant, *Practical Philosophy* (New York: Cambridge University Press, 1996)

Introduction

Jens Timmermann

Its 77 Academy pages make the *Groundwork of the Metaphysics of Morals* a short book, certainly by Kantian standards. Readers of the *Critique of Pure Reason* or the *Metaphysics of Morals* can easily get the impression – true or not – that they are looking at a 'patchwork' of previously existing material. The *Groundwork* is different. It was composed with great care. Moreover, Kant's technical language is absent from the first section, whereas the second employs resounding concepts like that of human beings as 'ends in themselves' or that of a 'kingdom of ends' that we are morally bound to create through our actions. These qualities explain its enduring popularity.

At the same time, the *Groundwork* claims to be as revolutionary in the field of ethics as the *Critique of Pure Reason* was in theoretical philosophy. Kant argues that all other ethical theories are fundamentally unsound because they fail to separate the rational and the natural elements of human volition. An unconditional moral command – a 'categorical imperative' – can only be grounded in pure reason. But this revolution concerns the level of ethical theory, not that of morality. Kant claims to re-establish what he claims are the insights of an uncorrupted common understanding of value and duty against the dangerous perversions peddled by his philosophical opponents. He emphasizes the capacity for self-determination or 'autonomy' that is located within individual human beings; and yet, the law that we impose upon ourselves is not arbitrary, it commands with unrelenting necessity.

As this brief overview indicates, it is hardly an accident that the *Groundwork* has inspired controversy ever since it was first published in 1785. The eleven contributions to this volume show that it still deserves and

The editor would like to thank the Netherlands Institute for Advanced Study for providing outstanding work conditions and support in 2007–8, Lucy Richmond for her help with the manuscript of this volume and an anonymous referee for many helpful comments.

receives careful philosophical, exegetical and historical attention from scholars that belong to remarkably different philosophical traditions.

One of the most striking features of the *Groundwork* is the idea that the final ethical system – a metaphysics of morals – should apply not only to human beings but to all rational beings as such. It is of the utmost necessity, Kant argues in the Preface, to 'work out for once a pure moral philosophy, completely cleansed of everything that may be only empirical and that belongs to anthropology' (*G* IV 389). In the first chapter of this collection ('Ethics and anthropology in the development of Kant's moral philosophy'), Manfred Kuehn traces the tumultuous relation of moral philosophy and the study of human beings through Kant's lecture notes from the 1770s and early 1780s and thus illustrates issues in the development of Kantian ethics in the period between the publication of the *Inaugural Dissertation* in 1770 and the *Groundwork* in 1785. At the time, the anthropology lectures served, at least in part, as an introduction to the moral sciences in general. The emergence of Kant's critical view, Kuehn argues, is of central importance if we want to answer modern critics of Kant's moral philosophy, which see it as too far removed from the complexities of human life. Kant is shown to possess an intricate notion of character; and it turns out that, on closer inspection, the categorical imperative concerns not so much the assessment of token acts but rather the evaluation of practical principles that individual actions merely exemplify. As a result, the pure principles of morality sit comfortably with our everyday manifestations of morality. They do not clash with the reflective views of moral agents – which in the *Groundwork* Kant declares to be his starting point. Kuehn pays particular attention to the impact of Johann Fürchtegott Gellert's thought on the development of Kant's ethical theory.

The next three chapters continue the theme of the moral versus the non-moral, which Kant seeks to define and distinguish on his way to the supreme principle of morality. In her 'Happiness in the *Groundwork*', Alison Hills discusses the moral status of the main rival, ancient and modern, of pure practical reason as the foundation of morality: happiness. In the opening paragraph of the *Groundwork* Kant famously seeks to put happiness in its place. Unlike a morally good will, even happiness, the sum of everything we desire, is not good unconditionally. Happiness is good only if the agent is worthy of it (*G* IV 393). Indeed, for the most part Kant uses happiness and related concepts like inclination and prudential imperatives as a foil to demonstrate what morality is not. At the same time, he concedes that all human beings by nature want to be happy. But what exactly is happiness? What is the status of prudential reasoning in Kantian moral theory? And how does his ethics of autonomy affect Kant's notion of happiness? Drawing on arguments in Mill and Nagel, Hills suggests that Kant's conception of happiness is an interesting and unusual variation on the standard modern desire-satisfaction model of wellbeing that merits careful philosophical scrutiny.

Perhaps the most notorious thesis put forth in the *Groundwork* is Kant's doctrine that an action possesses moral worth only if it is done solely from duty (e.g. *G* IV 399). In other words: actions motivated by inclination that coincide with moral commands but are not done for the sake of the moral law may be useful, welcome or amiable, but they can never be morally good. In 'Acting from duty: inclination, reason and moral worth', Jens Timmermann examines the underlying assumptions of this view. He argues that 'motivational rigorism' is a consequence of Kant's belief that moral and non-moral volition are different in kind: the latter is directed at some object or state of affairs, whereas the former is directed primarily at volition itself. This radical heterogeneity explains why inclination need not be frustrated if one acts on purely rational grounds (but not vice versa). Consequently, there is no need to relegate the motive of respect to the role of 'backup motive': it makes good sense to say that all moral action must be done for the sake of the law. Also, as morality shapes the life of the virtuous agent without determining the details, there is little danger that Kantian morality will unduly dominate his life. The motivational theory implicit in Section I of the *Groundwork* may thus be more attractive than initially assumed.

At the outset of Section II, Kant turns to examples in moral philosophy, which are portrayed as the central feature of the misguided, haphazard attempts of the popular moral theories of his day. One could not, he says, choose a worse method of moral enquiry than 'wanting to derive it from examples' (*G* IV 408). Examples of virtuous conduct merely illustrate moral principles. It follows that principles are prior. But this just means that examples should be banished from the foundations of ethics, not from moral philosophy as a whole. This is the theme that Robert Louden develops in 'Making the law visible: the role of examples in Kant's ethics'. He examines Kant's objections to examples in the *Groundwork* as well as the place of examples in the moral life of human beings, the distinction between imitation and emulation, and how the teaching of ethics by way of examples – though not as such sufficient – can supplement the cognition and motivational force of an abstract moral law in finite rational beings like ourselves. Drawing on texts such as the *Religion*, the *Metaphysics of Morals*, the *Anthropology* and Kant's lectures on moral philosophy and education, Louden demonstrates that Kant was not oblivious to the power of example after all.

The three chapters that follow also revolve around the same theme: the formulation of Kant's supreme principle of morals, the categorical imperative, and its various formulations. In 'The moral law as causal law', Robert Johnson examines the connections between rational agency and conformity with universal law, which for Kant is the hallmark of moral volition. After all, the first and basic formulation of the categorical imperative tells us to act only on maxims that we can will as universal laws (*G* IV 421). Johnson argues that the Kantian requirement to conform to laws valid for all rational agents is grounded in the fact not that all agency is *rational* but rather that it is *agency*, i.e. the exercise of a causal power. Whereas reason does not as such provide a universalization requirement, it does provide a spontaneity requirement. According to Johnson, the derivation of the first formulation of the categorical imperative relies on the thought that rational willing is a kind of causation. If so, the claim that the concept of causation contains the idea of conformity to universal laws is not – as many have argued – a trivial claim.

An alternative way of stating the principles of Kantian ethics focuses not on the formal requirement of universalization but on the idea that one should always treat human beings respectfully. This is articulated in the second variant formulation of the categorical imperative to use humanity, whether in one's own person or that of any other, 'always at the same time as an end, never merely as a means' (*G* IV 429). However, the precise reason why one should treat humanity in this manner is highly controversial among Kant scholars. Should we respect human beings because of some absolute inner worth or value that we all possess by virtue of some special capacity or characteristic, our 'dignity', as the standard interpretation has it? Does this turn Kantian ethics into a kind of teleology? Can the requirement to treat others with respect perhaps be justified with recourse to any value at all? In his 'Dignity and the formula of humanity', Oliver Sensen argues for the latter, less common view. One should respect others simply because it is commanded by the categorical imperative. Kant does not ground morality on any value. If so, Kantian ethics can perhaps be shown to be a kind of deontology after all.

Katrin Flikschuh's 'Kant's kingdom of ends: metaphysical, not political' takes issue with a widespread contemporary interpretation of Kant's third variation of the categorical imperative, which involves the notion of an ideal moral commonwealth. On the view in question, the 'kingdom of ends' is a semi-political entity that represents the normative ideal of a democratic order of mutually legislating and essentially equal citizens; and Kantian moral autonomy is aligned with liberal personal autonomy, understood as the competence of individuals to judge for themselves. In the course of this, the metaphysical elements of Section II of the *Groundwork* are played down or curtailed in the interest of a normative philosophical project. But Kant's 'kingdom of ends', Flikschuh argues, is an essentially metaphysical conception of a non-political order with God at the top that cannot be appropriated by political theory without distorting both Kantian ethics and Kant's basic doctrine of right, which concerns the much more confined notion of *Rechtsstaat*.

Jerome Schneewind's contribution returns to the historical context of Kant's *Groundwork of the Metaphysics of Morals*. Towards the end of Section II, as the categorical imperative has duly been revealed as a principle of autonomy, Kant rather unflatteringly lumps together the views of earlier moral philosophers and dismisses them because they are, one and all, expressions of the misguided assumption of heteronomy (*G* IV 441). In 'Kant against the "spurious principles of morality"' Schneewind considers the claim that Kant's argument for the categorical imperative as the supreme principle of morality succeeds in dismissing all rival principles by means of an 'only survivor' argument without begging the question. The final verdict is negative. Whereas Kant's objections to egoistic hedonism, Wolffian perfectionism and Crusius' divine command theory are telling, in other cases he has to rely on assumptions that his opponents are supposed to share while in fact they do not; there are some contemporary views that he does not consider, and more recent alternatives were not, of course, available to him to be dismissed in this fashion. Nonetheless, Schneewind concludes that only Hume matches Kant in trying to give fair-minded and often trenchant responses to the main rivals of his own theory.

The final three contributions again concern a single theme: that of the ambitious Kantian project contained in the last section of the book. John Skorupski discusses Kant's 'grand claim' that we can derive from the notion of free or rational action a principle of how all rational beings should act, which he equates with a peculiar kind of impartiality: the categorical imperative ('Autonomy and impartiality'). He breaks the Kantian argument down into two steps: the first leads from the notion of acting on a reason to autonomy, the second from autonomy to the impartiality of Kantian morality. If successful, this move would help us against the moral sceptic, who is unlikely to doubt the existence of practical reason. But whereas the first step is defensible, Skorupski argues, the second one fails: morality cannot be derived analytically from the mere idea of autonomy. If so, the 'grand project' pursued in the third section of the *Groundwork* fails.

Paul Guyer's 'Problems with freedom: Kant's Argument in *Groundwork* III and its subsequent emendations' centres on Kant's claim that Section III provides a rudimentary 'critique of the subject, that is, of pure practical reason' (*G* IV 440), which is meant to substantiate the analytic claims of Sections I and II. This critique, Guyer claims, is supposed to achieve this end by means of a metaphysical argument that depends on a claim about our real, 'noumenal' selves, and that is intended to prove that the moral law is a causal law of the 'real' self. He continues by showing how the problems raised by this conception of freedom occupy Kant in his later writings, notably the *Critique of Practical Reason* and *Religion Within the Limits of Mere Reason*.

By contrast, Fred Rauscher argues against the prevalent reading of the deduction of the categorical imperative in Section III, which assumes that Kant is trying to provide an argument for the validity of the moral law for human beings by drawing on a theoretical argument about the nature of reality – transcendental idealism – borrowed from the *Critique of Pure Reason* ('Freedom and reason in *Groundwork* III'). He contrasts this reconstruction with his own 'validation of reason' interpretation, which does not pretend to provide proof of the objective reality of morality but rather seeks to explain only the inevitability of the ascription of morality to human beings who take themselves to be rational agents. He argues that Kant invokes transcendental freedom not as a feature of the whole person or the choice, but only of the faculty of reason that we all possess as a way of explaining freedom of the will. In doing so, Rauscher emphasizes the limitations of the project of deduction that Kant himself stresses on the last page of the *Groundwork* (*G* IV 463).

CHAPTER I

Ethics and anthropology in the development of Kant's moral philosophy

Manfred Kuehn

In the *Groundwork of the Metaphysics of Morals* of 1785, Immanuel Kant sharply distinguishes moral philosophy from anthropology, claiming that the metaphysics of morals must precede practical anthropology, must be completely *a priori*, and must therefore be 'purified' or 'cleansed' of anything empirical, *a posteriori*, or belonging to mere anthropology (*G* IV 388).[1] The rudiments of the *a priori* moral philosophy expounded in the *Groundwork* are extensively explained and analysed in the two other major works that are explicitly concerned with moral philosophy, the *Critique of Practical Reason* (1787) and the *Metaphysics of Morals* (1797). The *a posteriori* or empirical doctrine of morals or what is 'called more specifically practical anthropology', by contrast, never really comes into focus in the published works. Even the *Anthropology from a Pragmatic Point of View* contains little that would directly concern moral philosophy. Reflections on the empirical and anthropological aspects of morality can, however, be found in the student notes of his lectures on moral philosophy given before 1785, that is, before the publication of the *Groundwork*, and, more importantly, in those of the lectures on anthropology, which Kant began to offer in the winter semester of 1772–73 with the hope of transforming the subject into a proper academic discipline. Kant's main goal in this new *collegium privatim* was, as he put it, to 'introduce all the sciences that are concerned with morals, with the ability of commerce, and the method of educating and ruling human beings, or all that is practical' (X 145). As such a general introduction into practical philosophy, the anthropology lectures had the closest relation to moral philosophy, which Kant always offered during the winter semesters. The anthropology lectures were conceived, at least in part, as a general introduction to or preparation for moral philosophy. But even if

---

[1] Compare also *MdS* VI 247: 'If there is any subject matter that allows of *philosophy* (a system of rational cognitions on the basis of concepts), then there must exist for this philosophy also a system of pure rational concepts independent of the conditions of intuition, i.e. a metaphysics.'

it were argued that Kant himself did not see the relation of anthropology and moral philosophy in this way, it is clear that there must have been some overlap and cross-fertilization between these two subjects taught so closely together.[2]

These early lectures contain, therefore, just the notions that characterized for Kant the kind of morality that was not yet 'carefully cleaned of everything empirical'. Therefore, a closer analysis of these lectures seems to me to be of central importance for understanding pure moral concepts, for we may assume that even something that has carefully been cleaned still has the contours of the object not yet cleaned or still encrusted with impurities. At the very least, one should expect that the cleaned object does not contain entirely new or different features than the one that has not as yet been cleaned. Furthermore, the cleaning process should only remove the impurities, not parts of the object to be cleaned; nor, one might argue, can the cleaned object have a shape that could not find its place within the object encrusted with impurities. In other words, the pure principles of morality must fit with the empirical manifestations of morality. Pure moral philosophy should not have a 'shape' entirely different from what most people would consider moral. If we take Kant's metaphor seriously, there should be no incompatibility between his metaphysics of morals and morality.

Many philosophers have argued just that. Kant's metaphysics of morals seriously misconstrues the moral domain. Bernard Williams is perhaps the most important of those who have done so recently.[3] Others have argued that Kant's moral philosophy does not only not involve fundamental metaphysical assumptions, but captures very well our common preconception of morality.[4] However, before we decide whether or not Kant's modern critics or defenders are right, it might be of interest to see what 'empirical concepts' of morality Kant actually started out from, and what it was that he thought it was necessary to cleanse or purify. If only for this reason, it should be rewarding to investigate in some detail the kind of morality from which Kant started out. In any case, this is what I intend to do in this chapter. I would like to investigate what the contents of Kant's anthropology lectures between 1772 and 1785 show about the origins of some of the

---

[2] Kant himself refers his students in the ethics lectures to the anthropology lectures. See XXVII 466, for instance.

[3] See, e.g., Bernard Williams, *Ethics and the Limits of Philosophy* (Cambridge University Press, 1985), pp. 174, 180, 190f.

[4] See, e.g., Christine M. Korsgaard, *The Sources of Normativity* (Cambridge University Press, 1996) or Barbara Herman, *The Practice of Moral Judgment* (Harvard University Press, 1993), or any number of contemporary American 'Kantians'.

central concepts of the *Groundwork*, hoping to illuminate certain issues of the development of his moral philosophy between, that is, the period that roughly lasted from the publication of the *Inaugural Dissertation* (1770) to the *Groundwork of the Metaphysics of Morals* (1785).[5] These issues concern the closely related concepts of 'moral sense', 'moral character', 'maxim' and 'the good will'.

Especially 'character' has received some attention lately. Barbara Herman, for instance, has pointed out in an influential paper 'some of the resources that might be drawn on to develop a Kantian idea of character and to indicate ... some of its advantages for moral judgment'.[6] Others, like Otfried Höffe, have argued for a relevance of Aristotle in this context.[7] Still others, like Nancy Sherman, have tried to show, while being 'more faithful to the texts' and 'responsive to debates in contemporary ethics', that Kant and Aristotle are closer on character because emotions actually play a central role for Kant as well.[8] While I will not directly engage these proposals here, it should be clear to anyone acquainted with the recent literature that my discussion provides an alternative to such views.

[5] Though I have written on Kant's moral development several times before, this chapter is very different in focusing more explicitly on the anthropology. See 'The Moral Dimension of Kant's Inaugural Dissertation: A New Perspective on the "Great Light of 1769?"' in *Proceedings of the 8th International Kant Congress in Memphis* (Milwaukee: Marquette University Press, 1995), vol. 1.2, pp. 373–92; 'Kant and Cicero' in Volker Gerhardt, Rolf-Peter Horstmann and Ralph Schumacher (eds.), *Proceedings of the 9th International Kant Congress in Berlin, April 2000* (Berlin/New York: de Gruyter, 2001), pp. 270–8; 'Einleitung' in Immanuel Kant, *Vorlesungen zur Moralphilosophie* (Werner Stark (ed.), Berlin: de Gruyter, 2004), pp. vii–xxxv; 'Introduction' in Immanuel Kant, *Anthropology from a Pragmatic Point of View* (Robert Louden (ed.), Cambridge University Press, 2006), pp. vii–xxxiii.

[6] Barbara Herman, 'Making Room for Character' in Stephen Engstrom and Jennifer Whiting (eds.), *Aristotle, Kant and the Stoics: Rethinking Happiness and Duty* (Cambridge University Press, 1996), pp. 36–62 at p. 37. Herman is responding in this context to McDowell, who claims that virtue is also a perceptive ability that allows us to see 'situations in a certain distinctive way' and make moral judgements. See John McDowell, 'Virtue and Reason', *The Monist* 62 (1979), 331–50.

[7] Otfried Höffe, 'Universalistische Ethik und Urteilskraft: ein aristotelischer Blick auf Kant', *Zeitschrift für philosophische Forschung* (1990), 537–63 and his 'Aristoteles' universalistische Tugendethik' in Klaus Peter Rippe and Peter Schaber (eds.), *Tugendethik* (Stuttgart: Reclam, 1998), pp. 42–68, which seems to be influenced very much by Martha Nussbaum's 'Non-Relative Virtues: an Aristotelian Approach' in Peter A. French, Theodore E. Uehling, Jr and Howard K. Wettstein (eds.), *Ethical Theory: Character and Virtue*, Midwest Studies in Philosophy 13 (Notre Dame, IN: University of Notre Dame Press, 1988), pp. 32–53, an expanded version of which is in 'Non-Relative Virtues: an Aristotelian Approach' in Martha C. Nussbaum and Amartya Sen (eds.), *The Quality of Life, Papers presented at a conference sponsored by the World Institute for Development Economics Research*, WIDER Studies in Development Economics (Oxford: Clarendon Press; New York: Oxford University Press, 1993), pp. 242–69.

[8] Nancy Sherman, *Making a Necessity of Virtue: Aristotle and Kant on Virtue* (Cambridge University Press, 1997), especially pp. 121–86.

I FROM MORAL SENSE TO MORAL CHARACTER: CHRISTIAN FÜRCHTEGOTT GELLERT AND 'IDLE IDEALS AND DESIRES' VERSUS 'GUTE DENKUNGSART'

It is well known that during the 1760s, Kant was very much influenced by Francis Hutcheson and considered the moral sense or 'moral feeling', as he and others also called it, as the foundation of morality.[9] It is also well known that he changed his mind some time after 1764, that is, after the publication of his Prize Essay for the Berlin Academy: *Inquiry concerning the Distinctness of the Principles of Natural Theology and Morality*. In that work, Kant still found that Hutcheson has provided 'the starting point for some nice observations about what he called the moral feeling' and leaves open the possibility that the 'first principles' of obligation may be found in such a feeling. If we can trust Adickes' dating of the reflections, then Kant had already abandoned by 1770 or 1771 the view that moral feeling or moral sense could play any foundational role.[10] For in the reflections of that period he found that the real question of morality is (XIX 135):

whether moral judgements are concerned with whether the actions [judged] are seen as good or as pleasant. If it is the former, then it is the quality of the action which is identical for every understanding that forms the basis of the judgement, and this is the effect of reason. If it is the second, then one judges on the basis of feeling, and this is not necessarily valid for everyone.

In these reflections, he also suggested that the moral sense may not be an original sense, but rather something derivative and instinctual. It does not lead to moral judgements, but to inclinations. Furthermore, he thought that the moral sense needs to be formed by education or by 'concepts and rules' (XIX 137).

This view can also be found in the lecture notes on anthropology called *Collins*, which were taken during the winter semester 1772–73. In a section that is concerned with pleasure and displeasure arising from the beautiful

---

[9] Thus Henrich has claimed that 'Kant became aware of the general situation of ethics at the middle of the eighteenth century through the opposition between Wolff's *philosophia practica universalis* and Hutcheson's moral philosophy, and his first independent formulation of an ethical theory resulted from a critique of these two philosophers' (Dieter Henrich, 'The Concept of Moral Insight' in *The Unity of Reason: Essays on Kant's Philosophy* (R. Velkley (ed.), Manfred Kuehn (trans.), Harvard University Press, 1994), pp. 55–88. Apart from the fact that there was no thorough opposition, but rather a perceived complementarity, this claim situates Kant's early theory correctly. See also Dieter Henrich, 'Hutcheson und Kant', *Kant-Studien* 49 (1957/58), 49–69, and 'Über Kants früheste Ethik', *Kant-Studien* 54 (1963), 404–31.

[10] See XXV 1–228. These notes are based mainly on a set of notes taken by Collins, but they are supplemented by materials from lecture notes, taken by others.

and the good, Kant argued that there is a fundamental difference between the pleasure we feel as a result of perceiving something we find beautiful and something that we find to be good. The one is concerned with 'appearance' and is 'subjective', the other 'pleases conceptually' (*gefällt im Begriff*) and is 'objective' (XXV 197). While he did not want to deny that there are also laws that govern our estimation of what is beautiful, these laws are not objective. They only determine how I feel. Moral laws, on the other hand, do not determine how I feel about something, but 'how the thing (*Sache*) is in itself' or '*an sich selbst*' (XXV 197). Therefore, he claimed, we can formulate '*principia a priori* of judging, i.e. maxims' about the latter, but not about the former (XXV 204). These have to do with the intrinsic value of the action or end pursued.

What we feel to be beautiful and judge to be good has, of course, a close connection with what we desire. But 'desire' can be taken in two senses. It is either an idle (*müßig*) or an active (*tätig*) desire, where the former implies that we do not have the power to do what we desire, while the second implies that we do have such power. Kant also identified idle desires with wishing and active desire with willing, and he seemed to think that one of the problems of his contemporaries was the confusion between the two. People read novels and allow themselves to become subject to passionate yearnings and be preoccupied by 'true ideals' that get in the way of active desires. One of the thinkers who not only endorsed idle desires, but actually encouraged them, was Johann Fürchtegott Gellert (1715–69).[11] He therefore became a target of severe criticism for Kant, who argued that he (XXV 206):

puffs up the mind with such moral vapours and yearnings, and creates the delusion that it is sufficient, if we simply have such feelings without having an active benevolence, nay he does not even inculcate true sentiments of humanity, but leads us only to admire such characters. Misled by such delusion, we may thus consider ourselves as good people if we have such wishes or even just such sentiments.

For Kant, this approach was closely connected with what he considered one of the 'most injurious religious delusions', namely the belief that sighing

---

[11] Gellert is not very well known today outside of Germany and even within Germany he is viewed as one of the minor poets of the eighteenth century, a mere transitional figure, who occupies a place somewhere between Gottsched and Lessing. He is usually considered to be a 'sentimentalist', i.e. someone for whom feeling and sympathy played a greater role than it did for thinkers like Gottsched or Lessing. His most famous writings are *The History of the Swedish Countess of G------* (1752), and a collection of hymns, *Geistliche Oden und Lieder* (*Spiritual Odes and Hymns*) (1757). His fables and parables have a clear didactic purpose, firmly rooted in more or less traditional Christian sentiments, that would strike many Christians today as naive and superficial, but his writings seem to have hit a nerve in this period.

and awe-inspired yearning amount to true religion, when, in fact, it is
characterized by actively serving our fellow creatures, inspired awe and
obedience to God.

Gellert, a professor of philosophy at the University of Leipzig and well-
known as a poet in the German tradition of *Empfindsamkeit*, had died about
three years earlier. Kant's remarks are clearly occasioned by his *Moral
Lectures* (*Moralische Vorlesungen*), which had appeared posthumously in
1770, and were selling at a record pace in Germany. It is said that the
work sold more than 100,000 copies, which was almost unheard of in the
eighteenth century. Johann Wolfgang von Goethe called the *Moral Lectures*
'the foundation of German moral culture'. Since Kant had known the work
of Gellert for a long time, and would have been close to Gellert's way of
thinking in many ways, the book must have been important to him.[12] Both
were influenced by Hutcheson and other authors who defended the moral
sense as a basic principle of morality, both considered reason and moral
sense to be equally important.

While the *Moral Lectures* do not pretend to be a systematic treatment of
the metaphysics of morals, and while Gellert himself admits that he does not
possess enough philosophical depth to provide such a work, promising only
an easily comprehensible and practical account of some of the most important moral doctrines for the moral orientation and education of his students,
he does offer an interesting theory. He claims to have relied mainly on the
writings of Mosheim, Baumgarten, Crusius and Jerusalem, as well as on
Hutcheson, Fordyce and other 'acute and well-spoken men'.[13] This list is as
interesting for the names that are in it as for the names that are not included
in it. The complete lack of any reference to Wolff or other Wolffians or
Leibnizians is certainly significant. Baumgarten, Crusius and Hutcheson are
perhaps not surprising, but Mosheim and Fordyce are. Christian August
Crusius (1715–75) is not surprising, as he was one of Gellert's predecessors
and colleagues at the University of Leipzig. Kant's colleagues at Königsberg,
who admired Crusius, also read moral philosophy in accordance with
Gellert.

The first sentence of the lectures reads: 'Morals or knowledge of the duty
of man should educate our understanding to be wise and our heart to be

---

[12] See XX 6 ('Remarks on the Observations on the Beautiful and Sublime'): 'The motion of the fine
moral sentiments or refinements can hardly be a replacement for the domestic occupations (moral
yeomen; the Gellert right beside the brilliantine box); and the woman who weaves a coat for her man
always puts the *galante dame* to shame, who reads a tragedy instead.'
[13] C. F. Gellert, *Sämmtliche Schriften. Neue verbesserte Auflage* (Leipzig: M. G. Weidmanns Erben und
Reich, und Caspar Fritsch, 1775), pp. ix and 5 (hereafter Gellert, *Moralische Vorlesungen*).

virtuous and thus lead us to happiness by means of both.'[14] This means, first of all, that to be truly virtuous is also to be truly happy. The highest goal of morality can only be 'the lasting and general satisfaction [*Zufriedenheit*] and happiness of human beings through their freely willed obedience to God', who is our master and creator.[15] Indeed, the fifth lecture deals exclusively with the question of how morality and happiness go hand in hand. Gellert claims that happiness (*Glückseligkeit*) consists 'in the enjoyment of the highest and most durable good that human beings are capable of as well in the liberation of the smaller and larger evils, which are in our power', and if that is so, then:

our reason, our heart and our experience teach us that virtue is the only secure way towards happiness; or that the possession of virtue gives us the highest and most lasting pleasures [*Freuden*] and either averts the greatest evil or at least allows us to carry their load more easily.[16]

Secondly, there is, according to Gellert, no tension between the 'heart' or feeling and the understanding. The understanding and the heart, if understood correctly, aim at the same thing. However, the relationship between inclination and reason is not quite so simple, for we 'feel inclinations towards the good, which conscience gives to us and reason justifies and we feel inclinations of the heart towards evil, whose ignominy conscience points out and reason proves'.[17] Thus, we must say that while moral sense or 'moral taste' (*moralischer Geschmack*), as he sometimes also calls it, and reason are complementary, this kind of moral feeling is not identical with mere desire or raw sensibility. It is something that is due to culture or the influence of the understanding on sensibility. Gellert is very clear on this, that understanding or reason must rule over sensual impulses and desires. It guides our feeling in perfecting itself to become a truly moral feeling. The understanding must 'rule' over the passions. Accordingly, Gellert advises his students: 'Guard your passions and your sensibility [*Sinnlichkeit*], they do lead you astray; place a wise mistrust in yourself and examine your heart and your behaviour daily with honesty [*Aufrichtigkeit*].'[18] Gellert also often speaks of 'conscience' or the 'sentiments of conscience' (*Empfindungen des Gewissens*), but this does not appear to be a separate kind of faculty. It is just another way of speaking about the moral sense or the heart.

[14] Gellert, *Moralische Vorlesungen*, pp. 6, 9.   [15] *Ibid.* p. 12.   [16] *Ibid.* p. 109.   [17] *Ibid.* p. 20.
[18] *Ibid.* p. 29.

Even though Gellert constantly talks of 'virtue', he seems to be offering a duty-based ethics, or an ethics in which virtue is ultimately based on duty, for morals is ultimately 'knowledge of the duty of man'. Indeed:

the source of the natural doctrine of morals is reason and the natural feeling of good and evil. What agrees with the truths of reason and the sentiments of conscience, with the nature of man and the welfare of the world, is right and good; and everything that can be correctly deduced from these is duty.[19]

So duty is based directly or indirectly on the natural doctrine of morals. Virtue, by contrast, consists in 'the purposive [absichtvolle] pursuit of this duty from obedience to God'.[20] To be virtuous means to do one's duty in a certain way, namely to do it 'from the obedience to God'.

Gellert thinks 'there are not many laws of wisdom and morals', even though there are many proofs and applications. Indeed, there is only *one* fundamental law of morals (*das Hauptgesetz der Moral*), and this is:

Do everything that is in accordance with God's perfections, your own true happiness and the welfare of your fellow human beings from obedience and with honesty [Aufrichtigkeit] in your heart towards your almighty creator and desist from the contrary.[21]

This fundamental law of morals says, in other words, that an act has moral worth only if it is done 'from obedience and with honesty towards God'. It emphasizes how important the concept of 'disposition' or 'Gesinnung' is for him. According to Gellert, it is also 'a law of healthy reason' or common sense (*gesunde Vernunft*) that we must do our actions from a certain motive and that it is this motive that makes the act moral. All other duties are rooted in this fundamental duty, as a tree and its branches can be traced back to its roots.[22] It is our duty to do our duties in this particular way or from this motive and if we consistently pursue our duties in this particular way, we also possess the most fundamental virtue, the 'virtue of the heart'. And the:

heart has really only one virtue, and this is the lively, powerful intention [Vorsatz] that has been conceived by conscience and reason and that says that we should always do the good and act in accordance with God's determination without exception because there is nothing holier [seliger] than that. From this virtue of the heart flow, like from a rich spring as it were, the many streams of particular virtues and duties.[23]

---

[19] *Ibid.* p. 91.   [20] *Ibid.* p. 91.   [21] *Ibid.* p. 19.   [22] *Ibid.* p. 145.   [23] *Ibid.* p. 20.

All particular duties and virtues are secondary to the primary law of morals, and the primary law of morals is a law that concerns the intention with which these other duties and virtues are done. One might therefore say that the particular duties and virtues are derivable from the primary law of nature, even though this derivation cannot be straightforward and direct or without further input from reason and moral sense. One might even say that this fundamental law is merely formal in the sense that it does not say anything about the content of these other duties, but only claims that they all must be done from honest obedience to God.[24]

So, it might be said that Kant is somewhat unfair in his criticism, for Gellert did not reduce morality to idle wishes. Just as Kant does, he emphasized the necessity of duty. However, the two are fundamentally different concerning the foundation of duty. Whereas Kant finds that the 'virtue of the heart' is central and emphasizes the role of the understanding and concepts at the expense of inclinations and feelings, Gellert argues that the understanding and feeling coincide with one another. It is our task to cultivate our feelings so that they become true moral feelings. Kant claims that feelings cannot be so cultivated, that they are at bottom a gift of nature that one either has or has not received. For this very reason, feelings cannot form the basis of our judgements of good and evil.

In the anthropology notes 'Parow' that were also taken in 1772–73, Kant also claims that 'Gellert's *Morals* teaches us to do all good things from a good disposition' (a good heart or *Gutherzigkeit*) and argues that such a good disposition has 'no rule'. Thus good-hearted people can do evil things: 'it is not good that the human being is ruled by the heart alone' (XXV 629). We need rules and firm principles.[25] This means that we need character, for 'character is the use of our will [*Willkühr*] in accordance with rules and basic principles' (XXV 629). Character is what gives a human being worth. Indeed, character seems to be the most important notion for his conception of moral philosophy in these sections.

We might say that character is Kant's alternative to Gellert's virtue of the heart. It is not something we are born with. It is not a gift of nature (or God), but it is our own creation. We make or adopt our character. And to have a good character is the ultimate moral achievement. Only insofar as we

---

[24] Gellert's morality is ultimately a divine-command theory of ethics. The obedience to God is the beginning and end of all of morality.

[25] Kant, on the other hand, does everything to show that feeling cannot form the basis of morality. He notes a 'nice gradation' from 'inclination', 'affect', to 'blind affect', saying that while 'all inclination is opposed to morality', affect is 'also opposed to prudence', and blind affect is 'not just opposed to morality and prudence but also to practicality [*Geschicklichkeit*]' (XXV 412).

have a character do we have moral worth. This is as true of our empirical character as it is of any intelligible character we may or may not have. Put somewhat anachronistically, Kant's moral psychology is a psychology of character. We could say that it is our duty to form a character in the moral sense, and it is this character that is the focus of Kant's concern in those sections of the anthropology lectures that have moral concerns.[26]

Now, the notion of character is closely bound up in these lectures with the concept of maxims. Indeed, character is based on rational maxims that have been adopted by the individual agent. Maxims, at least 'maxims' in the anthropological sense, are *Lebensregeln* or rules to live by. They are therefore not to be understood on the basis of 'free-floating, isolated decisions ... that stand in no connection with an enduring moral agent with a determinate nature and interest', as Allison suggests at one point.[27] Maxims always already have reference to such an enduring moral agent. Indeed, they only make sense, if we assume a moral agent. They are expressions of rational agency. If we truly knew the maxims of a rational agent, we would also know a great deal about the moral agent. Since the maxims are the very rules

[26] It might perhaps be said that philosophical scholars of Kant have not paid enough attention to character and anthropology in the sources that are available in English today. A cursory look at the way in which 'character' is treated in a more or less random selection of important books on Kant's moral theory is instructive. In many, both in older and more recent discussions, it simply does not occur. It is not even in the Index of Thomas E. Hill Jr's *Autonomy and Self-Respect* (Cambridge University Press, 1991); it does not occur, and it does not play a larger role in his 'Dignity and Practical Reason' in *Kant's Moral Theory* (Ithaca, NY: Cornell University Press, 1992). Nor can it be found in H. J. Paton's book on *The Categorical Imperative: A Study in Kant's Moral Philosophy* (London: Hutchinson's University Library, 1947), in Bruce Aune's *Kant's Theory of Morals* (Princeton University Press, 1979), or in Onora O'Neill's *Acting on Principle* (Columbia University Press, 1975). In other books, it occurs, but is restricted to character in the sense of characteristic property of a free being, as in Lewis White Beck's *Commentary on Kant's Critique of Practical Reason* (University of Chicago Press, 1960). Henry Allison also places special emphasis on this passage in his *Kant's Theory of Freedom* (Cambridge University Press, 1990), and at least in part as a result of this, the distinction between 'empirical' and 'intelligible' character has become very important in discussing freedom. While this discussion is extremely important for understanding Kant's conception of freedom, it does not tell us much about character proper in Kant. Character in its specifically moral sense does not appear to have received the same attention. Roger J. Sullivan's *Introduction to Kant's Ethics* (Cambridge University Press, 1994) has a chapter on 'Moral Character', but the chapter does not deal with Kant's view of character. Rather, it starts from a notion that is 'typically taken in the social sciences' (p. 130). His earlier *Immanuel Kant's Moral Theory* (Cambridge University Press, 1989) seems to do better. Referring to the *Anthropology* and the first *Critique* he differentiates between 'psychological' or 'empirical' character, claiming that 'the "empirical" self or character consists of inherited dispositional or temperamental traits modified by complexes of acquired habits as well as by the influence of a wide variety of external influences, such as one's family and education' (p. 127). But character in this sense is just what he later describes as the notion 'typically taken in the social sciences'. It is precisely the opposite of the Kantian notion. Character in any sense, even character in the anthropological or empirical sense, is more than inherited traits, acquired habits, or external influences.

[27] Allison, *Kant's Theory of Freedom*, p. 136.

she lives by, the maxims would tell us what kind of person she is. Nor would we have to observe every action of the agent, the patterns of her behaviour would be enough to tell us something about the rules she has chosen to live by. But this is not all. Maxims are not just expressing what kind of a person one is, but they actually constitute that person in some sense, for they constitute the person as character. In other words, to have a certain set of maxims and to have character (or to be a person) are one and the same thing. Maxims represent the origins of the enduring traits of a person. Maxims are character-building devices.

Character is not the result of habit either. It is not *ethike* in the Aristotelian sense, constituted by exercising the right decisions. This means that Kant, like Aristotle, can claim that character does not arise from nature. It also means that Kant does not necessarily agree with Aristotle that it cannot be 'contrary to nature'. It is not important whether we 'are adapted by nature to receive the virtues of character'. It is more important that we have adopted them ourselves as maxims and that we stick by them. This is perhaps the most important result of the discussion of maxims in the anthropological context. Maxims are character-constituting principles. They make us who we are, and without them we are, at least according to Kant, nobody.

Still, even if one has character, one does not necessarily have a morally good character. One might have a good character or a bad character. And while Kant believes that it is better to have character in either sense rather than to have no character at all, which would basically make us into instruments, good character or moral character is better. Indeed, the good character is what moral philosophy is ultimately all about. And we judge whether character is good or bad by the maxims, of course. Maxims are decisive for judging the goodness of our character because it depends upon the goodness of the maxims. If someone has a good character, then she also has good maxims, and if someone has good maxims then she has a good character. Someone without a character is not moral at all, but simply ruled by his animal instincts. And this is what Kant's objection to Gellert ultimately amounts to: his moral ideal is a man of mere feeling without any character. Kant's own theory of the centrality of a good character for morality is formulated in conscious opposition to Gellert's morality of the heart.[28] Our moral

---

[28] Gellert is also discussed in the lecture notes on moral philosophy by *Collins* (XXVII 340), where he is chided for not having talked about duties towards oneself; see also Kant, *Vorlesung zur Moralphilosophie* (Stark (ed.)), p. 169 for the corresponding passage; in the anthropology lecture notes 'Friedländer' (XXV 583, 629–30); and the anthropology lectures 'Mrongovius' (XXV 1390) of 1784–85, where Kant notes that the doctrine of the soft heart or of sympathy is not based on principles and is opposed to character. Gellert's morality is too much based on inclination, as is that of Hutcheson.

judgements ultimately concern the moral character of a person, and since the moral character of a person depends on his or her maxims, we also must judge a person's maxims. Since Kant's moral philosophy around 1772–73 is based on his conception of a good character, his discussion of Gellert is not unimportant.[29] Whether Kant's critique of Gellert is fair, is quite a different matter.

Furthermore, Gellert's morality of the heart emphasizes the importance of a good disposition for morality; and Kant, just like Gellert, ultimately reduces the morality of the person to the morality of her disposition. 'The goodness of the character ... is based on the goodness of the dispositions [*Gesinnungen*]', but, unlike Gellert, he claims that these dispositions have to be based on our cognitive faculties alone, and that Gellert's dispositions must reduce to merely innate characteristics of human beings (XXVII 632). Seeing Gellert's position as belonging entirely in the tradition of Hutcheson, he objects that the presence or absence of a strong moral sense cannot provide us with a criterion for judging human beings. But Gellert's entire project is designed to 'form' (*bilden*) the human heart and human virtue by his lectures, as he says at the very beginning of the lectures. And whatever Kant claims about Gellert's view, Gellert himself thought that morality '*forms* and *improves* the heart', and his '*Aufrichtigkeit des Herzens*' towards God is not an innate characteristic either. Kant's own view during the time we just considered was different from Gellert's, as one might expect from his devastating criticisms. Indeed, a significant part of his vehemence may have had more to do with the fact that Daniel Weyman, a declared enemy of Kant in Königsberg, seems to have liked Gellert almost as much as he did Crusius.[30]

2 FROM GOOD CHARACTER TO THE GOOD WILL

As we saw, character was for Kant already in 1772–73 closely bound up with active desires or willing. But he seems to have talked in these lectures only of

---

[29] Gellert's *Moral Lectures* actually end with a number of character sketches that might be loosely characterized as belonging in the tradition of Theophrast's *Characters*. They are found under the heading 'Moral Characters'. Some of the characters Gellert presents are 'Consistent [*regelmäßig*] Sensibility', 'The Man with One Vice and Many Virtues', 'The Consistent Idler or the Man without Vice or Virtue', 'Character of a Noble Betrayer', etc. Gellert was thus not unaware of the importance of character. It is just that he did not develop a theory of character, as Kant did. We should also note that the notion of constancy or consistency (*Regelmäßigkeit*) does play a fundamental role in Gellert's sketches, and that Kant's own insistence on the importance of this notion does not seem unrelated to Gellert's.

[30] He later even offered lectures on moral philosophy, based on Gellert.

the necessity of a good character, not of the necessity of a good will that plays such an important role in his later work. In 1775–76 this changes. Kant notes in the anthropology lectures of this semester that 'the character is in human beings the most important thing. Everything depends on whether it is good, and therefore we must investigate the source of the character' (XXV 648). Again, Kant opposes feelings, which he characterizes as merely natural, with firm principles of action. But now he identifies the good moral character with the good will. 'The good character would be [*wäre*] the good will' (XXV 648), or better, the good will is the basis (*Grund*) of the good character (XXV 649).[31] And a good will is characterized by good maxims. It is for this reason that he identifies character with our 'way of thinking' (*Denckungs Art*) or disposition (*Gesinnung*), as opposed to the 'way of sensing' (*Sinnesart*).It is the good will that is good in itself. While some people do good on the basis of inclination, they should act on the basis of their *Denckungs Art*, which is 'the *principium* to act in accordance with principles' or the ability to act in accordance with 'maxims' (XXV 649).

For Kant, our will or *Denkungsart* shows that we are rational creatures. He also says that it is the faculty that allows us to act in accordance with concepts. To sum up, Kant claims in the anthropology lectures from the middle of the 1770s that the good character is the foundation of the good will.[32]

In the notes from the anthropology lecture 'Menschenkunde' of 1781–82, we do not hear so much about the will, but we hear much about the relationship of character and maxims. Thus, Kant finds (XXV 1171):

A man of character has his maxims in all things: in friendship, action and religion ...
The maxims of a true character are:
(1) Love of truth. All lying makes [us] despicable, and a liar has no character.
(2) If someone promises something, he must keep his word, i.e. faithfulness to his enemies.
(3) He does not flatter, for flatterers have a very small worth.

A good character may not make us happy, but it does make us worthy of happiness (XXV 1174). He also maintains that people of character have an inner worth, while people of talent have a market value (XXV 1174), and emphasizes that this worth is created by the person himself. Most importantly, however, he claims that character 'consists in the basic characteristic [*GrundAnlage*] of the will' (XXV 1174).

---

[31] I think the note-taker meant to indicate indirect speech by the subjunctive, meaning something like 'Kant said the good character was the good will'.
[32] Some of this material can also be found in the *Anthropology from a Pragmatic Point of View*, especially VII 292–6, 225–38.

In the lecture notes 'Mrongovius' of 1784–85 we find Kant argues that character presupposes three things, namely (i) that we have a will; (ii) that we have our own will that allows us to resist our temptations; and (iii) that we have a constant will and are not subject to whims. In fact, it is the constancy or endurance of the will that forms the main characteristic of a character (XXV 1386), thus again emphasizing the same close relationship between will and character that he had emphasized before.

While there is not much talk in Kant's published work on moral philosophy about character, there are two crucial passages that suggest that the basic relationship of the dependence of character on will has not changed. Thus, he speaks in the *Critique of Practical Reason* of character as 'the practically consistent way of thinking in accordance with unchangeable maxims' (V 152). And in the first sentence of the first section of the *Groundwork* he claims (*G* IV 393, bold emphasis added):

There is no possibility of thinking of anything at all in the world, or even out of it, which can be regarded as good without qualification, except a *good will.* Intelligence, wit, judgement, and whatever *talents* of the mind one might want to name are doubtless in many respects good and desirable, as are such qualities of *temperament* as courage, resolution, and perseverance. But they can also become extremely bad and harmful *if the will,* which is to make uses of these gifts of nature and *whose special constitution is therefore called character* is not good.[33]

This passage is found at the beginning of the 'Transition from the Ordinary Rational Knowledge of Morality to the Philosophical', i.e. also at the very beginning of his fundamental project in the *Groundwork*. It appears to me that this gives it a special significance. Using Kant's critical terminology, we may say that 'character' is the appearance of the will; that a good character corresponds to the good will, and an evil character to an evil will. If this is true, then almost everything that Kant says about the will in his pure moral philosophy can be translated into language about character as used in his anthropology. Put differently, 'will' is 'character', but it is character 'completely freed from everything which may be only empirical and thus belong to anthropology'. If we can assume that this is correct, we can make almost immediate sense of Kant's claim that the good will is of the most central importance in the metaphysics of morals. It is central because it is the rational analogue of character and virtue.

This would mean that the relationship between character and will has changed from the way it is represented in the lectures. They both seem to

---

[33] This is the only time the term occurs in the *Groundwork*.

belong to the same order of explanation, whereas in the later works they belong to different worlds or are different aspects of one and the same person who belongs to two different worlds. The one names a phenomenon of the world of experience, the other its analogue in a rational account of morality. The fact that in the lectures character and will belong to the same explanatory context, and are thus related to each other in a more straightforward way, may help us in better understanding how the moral theory that is 'completely freed from everything which may be only empirical and thus belong to anthropology' is relevant to the more mundane matters of day-to-day morality. But however that may be, it might also shed some light on the motives that led Kant to formulate the categorical imperative.

3 FROM THE GOOD WILL TO THE CATEGORICAL IMPERATIVE

Another important issue that Kant raised in 1775–76 is how the concepts that characterize the *Denkungsart* or the moral will could ever become motives for us, because in and of themselves (or *qua* concepts) they cannot be motivating factors or *Triebfedern*. Only feelings can be, or so Kant thought at this time. Therefore, he also thought that it is essential that the concepts of good and bad themselves 'create the feeling to act in accordance with these concepts', for when we 'act in accordance with concepts, then we act in accordance with principles and maxims' (XXV 649). Alas, he had to admit, few people are capable of being moved by concepts in this way, and we don't know why this is so. Nevertheless, he entertains an interesting idea as a possibility of how this might work after all (XXV 650):

The motivation [*Triebfeder*] to act in accordance with good principles could perhaps be the idea that, if all would act in this way, the world would be a paradise. This moves me to contribute, so that it is at least not my fault, if this paradise is not realized. As far as I am concerned, I am still a part [*Glied*] of this paradise. Now it is important that everyone should also be this way. Thus the concept of the good can be the motivation here, and then we have a good character.

The notes from the lectures on moral philosophy *Collins* of 1774–75 or 1775–76 contain similar musings, but in this context are entirely negative. In the section entitled 'Of the Supreme Principle of Morality' he finds that there are ultimately two fundamental principles of morals, namely the so-called *principium diiudicationis* that tells us when a maxim is a moral maxim and a *principium executionis* that moves us to act on a principle or maxim that has moral worth, and he then asks the question: What moves me to live according to what I recognize to be the moral law? (XXVII 1425 f.):

Appraisal of the action is the objective ground, but not yet the subjective ground. That which impels me to do the thing, of which the understanding tells me that I ought to do it, is the *motive subjective moventia*. The supreme principle of all moral judgement lies in the understanding, the supreme principle of the moral impulse to do this thing lies in the heart ... the motive is in the moral feeling. The motive does not take the place of the norm.[34]

After spending some time arguing that the principle of judgement is objective and not subjective, that there are at least two '*principia pathologia*', that God is not the solution, and that 'morality is the conformity of the action to a universally valid law of free choice' (XXVII 1427), Kant returns to the relation of the principle of appraisal of the action (or the *principium diiudicationis*) and the principle of its performance (or the *principium executionis*), saying that 'no one can or ever will comprehend how the understanding should have motivating power' (XXVII 1428), and affirming again that appraisal and action are far apart and that we need a moral sense to bridge the gap. The solution to the problem of how universal moral principles can move us to do what is moral would be 'the philosopher's stone'.

It is difficult to resist the idea that these musings represent at least a germ of the idea that later became the categorical imperative. As I have argued elsewhere, Kant's categorical imperative is an attempt to combine what he had kept separate in his lecture courses on ethics from the middle of the 1770s, that is, the principle of the appraisal of actions and the principle of motivation. The former principle looks in all essential respects like the categorical imperative, the latter principle is identified as the moral sense (that God has implanted in us). It seems to me an interesting question to ask what made him change his mind and why he conceived of the categorical imperative as both a *principium diiudicationis* and a *principium executionis*. Kant must have seen in Gellert's theory some of the excesses that reliance on feeling may lead to, and he must have tried to remedy these situations by trying to find a more rational account of these matters. Clearly, this account eluded him in the 1770s, but just as clearly, the later view pursues in a different way the basic idea of the 1770s that the motivating factor of morality must have something to do with universalizability.

The idea of a paradise on earth, realized by the moral effort of human individuals, has clearly also a relation to what Kant argued in the *Idea for a*

---

[34] The 'heart' should remind us of Gellert, of course.

Universal History from a Cosmopolitan Point of View of 1784, which has the closest connection with the discussion of the infinite perfectibility of human beings and 'the vocation of man' (*die Bestimmung des Menschen*) that originated with Johann Joachim Spalding, Thomas Abbt, Moses Mendelssohn, Gotthold Ephraim Lessing and other Enlightenment thinkers during the 1750s and 1760s, and found a late echo in Lessing' *Education of the Human Race* (*Von der Erziehung des Menschengeschlechts*). And it is interesting to note that during the 1760s these issues were closely connected for Kant.

But however this may be, it appears to me that these passages suggest that there is a similar relation between maxims 'as subjective principles of volition' (carefully cleansed of anything empirical) and maxims as *Lebensregeln* in the context of anthropology. The two conceptions of 'maxim' correspond to the differences between 'good will' and 'good character'. And just as the maxims in the anthropology lectures are not so much rules that govern us in doing individual acts, but rules that constitute possible (moral) character, the subjective principles of volition are tested in the categorical imperative for their suitability for constituting a good will. Without getting into the details, it appears to me that we must say that Kant's categorical imperative is not so much concerned with the evaluation of particular acts, but rather with the evaluation of the enduring principles which these actions merely exemplify. Thus, the categorical imperative does not and should not be required to tell us what we must do in particular situations. Rather, it is about rules that are to be permanent characteristics of a good will. Maxims do not represent 'willings' in general (as Herman has claimed), but a highly generalized form of willing within a definite context. In other words, maxims are rules as they are willed when we adopt a certain character.

The categorical imperative is to tell us which moral rules we should adopt. It is ultimately a specific response to a fairly specific situation – a situation which most people today do not seem to find themselves in any longer. Since maxims are character-constituting devices or, if you prefer, 'good will con-stituting devices' and the categorical imperative evaluates maxims, it is ultimately a means to evaluate our will or character. It regulates the evaluation of which character we should choose. It contributes to the answer to a question that is rarely asked in that particular way today. It is not the question: What is the right way to act? Or: How do I live in the best possible way? But the question: What kind of character should I adopt? Or: How do I become a good person? Or: What does it mean to live a virtuous life?

Let me use the example of a certain young man – I'll call him Ben – who finds himself pondering what is the purpose of living. Soon he realizes that whatever the purpose of living may be, it must have to do with living morally. Not inclined to do anything half-heartedly, Ben conceives 'the bold and arduous project of arriving at moral perfection', and that he would 'conquer all that either natural inclination, custom or company might lead [him] into'. Now, he thinks he knows what is right and wrong, and therefore he starts to draw up a list of virtues to live by. This turns out to be difficult, but he ultimately ends up with a list of twelve. They are Temperance, Silence, Order, Resolution, Frugality, Industry, Sincerity, Justice, Moderation, Cleanliness, Tranquillity and Chastity. Under these virtues, he lists certain precepts, which we may also call maxims. Kant would have. Thus we find under Chastity the rather curious maxim: 'Rarely use venery but for health or offspring, never to dullness, weakness, or the injury of your own or another's peace or reputation.' And under Order: 'Let all things have their places, let each part of your business have its time.' Ben wants to build his character using maxims such as these. But before he engages on the project, he asks a friend, who on the whole approves, but tells him that he has forgotten to include another important maxim, namely Humility. Ben is not sure about Humility, but includes it against his better judgement. Late in life, after having meticulously kept a book on his progress towards his character, it turns out that humility is unachievable for him.

Benjamin Franklin, for that is who 'Ben' was, never took to being humble. Should Humility have been included? Indeed, should all the virtues and their corresponding maxims have been included as specifically moral maxims? Probably not! Some of them are maxims of dietetics, others are maxims of social intercourse, while some are indeed moral maxims. Kant's categorical imperative is concerned first and foremost with evaluating maxims of this sort. And the list Kant himself formulated was rather shorter than that of Ben. Indeed, as he says in his *Anthropology from a Pragmatic Point of View* (VII 295):

The sole proof a man's consciousness affords him that he has character is his having made it his supreme maxim to be truthful, both in his admission to himself and in his conduct toward every other man. And since having character is both the minimum that can be required of a reasonable man and the maximum of inner worth (of human dignity), to be a man of principles (to have determinate character) it must be possible for the most ordinary human reason and yet, according to its dignity, surpass the greatest talent.

Kant gives in his lectures other lists of maxims that will make for a good character, but they are always rather short, and truthfulness, or perhaps better, integrity, is always central in them. In any case, there appears to me little reason to suppose that for Kant there are thousands of maxims necessary, and that we cannot act rationally without worrying about the moral worthiness of every act we commit. His focus is not on the particular acts. Rather, it is on character as 'the practically consistent way of thinking in accordance with unchangeable maxims' (V 152).

Kant, while not trying in his metaphysics of morals to help someone like young Benjamin, intends to spell out the principle that any such evaluation must follow. No less, no more. Franklin probably would have been appalled by Kant's rigorism, but I believe he would have learned from his discussion of the moral principles. Perhaps we are in a similar situation.

4 SOME CONCLUSIONS

If we wish to translate Kant's pure moral philosophy into something more practical, that is, if we wish to do moral psychology of the Kantian sort or apply his pure moral philosophy, we should pay heed to what Kant says about character and therefore also to his lectures on anthropology. Kant's philosophical development can thus tell us something about Kant's 'applied' ethics. And one of the conclusions we seem to have to draw is that Kant's ethics is fundamentally an ethics of character or a virtue ethics, for this would appear to be just the converse of saying that the ethics Kant started out from is a type of ethics of character or virtue ethics.

However, it appears to me that this would be a mistake. Kant's published texts were neither intended to offer nor do offer a theory that can usefully be described as 'virtue ethics'. They were intended to offer something much more general, namely the beginnings of a 'metaphysics of morals' or a fundamental discussion of the general framework of morals. This is a claim that is per se neither new nor startling. It only needs to be emphasized in this context.[35] Indeed, contemporary discussions which ascribe to Kant's published writings on morals a kind of virtue ethics confuse different levels of discourse that Kant meant to keep separate, namely the level of everyday morality and the rational and *a priori* account of morality, which is freed of anything that might be empirical and anthropological. For this reason, they distort his view of the virtues.

---

[35] Whether or not Kant succeeded in the task he set for himself is a difficult question (and one that I will not address). See also what I say about the presuppositions of this chapter. In some sense, claim (i) follows immediately from these premises.

'Virtue' or '*Tugend*' does not play a significant role in Kant's *Groundwork*
While it does play a role in the *Critique of Practical Reason* within the limits
of the discussion of the postulates, it is not itself a specific topic of
discussion. While Kant explicitly claims that 'virtue is the greatest that
finite practical reason can achieve', it would be a mistake to interpret this as
evidence for the view that virtue should have played a more important place
in his books, for it is just because virtue is (only) the greatest good for
a specific kind of reason, namely our own, that it is not a topic of pure
philosophy.[36] Kant makes this very clear in the early lectures on moral
philosophy, where he argues that any kind of doctrine of virtue cannot
capture moral philosophy as a whole:

> Ethics explained by a *doctrine of virtue* is good inasmuch as virtue belongs solely to
> the inner tribunal; but since virtue entails not just *morally good* actions, but at the
> same time the possibility of the opposite, and thus incorporates an inner struggle,
> this is therefore too narrow a concept, since we can also ascribe *ethics*, but not virtue
> (properly speaking) to the angels and to god, for in them there is assuredly holiness
> but not virtue.[37]

In this respect, virtue is similar to piety. Both concern internal matters and
consist in dispositions. They differ 'not in actions, but in their motivating
grounds'. In virtue the motivating ground is morality or the 'good disposition' alone. In piety there are other reasons. But piety does not only not
exclude virtue; it actually demands it (XXVII 300). Virtue is something
essentially human, and just for this reason it cannot serve as a central
concept in a 'pure moral philosophy that is completely cleared of everything
which can only be empirical and anthropological'.

There is also a less theological argument that can be found in his
reflections on moral philosophy. Virtue cannot express 'quite accurately
the notion of moral goodness' because it has to do with the 'strength in
mastering and overcoming' ourselves, i.e. with our moral disposition
(XXVII 300). But this effort presupposes that we know already what it is
that we must do, or as Kant would say: what our duty is.[38] Virtues lead to
duties of virtues (*Tugendpflichten*) and, as should be clear from premise
(ii) referred to above, the duty is more fundamental. Ultimately morality is a

---

[36] *CpV* V 33; in the *Groundwork* the word appears only ten times. In the second *Critique* Kant addresses
the question of the relation of happiness and virtue.

[37] XXVII 13; see also *MdS* VI 379 and VI 383, where Kant argues that for finite holy beings there is no
doctrine of virtue but only a doctrine of morals.

[38] XXIII 375: 'Since virtue is only the moral strength of the human being in following his end that is at
the same time his duty, it already presupposes the knowledge (*Erkenntnis*) of his duty and needs thus
no metaphysical foundation. It lies already in the doctrine of morals in general.'

function of duty, not of virtue. Still, it is important to insist here that they are duties of virtue, i.e. duties that have an essential relation to the virtues, and one might say that one of the criteria of success of this chapter consists in whether I am able to show why the duties of which Kant speaks in the *Groundwork* and the second *Critique* are duties of virtue.

In any case, just as 'a science of customs is not yet a theory of virtue', so 'virtue is not yet morality' (XXVII 300). On the other hand, virtue is not unimportant, because it is the ability to overcome the inclination of evil 'on moral principles' (XXVII 463). It is 'the moral perfection of man. To virtue we attach power, strength and authority. It is a victory over inclination' (XXVII 465). It is also 'the greatest worth of the person' (XXIX 600). For this reason Kant claims it is important that we believe in the reality or possibility of virtue and do not simply suppose that it cannot exist. To argue that virtue is impossible would just be misanthropic and amount to what he calls 'moral unbelief' (XXVII 316). Still, in another passage he characterizes virtue as an idea, saying that 'nobody can possess true virtue' and that it is just as uncommon to hear someone called virtuous as it is to hear someone called wise (XXVII 463). The claim seems to be that it is not just an idea.

To sum up: virtue is something human, perhaps even all-too-human. It is a notion that gives us a preliminary idea of morality that must be discussed in anthropological contexts. Already in his announcement of his lectures in 1765 Kant said as much when he proclaimed that he intended to make clear what his method is 'by historically and philosophically considering within the doctrine of virtue always what actually takes place before indicating what should happen'. The customs and virtues introduce his truly ethical concerns, which have to do with moral principles. In the terminology of his mature works this means: first comes anthropology and then comes morality. Indeed, Kant worries as late as 1785 that 'morality' may not be the best word for indicating what he is after, but he is sure that 'we cannot take virtue to do so' (XXVII 300). Put differently, the concept of 'virtue' does not belong among those concepts that have been sufficiently cleansed of everything that may be only empirical in nature. In fact, it may belong among those that cannot be so cleansed. Being closely related to 'character', it also finds its rational analogue in the good will.

On the other hand, Kant's published texts do presuppose or start out from a particular kind of virtue ethics. Put differently, his general discussion of the framework of morals is based on a certain conception of morals in which virtues played a fundamental role. The doctrine of the virtues is important in describing the common moral praxis but it is not part of the science of morals. Only beings like us can or need be virtuous. Therefore we may hope that Kant's theory has some relevance for the virtues.[39] However, the virtue ethics presupposed by Kant is most definitely not Aristotelian in character.[40] Rather, it is a variety of the kind of ethics prevalent in Europe and North America during the eighteenth century. It possessed (almost inevitably) some Aristotelian features, but it was much more influenced by Christian and Stoic doctrines and imbued with local Prussian and German convictions, such as those of Gellert, for instance. Not all of these influences were philosophically desirable. In any case, an investigation of the relations of Kant's moral philosophy to his minor contemporaries remains a *desideratum*.

One of the lessons of this historical look at Kant's development should be that we must be careful when we translate Kant's 'metaphysics of morals' into 'Kantian morality'. Thus, Bernard Williams' accusation that Kant neglected character turns out to be simply false. Kant did not ignore it, but started out from it, even if his view of character was in important ways different from that of Williams because he thought, like many eighteenth-century thinkers, that the fundamental project of any human being had to include as an important part a moral dimension. I don't think that he was wrong in this.

---

[39] How could this be otherwise in an author that wrote a book on the '*The Primary Metaphysical Grounds of Virtue*'? Also, the very structure of the *Groundwork of the Metaphysics of Morals* makes clear that he starts from 'ordinary rational knowledge of morality', goes on to a certain kind of 'moral philosophy' and its relation to 'metaphysics of morals', and ends in a critique of pure practical reason. However, the description of the 'ordinary rational knowledge of morals' covers up the importance of virtue somewhat by emphasizing 'will' and 'duty'. One of the tasks of the chapter will be to show that there is no real opposition between talking about 'will' and 'duty' while at the same time talking of 'virtue'.

[40] I would suggest there are also the bare beginnings of a new version of a universalist virtue ethics that would be appropriate for a cosmopolitan or a citizen of the world. The germs of it can be found in Kant's writings on history. It would not be entirely inappropriate to call these 'virtues of the Enlightenment'. However, Kant himself failed to develop these because he believed not in the progress of individuals but the progress of the human race. But this is the subject of another paper.

Happiness in the Groundwork

Alison Hills

I WHAT IS HAPPINESS?

Kant begins the *Groundwork* by putting happiness in its place. Happiness is not unconditionally good. Your happiness is not good unless you are worthy of happiness, and you are not worthy of happiness unless you have a good will. Right from the start, Kant has made it clear that the most important concept in ethics will be the good will, and he devotes the remainder of the *Groundwork* to elaborating and explaining what it is. This does not leave much room for happiness. But Kant does not neglect it altogether. In fact, he makes a number of intriguing suggestions, both about what happiness really is and the reasons, if any, we have to pursue it.

Kant first introduces happiness in the *Groundwork* as 'that complete wellbeing and satisfaction with one's condition' (*G* IV 393), and a little later links it with 'enjoyment of life' (*G* IV 396). What is satisfaction? We might think of it as a mental state of pleasure: a life of happiness is then a life of pleasure. Kant never explicitly explains what he takes satisfaction to be, but he does introduce a second conception of happiness, on which he concentrates in the rest of the *Groundwork*. On this second view, happiness is getting what you want, or more precisely, the idea of happiness is the idea of the sum total of inclinations (*G* IV 399, see also *G* IV 405, *G* IV 418). Obviously, getting what you want is not the same as a mental state of pleasure, so Kant's two conceptions of happiness are not equivalent if we understand satisfaction in that way. But instead, we might think of satisfaction as a state in which you are satisfied, in the sense that your desires are fulfilled, and there is nothing further that you want. You would not change your state or your circumstances, even if you could. Understood in this way, the two ideas of happiness do turn out to be the same: happiness is satisfaction, where this is precisely having all your desires met.[1]

---

[1] Kant has an interesting conception of the relationship between pleasure and desire. He believes that there is an important connection between pleasure and the formation of new desires; for example, you

Kant's conception of happiness is not unusual: many philosophers have espoused 'desire-satisfaction' theories of happiness or wellbeing, though many believe that the satisfaction of only some, rather than all of our desires, contributes to happiness, namely those that are in the right way 'connected' with our life. For example, the satisfaction of your desire that some distant stranger's life goes well might not contribute to your happiness. Kant does not restrict his account in this way. Kant is not typical, however, in his deep pessimism about our prospects for happiness. We cannot, for a start, know what will make us happy. Of course, we cannot know *a priori* what desires we will have, and so what will count towards our happiness. But even when we have experience of life and of the kind of things that we like, we still are at a loss (*G* IV 418):

> Now, it is impossible for the most insightful and at the same time most powerful but still finite being to frame for himself a determinate concept of what he really wills here. If he wills riches, how much anxiety, envy and intrigue might he not bring upon himself in this way! If he wills a great deal of cognition and insight, that might become only an eye all the more acute to show him, as all the more dreadful, ills that are now concealed from him and that cannot be avoided, or to burden his desires which already give him enough to do, with still more needs. If he wills a long life, who will guarantee him that it would not be a long misery! If he at least wills health, how often has not bodily discomfort kept someone from excesses into which unlimited health would have let him fall, and so forth.

There are many things that we might think are sufficiently important so that, if only we could achieve them, we would arrive at a state of contentment and would want for nothing more. Kant is sceptical that we are ever right about this. When we actually gain these things – long life, health, knowledge, wealth – we typically find them disappointing, and immediately acquire further, as yet unsatisfied desires, for something different.

Our conception of happiness is subject to change throughout our life, Kant thinks, as we change our mind about what we want, and acquire new desires. So genuine happiness, complete contentment, is always out of our reach.

2 THE VALUE OF HAPPINESS

The good will is unconditionally valuable, esteemed beyond all comparison, according to Kant. It is the condition of the value of happiness: your

---

normally form a desire that p when you expect pleasure if p; you normally desire pleasures to continue, and if you find a state unpleasant, you normally desire it to cease (*CpV* V 22–3, *CpV* V 25; *CU* V 231; *Anth.* VII 230–5). In contrast to some commentators, I do not think that Kant believes that all desires are desires for pleasure, however. See A. E. Hills, 'Kant on Happiness and Reason', *History of Philosophy Quarterly* (2006), 243–62.

happiness is good provided that you are indeed worthy of it.[2] In the *Critique of Practical Reason*, Kant goes further, claiming that happiness together with virtue is in fact the highest good (*CpV* V 110–13). Why does Kant think that happiness by itself is not good? He says that happiness can produce 'boldness' and 'overboldness', concerned that it can lead one to complacency and wrongdoing. Moreover, he suggests that no impartial observer would approve of a person's being entirely happy if that person was not good.

Kant also appeals to a teleological argument to try to show that happiness is not the highest good in human life and the purpose to which we should all strive. The purpose of reason cannot be to pursue our happiness, he argues, since reason is so poorly designed for that task.[3] Instinct would be a much better guide to happiness. Since the function of reason cannot be to pursue happiness, it must have some other role, and that is, he claims, to become a good will. Virtue, not happiness, is the ultimate purpose of human life (*G* IV 395–7).

This argument obviously depends on a number of highly controversial claims. In the first place, Kant has to establish that using reason is not a good method of becoming happy. There are perhaps a number of considerations that Kant might have had in mind here. First, he might appeal to the 'paradox of hedonism'. It is widely believed that the best way to become happy is to aim at some specific goals – to have a successful career, or to enjoy yourself with your friends, for example – and as a consequence, you will find yourself happy. By contrast, aiming directly for happiness and reasoning with that purpose in mind tends to be counter-productive. The harder you try to be happy, the less successful you will be. In fact, Kant might well insist that aiming directly for happiness and reasoning with that aim in mind is not really possible for us in any case. For, as we have seen, he thinks that happiness is not a clear aim at all (see *G* IV 399 and IV 418). We may have some idea of what will make us happy, but we cannot be certain of it, and our conception of what happiness consists in for us almost inevitably changes through time, as we come to want different things. It is not surprising that success in achieving this protean, indeterminate goal eludes us.

---

[2] I take Kant to mean that happiness is not objectively good unless it is deserved; he thinks that we all want our own happiness whether or not we deserve it.

[3] Interestingly, this seems to be something about which Kant changed his mind. Initially, he thought that freedom and reason were valuable because they provided a more secure basis for happiness, as Guyer notes (P. Guyer, *Kant on Freedom, Law and Happiness* (Cambridge University Press, 2000), p. 108). Kant believed that reason could be useful in achieving happiness through the process of eliminating unattainable desires, though later he realized that desires can and often do persist despite the fact we have decided that we will not or cannot fulfil them.

Secondly, Kant insists that the more we reason, the worse the problem becomes. For it is undeniable that anyone who cultivates their reason tends to develop new desires. Whilst all of us have the most basic desires, for food, for shelter, perhaps for money, if we did not have or use our reason, we would have no further desires. And though we would not always be able to satisfy these more basic desires, of course, they are not too demanding. The kinds of goods needed to satisfy them are not complicated nor are they, except in unfortunate circumstances, particularly difficult to find. So it is not unreasonable for Kant to suggest that, in the absence of practical reason, we would have a few fairly simple and basic desires, and that we might have had instincts that enabled us to do whatever we needed to satisfy them (G IV 395). Whilst we would certainly not be guaranteed happiness, for we might be faced with disease or a shortage of food, nevertheless, happiness would not be too distant.

But having reason, especially practical reason, changes everything (G IV 418). In the first place, it can transform our original basic desires. For reason enables us to make comparisons with others, and we see not just whether we have food or money and whether they do, but whether we have more than them. And this enables us to form a new set of desires, not just desires for food or money, but for more food or money than others. We are now competitive; we have formed new desires that are less easy to satisfy than those basic desires with which we began.

In addition, cultivating reason can gives us desires in wholly new areas. We may well become interested in the arts and sciences, either in understanding complex and sophisticated works of art and scientific theories, or more ambitiously, in contributing towards the arts and sciences ourselves. It is, of course, extremely difficult to make a genuinely valuable work of art or scientific advance, so many of those who would like to do so will finish disappointed and frustrated. Appreciating the work of others is less demanding, but is still not an easy task. Once again, we have gained new desires that are not easy to satisfy.

According to Kant's conception of happiness, complete happiness is the satisfaction of all of your desires. As you acquire more desires that are less easy to satisfy, happiness eludes you. Even if, by cultivating reason, overall the number of desires that you satisfy increases and you begin to satisfy some more sophisticated desires, this need not make you happier, according to Kant, because you will have many unfulfilled desires that remain. Those of us who reflect on this state of affairs, Kant thinks, have a tendency to hate reason and to envy those who have not cultivated their reason at all but have remained more or less under the guidance of instinct, with a few straight-forward and easily satisfied goals (*G* IV 395).

It is illuminating to compare Kant's argument that happiness is not the sole purpose of our lives with Mill's defence of happiness in chapter 2 of *Utilitarianism*.[4] Mill tries to answer critics who say that happiness cannot be our ultimate goal by arguing that they mistake what happiness really is. Our higher faculties, our capacity to reason, mean that many types of pleasure are available to us that animals could not appreciate. These may be 'higher pleasures', pleasures that those who have experienced more than one type of pleasure prefer. Kant, of course, would be sceptical that higher pleasures play an important role in our happiness, given his view that reflection on types of pleasure and our forming desires for some rather than others is not a particularly good guide to what will make us happy in the end. We may prefer poetry to pushpin, but there is no guarantee that a life of poetry will make us happy.

Mill is well aware that having higher faculties can be a double-edged sword. They may open up to us the potential for higher pleasures, but they make us vulnerable to extra types of suffering: the pains of anticipation, of memory, of failure. But he insists that no one who had higher faculties would choose to be without them: 'No intelligent human being would consent to be a fool, no instructed person would be an ignoramus ... It is better to be a human being dissatisfied than a pig satisfied; better to be Socrates dissatisfied than a fool satisfied' (Mill, *Utilitarianism*, pp. 9–10).

Kant would agree. Although reason is not particularly useful in the pursuit of happiness, he thinks, it does not follow that we would be better without it or that we would choose to get rid of it if we could. He might well concede that those who have cultivated their reason do not, all things considered, envy those humans who tend to act more on instinct. What he emphasizes, however, is that our judgement that it is better to be Socrates than a fool is not based on which of the two we consider happiest. We would choose reason, but not for the sake of happiness. What follows, in his view, is that we have a purpose in life that is more important than happiness, namely to produce a good will that is the condition of the value of happiness and which, when the two conflict, is always more important.

Mill responds that there is more than one sense of happiness here: the pleasure or contentment of which a fool is capable and a second conception by which we judge Socrates to be happier than the fool, even though he is

---

[4] J. S. Mill, *Utilitarianism* (originally published in *Fraser's Magazine*, London, 1861; reprinted Hackett, 1979).

dissatisfied. So the dispute between Kant and Mill turns on whether we should accept this second sense of happiness, and agree that, in that sense, human beings are happier than pigs. There are problems with this suggestion. The first sense of happiness, understood as pleasure (Mill) or contentment where this is explained as the satisfaction of all one's desires (Kant), is perfectly clear. What exactly is the second sense? Mill does not elaborate, except by means of the idea of 'higher pleasures'. But it is not obvious that a life of higher pleasures will really make us happy, in Kant's sense of leaving us without unfulfilled desires. Kant can properly claim that the first sense of happiness is closer to what most people understand by happiness, that it is conceptually clear, and that nothing is gained by trying to extend the concept to cover anything in our lives that could conceivably be of value or worthy of choice. Once we limit happiness in this way, we are forced to concede that if it is indeed better to be a human being than a pig, this need not be because human beings are happier, but because there is something other than happiness that is valuable.[5]

3 THE PURSUIT OF HAPPINESS

Since happiness is not unconditionally good and it cannot be known *a priori*, it cannot ground categorical imperatives.[6] So your prudential reasons, your reasons to pursue your own happiness, cannot yield categorical imperatives. Kant in fact suggests that they are expressed as a special form of hypothetical imperative. Most hypothetical imperatives require you to take the means to some end that you have set for yourself, where this end is contingent: it is one that you might not have chosen, and similarly, other people may or may not set themselves the same end. So you should go to the theatre because you want to see that latest production, but you might have chosen instead to stay at home and others might never adopt this end or pursue it in their whole lives.

---

[5] This is, of course, the conclusion that Kant wanted to reach, and the argument is quite convincing. But it is not the argument that Kant himself uses. Instead, as we have seen, he makes an appeal to teleology. The teleological argument is problematic, insofar as we might question the crucial assumption that reason has a function, or that, if it does, its function is anything other than to help us to stay alive and to reproduce. Kant clearly endorsed the argument, however.

[6] Kant actually gives a number of different arguments against the possibility of categorical imperatives based on happiness, including that happiness is desired, and that the components of happiness, desires, are empirical or 'sensuous'. I discuss in much more detail the strengths and weaknesses of all of Kant's arguments that happiness-based reasons for action are not categorical in my 'Kant on Happiness and Reason'.

According to Kant, happiness is different (*G* IV 415):

There is, however, *one* end that can be presupposed as actual in the case of all rational beings (insofar as imperatives apply to them, namely as dependent beings), and therefore one purpose that they not merely *could* have but that we can safely presuppose they all actually *do have* by a natural necessity, and that purpose is *happiness*.

Since we all do aim for happiness, our prudential reasons are *assertoric* imperatives, a hypothetical imperative requiring us to take the means to some end which all of us have set for ourselves.

Why does Kant think that happiness is a 'naturally necessary' end for all of us? Most commentators on Kant have been bemused.[7] The problem is that the most obvious ways of interpreting the claim conflict with other views that Kant holds. For example, happiness might be a naturally necessary end for us in the sense that, necessarily, we all desire happiness. Kant does think that there are some universal natural desires, such as a desire for power. But Kant is not speaking of desires here, but of ends that we have willed: the hypothetical imperative governs our will, not our desires. Willing an end is something that we can freely choose to do, or not to do. It simply does not make sense to say that we might will an end by natural necessity (*MdS* VI 385). So, in particular, happiness cannot be an end that we will as a matter of natural necessity.

An alternative reading has been proposed by Allen Wood.[8] Perhaps happiness is a *rationally* necessary end for us. We would be free to choose to pursue happiness, or not, but not to do so would be irrational. In this regard Wood's suggestion is an improvement on the natural necessity interpretation, because it does not imply that we are impelled by nature to choose happiness. But it obviously fits badly with Kant's emphatic assertion that happiness is not an end of reason.[9]

In other work, I have argued that we can make sense of Kant's conception of assertoric imperatives by thinking of the pursuit of happiness as a way that someone who chooses to try to satisfy her desires can unify herself as an

---

[7] C. M. Korsgaard, 'Reply to Ginsborg, Schneewind and Guyer', *Ethics* 109 (1998), 49–66; A. Wood *Kant's Ethical Thought* (Cambridge University Press, 1999), p. 67; R. Johnson, 'Happiness as a Natural End' in M. Timmons (ed.), *Kant's Metaphysics of Morals: Interpretative Essays* (Oxford University Press, 2002); H. J. Paton, *The Categorical Imperative* (4th edn, London: Hutchison, 1963), p. 127.

[8] A. Wood, *Kant's Ethical Thought* (Cambridge University Press, 1999), p. 66.

[9] *G* IV 18–19. See also C. M. Korsgaard, *The Myth of Egoism*, The Lindley Lectures (University of Kansas, 1999), p. 17; Johnson, 'Happiness as a Natural End'.

agent through time.[10] Here, I want to consider a slightly different route to a similar conclusion, using Nagel's argument in *The Possibility of Altruism* that prudence is based on the generality of reasons.[11]

4 WILL, DESIRE AND THE GOOD

According to Kant, action is based on maxims, subjective principles that the agent wills. A maxim consists in an end that the agent has set for herself, and an action that aims to make progress towards achieving that end. If a will were entirely determined by reason, that agent would always do what was morally required and would never feel any contrary impulses at all. Doing what was morally right would not feel like a duty, in the sense of an action one is compelled to do no matter what one desires, for she would never want anything else. So the moral law would not consist of genuine imperatives for her. Someone like this would be what Kant calls a holy will.

We are quite different from holy wills, for we have many inclinations that conflict both with one another and with what we are morally required to do. We do not ever directly act on these desires, according to Kant. Instead, we choose whether or not to set the object of some desire as an end and pursue it: our action is always based on willed maxims, not desires. But desires are incentives for us to act, so when there are no competing considerations, no moral requirements, for example, we usually do choose to try to get what we want (sometimes we even do so when we ought to be doing our duty instead).[12]

Some commentators interpret Kant as claiming that whenever we will an end as part of our maxim, we regard that end as good.[13] In the *Groundwork*, however, Kant emphasizes the difference between determining your will by reason and determining it by desire, suggesting that in the former case alone do you determine your will by the good (*G* IV 413): 'Practical good, however, is that which determines the will by means of representations of reason ... It is distinguished from the *agreeable*, as that which influences the will only by means of feeling from merely subjective causes, which hold only for the senses of this or that one, and not as a principle of reason, which holds for everyone'.

---

[10]   Hills, 'Kant on Happiness and Reason'.
[11]   T. Nagel, *The Possibility of Altruism* (Princeton University Press, 1978).
[12]   In fact, in the *Critique of Practical Reason*, Kant makes an even stronger claim, that our desires, which ground our needs, must be acknowledged (*CpV* V 61): 'The human being is a being with needs, insofar as he belongs to the sensible world, and to this extent his reason certainly had a commission from the side of his sensibility which it cannot refuse, to attend to its interest, and to form practical maxims with a view to happiness in this life.' This does not mean, of course, that we are forced to act on our desires, but that, other things being equal, we will do so.
[13]   Wood, *Kant's Ethical Thought*, pp. 50–5.

But though we may in one case choose our maxims with reference to what is (morally) good, and in the other with reference to pleasure or desire-satisfaction, it does not follow that we regard only those ends chosen in the first way as good or worth pursuing. When we choose to adopt as an end either the object of a desire or what reason requires of us, we might regard each as worth pursuing.

In the *Critique of Practical Reason*, Kant makes his position clearer (*CpV* V 63):

The end itself, the gratification we seek, is in the latter case not a good but a wellbeing, not a concept of reason but an empirical concept of an object of feeling; but the use of means to it, that is, the action, is nevertheless called good (because rational reflection is required for it), not, however, good absolutely but only with reference to our sensibility, with respect to its feeling of pleasure or displeasure.

When we choose to set the object of our desire as our end, Kant thinks that we regard the action that we take to try to achieve that end as good, not good absolutely, but good with respect to getting what we want (we tend to expect pleasure when we get what we want). But if the action is good because it will satisfy a desire, then we must regard satisfying that desire as worthwhile also (though of course, we need not think that it is uncondi-tionally good, or worth pursuing in all circumstances). A means to an end cannot be good unless the end itself is worth pursuing. So it seems to be true in Kant's view that when we set the objects of our desires as our ends, we regard those objects as worth pursuing and ourselves as having some reason to do so.[14]

But, of course, you can pursue some desire and regard satisfying that desire as good without thinking that it is good to satisfy your other desires, either ones that you now have or ones that you will have in the future. So even if you choose to act on your desires, it does not seem to follow that you must set happiness as one of your ends. Of course, you might choose to set it

---

[14] Kant does not say much about reasons for action and their connection with maxims. But I assume here that if you regard the end that you have set for yourself as good, then you are committed to there being some reason at least for you to pursue that end. So on my interpretation, whenever you act on a maxim, you must regard yourself as having some reason to pursue the end you have set for yourself, and some instrumental reason to take action to achieve that end. As I have indicated, this is a common interpretation of Kant's action theory (see, e.g. Wood, *Kant's Ethical Thought*, pp. 50–5), but there is an obvious objection to the combination of claims: first, that action is always based on a maxim, and secondly, that we always regard the end of our maxim as (in some sense) good. For is it not possible to act in a way that you yourself regard as utterly worthless or pointless? This is a controversial matter, and though I have some sympathy with the objection to Kant, I cannot pursue it further here. Instead, I will continue to set out my interpretation of Kant's conception of happiness and of our reasons to pursue happiness, making the same assumptions as he did about the nature of action.

as an end, and therefore acknowledge that you are required to take means to become happier. But it is still difficult to understand why such hypothetical imperatives have a special status, why they are assertoric imperatives.

5 REASONS, DESIRES AND THE FUTURE

In *The Possibility of Altruism*, before turning his attention to altruism, Nagel focuses on prudence, which he understands as 'practical foresight'. Prudence, therefore, is a matter of anticipating and acknowledging reasons for action that you will have in the future (whether based on your own interests or other considerations). Nagel argues that this prudential concern need not be explained by a specific desire that you have right now, a desire to pay attention to the future. Instead, he argues that prudential reasons depend on the connection between the present and the future, and in particular, that your future forms part of your own life.[15]

Reasons for action must be general. It is impossible for something to be a reason that in principle has force only at particular times, addressed to particular people. You, here and now, cannot have a reason to brush your teeth before going to bed, for example, unless it is the kind of consideration that can have force more generally: other people may also have reason to do the same, for example. Nagel emphasizes this aspect of reasons, but it is also something with which Kant would be sympathetic, given his views that permissible maxims must be universalizable (*G* IV 421). Usually this is understood as a requirement that others must be able to adopt that maxim at the same time as oneself, but of course it also includes the requirement that you must be able to adopt that maxim at another time.

The generality of reasons with regard to time is, according to Nagel, the source of prudential reason. Suppose that in the future you will have a reason for action, for example, you will have a reason to be a policeman, since this an important job which you will find more rewarding than any other career open to you. You cannot be a policeman then, however, unless you join up now and go through a rigorous training programme. Do you have reason to apply to the programme? Nagel suggests that you do. It is tenselessly true, he claims, that in the future, you have a reason to be a

---

[15] Nagel, *The Possibility of Altruism*, pp. 33–46. Nagel argues that appeal to a present desire to explain prudential reasons for action cannot be correct, in the first place because the desire could be missing, yet people would still have prudential reasons for action, but also because it is not clear what the content of such a desire would be. It would also, in Nagel's view, have counter-intuitive consequences (for example, present desires with future objects would be weighed against the desires that you will have in the future, which he takes to be a mistake).

policeman. As a consequence, he thinks, you have a derivative reason now to promote your being a policeman then. Since going through the training programme is a necessary condition for that, you have a derivative reason to do so.[16]

Suppose that you do not consider yourself to have any reason whatsoever to go through a boring and lengthy training programme. This is not because you have no idea that in the future you will want to and have good reason to be a policeman. You are perfectly well aware that this is the best career for you. You know that in the future, you will have a reason to be a policeman. And you know, too, that you cannot be a policeman without training. But you cannot see either of those facts as giving you a reason to do anything now. You know that you will regret not going on the programme, and that later on when joining the police force is closed to you, you will wish you had acted differently. But future regret and future wishes are not, you think, of any significance with regard to reasons for action in the present.

What is wrong with this? There is a very clear sense in which you are not taking seriously a future reason that you have. You are not allowing it to influence your decisions or actions, nor acknowledging that it generates derivative reasons, such as reasons to take means to satisfy it. You fail to regard that future reason as a real reason, in the sense in which you regard present reasons for action as real.

But reasons have to be general, they have to apply at least in principle to times other than the present, if they are to be genuine reasons for action. It follows that reasons that will apply to you in the future are genuine reasons. Failing to treat them as such, not through ignorance of the reasons that apply to you in the future, but simply from a failure to acknowledge that they are binding on you, conflicts with your recognition of and response to present reasons. If you treat reasons that currently apply to you as considerations that should influence you, you should treat reasons that will apply to you in the same way.

If you do not do so, you must either have failed to recognize that reasons are general in the appropriate sense, or you must think that there is something about reasons that will apply to you in the future that means that they do not and should not really influence you. Why might you treat future reasons as insignificant? One possibility is that you do not regard these reasons as genuine because you do not think that they will apply to you, because the person in the future that they bind will not be you. In other words, you might not regard yourself as a persisting individual, who is alive

16 Nagel, *The Possibility of Altruism*, p. 48.

now and who will be in the future. There are interesting and difficult metaphysical questions to be raised about persistence through time, but I will leave this problem aside, as it is not the basis of most people's imprudence.

On the other hand, even if you do think of yourself as persisting, you might think that the present has some special significance, such that reasons applying to you now have a weight and force that reasons applying to you in the future do not. There is clearly something peculiar about such an attitude. Nagel argues that since you are an individual that persists through time, you should identify with yourself in the future (and the past), since these are simply later (or earlier) stages of yourself. Furthermore, you ought to accord equal status in practical terms to these different times. There is no interesting difference between you right now and you later, except for the temporal difference, which ought not to make a difference to your status.

What does it mean, to accord equal status to different times in practical terms? It must be the case that what is true or false of the present can be true or false of other times too, in the same sense.[17] Suppose that you now want to eat some ice cream today. There are no relevant moral considerations, you have competing desires, such as not to eat between meals, but you choose to set eating ice cream as your end. Then you must regard your getting the ice cream and eating it today as in some sense good, according to Kant. Now suppose that you confidently predict that you will want to eat some ice cream tomorrow. Does anything follow about what you should will? You have committed yourself to the claim that your eating ice cream today is good, having set that end for yourself on the basis that you wanted

---

[17] Nagel sets out his conception of this as follows. In practical terms, statements about reasons for action in the future must have the same sense as statements about reasons in the future. We can make statements about future reasons for action that are tenseless or that are tensed. A tensed statement might be: 'You will have reason to be a policeman in four years.' The same content can be expressed with a tenseless statement about that time, together with a statement connecting that time with the present: 'At the age of 25, you have reason to be a policeman. You will be 25 in four years.' Nagel argues that any tensed statement which cannot be understood as implying a tenseless statement about the same subject, plus a condition which makes the tense appropriate, suggests the existence of an area in which the sense of one's equal reality over time is defective. Nagel emphasizes that it should be possible to accommodate practical judgements to the standpoint of temporal neutrality. But present tense practical judgements possess motivational content, that is, the acknowledgement of a justification for promoting a certain end. But then the tenseless judgement must have motivational content too. It must include an acknowledgement of a justification for promoting the relevant end, tenselessly specified. (Nagel, *The Possibility of Altruism*, pp. 47–76). I do not intend to defend the details of Nagel's account of prudence here, in particular, whether it is really part of the generality of reasons that in the present you must recognize reasons that will bind you in the future as having some force on you. If this basic idea is right, however – and it is, I think, very similar to Kant's conception of the universalizability of reasons – it can help us understand Kant's conception of prudence.

ice cream today. You must therefore regard yourself as having reason to eat ice cream today. But if you think that it is worth eating ice cream today because you want to, then surely you cannot claim that eating ice cream tomorrow, on the basis that you will want to do that then, is entirely worthless. Reasons are general, and must apply to times other than the present, and so if you do regard yourself as having reasons for action that are based on your desires, it is not consistent to regard them as based on your current but not your future desires.[18]

It follows that you should at the least try not to rule out the possibility that you can satisfy the desire for ice cream that you anticipate having tomorrow: you might, for example, deliberately refrain from eating all your ice cream supplies today. Do you need to go further and ensure that you can satisfy that desire, or more ambitiously, that you will maximally satisfy your present and future desires? This depends on how we understand the thesis that reasons are general. In the strongest sense, it follows that if you regard yourself as having reason to satisfy any desire, you have equal reason to satisfy any other desire, and you ought to decide what to do by working out what will maximize your desire-satisfaction. A much weaker claim would be that if you regard yourself as having reason to satisfy a desire, you should acknowledge that other desires, both now and in the future, have some normative claim on you as well. You should try not to pursue your current desires in such a way that this rules out satisfying the desires that you think that you will have in the future. But you need not be committed to treating them equally, or satisfying them maximally. This weaker claim is more plausible as an interpretation of Kant's views about prudence, since he never suggests that one must attempt to satisfy as many desires as possible.[19]

In most cases, however, the question of what you should do is much more complicated. It may be difficult or even impossible to satisfy all of your present desires, let alone desires that you may have in the future. So you will have to decide which to pursue, thus constructing a conception of your

---

[18] Unless, of course, there is some feature that distinguishes your desires in the future and your desires in the present that is normatively significant. If you did not really persist into the future, for example, that might be such a feature, since the future desires would not really be yours. But in the absence of such a feature, you should acknowledge that your future desires ground reasons for action if your present desires do.

[19] It follows that the satisfaction of your desires, or happiness, is not a first order end that you pursue directly, as you might pursue ice cream or a career in the police force. Instead, it is a second order end, that limits your pursuit of the first order ends you set for yourself. This is analogous to the role that duty plays in regulating your action, according to some recent interpretations of Kant by Herman and Baron (B. Herman, *The Practice of Moral Judgment* (Harvard University Press, 1993), pp. 14–22; M. Baron, *Kantian Ethics Almost Without Apology* (Ithaca, NY, London: Cornell University Press, 1995), pp. 129–32).

happiness: those desires whose satisfaction is most important to you. Moreover, you may not be at all certain what desires you will have in the future: will you really want ice cream every day? Sometimes you may predict that you will have a particular desire, but when the time comes you want something completely different. But without a clear and accurate picture of your future desires, it is not obvious how you should constrain the pursuit of your current desires. In other words, it is not clear what prudence requires of you. Which is just as Kant says.[20]

6 THE STATUS OF PRUDENTIAL REASON

If you accept Nagel's claims about the generality of reasons, think of yourself in practical terms as persisting through time, and choose to set the objects of your desires as your ends, then you are committed to constraining the pursuit of those desires with the remainder of the desires that you now have or expect to have. According to Kant, happiness is the total of your inclinations. Therefore, you are committed to regulating those of your actions based on your desires with your idea of happiness.

Happiness therefore has a special status compared with other desires you might have. In most cases, you are free to choose whether or not to set the object of any of your desires as your end. You do not have to will a maxim of eating ice cream or becoming a policeman unless you choose to do so. But you do have to acknowledge happiness as your end if you set the object of any desire as your end. Happiness is not usually an end that you directly pursue, on this view, but it is an end that constrains the pursuit of your other ends: it is not prudent to pursue ice cream without consideration of everything else you do or will want, even if right now you want a chocolate sundae very much indeed.

Prudential reasons do not generate categorical imperatives, because the requirement to set happiness as your end is only conditional, specifically, it is conditional on whether you set the objects of your desires as your ends. You are not required by reason to do that, though you are by no means forbidden from doing so either. Since the moral law is the law of reason, according to Kant, and moral duties are expressed in categorical impera-tives, happiness cannot be the basis of the moral law, and there must be a fundamental difference between happiness-based prudential reasons and moral reasons for action. Prudential reasons generate a kind of hypothetical imperative, since they are requirements that depend on your setting an end

---

[20] There are laws of morality, but there can be only 'counsels' of prudence (*G* IV 416).

for yourself. They are not the typical kind of hypothetical imperative, which requires you to take the means to an end that you have chosen, however. Instead, they are requirements to make happiness your end, in the sense that you ought to constrain the pursuit of the objects of your desires with regard to happiness, whenever you set the object of your desire as your end.

Kant claims that happiness can be presupposed as an end in all of us. But we are not required to set it as an end by nature (indeed this suggestion is incoherent), nor are we required by reason to pursue it. But we are required to do so if we set the objects of our desires as our ends. Not all rational agents will set the objects of their desires as their ends; in fact according to Kant, some rational agents do not even have desires that are separate from and can conflict with laws of reason. But any agent for whom the moral law grounds duties that they experience as genuine normative imperatives does, for it is their recognition that they must do what is morally right even if they want to do otherwise that gives moral duties the feel of requirements for them. So any agent who, like us, experiences moral duties as categorical imperatives will have ordinary desires whose objects they are likely to set as their ends.

It is therefore a reasonable assumption that creatures like us, who are subject to imperatives because we must obey the moral law whether or not we have conflicting desires, will have set happiness as our end. This is not strictly a matter of necessity, however. Kant was mistaken about that, or more generously, he wrote in a very compressed way that was very misleading. We are not required to set happiness as our end, but if we set the objects of desires as our ends, and it is reasonable to assume that we will, then we must set happiness as our end too.

7 CONCLUSION

Kant does not regard the pursuit of happiness as the central purpose of our life, and as a result he spends little time in the *Groundwork* explaining his conception of happiness and what really is its role. Nevertheless, the little that he does say is both interesting and suggestive, though it certainly cannot be easily understood. It requires the help of other texts, and even then there is need for some rational reconstruction of what Kant might have meant by his claim that happiness grounds assertoric reasons and is our end by natural necessity.

The interpretation of Kant's conception of happiness presented here suggests that it is a coherent and unusual variant of the common 'desire-satisfaction' theory of wellbeing. Kant's theory is untypical in that he allows that the satisfaction of any of one's desires can contribute to happiness, and he is more pessimistic than many about the role that reason can play. He regards happiness as contentment, having no further unfulfilled desires, and he is keenly aware that we have no real idea of what such a state would be like or how we could possibly achieve it. Happiness is also not something that we can or should pursue directly; rather its purpose is to regulate our pursuit of the objects of our desires that we have chosen as ends.

Nevertheless, he does not play down its significance altogether. For he still regards happiness as a good, if a conditional good, and one particularly important to creatures like ourselves who have many powerful desires. We set the objects of our desires as our ends and thereby regard them as good; as a consequence, we commit ourselves to regarding happiness too as good, and to setting that as an end as well. So prudential reasons have a status different from ordinary hypothetical imperatives. Though not every rational agent must pursue her happiness, it is nevertheless an extremely important end for dependent rational beings like ourselves.

CHAPTER 3

Acting from duty: inclination, reason and moral worth

Jens Timmermann

I MOTIVATIONAL RIGORISM AND KANT'S SEARCH FOR THE MORAL LAW

Section I of Kant's *Groundwork of the Metaphysics of Morals* is meant to lead us from our everyday conception of morality to the supreme principle of all moral action, officially christened the 'categorical imperative' some twenty Academy pages further into the treatise. It is quite striking that in this first section Kant dispenses with the notorious technical language that pervades not just other parts of the *Groundwork* but also most of the remaining philosophical writings of the critical period. The mere fact that *Groundwork* I is comparatively accessible does not, of course, make it straightforward or uncontroversial. Kant's readers are faced with, amongst other things, four unconvincing paragraphs on the natural purpose of practical reason (*G* IV 394–6), a crucial change of topic from good volition to acting from duty (*G* IV 397), an unstated 'first proposition' about moral value that has baffled generations of interpreters (presumably *G* IV 397–9), and a contentious shift from an allegedly unproblematic principle of practical universalizability to a substantive moral command (*G* IV 402).

Moreover, the first section features the most famous examples of what critics have dubbed Kant's 'motivational rigorism': the thesis that actions are morally good[1] only on condition that they are motivated by a sense of duty, rather than inclination.[2] The first case – the example of the 'shop-keeper' (*G* IV 397) – concerns a *higher-order* inclination that leads to action in conformity with duty. In the other three examples – the 'suicide', the

I should like to thank audiences at the universities of Bremen, California (Riverside), Cambridge, Göttingen, Halle/Wittenberg, Leiden, Notre Dame, St Andrews, Trier and Zurich for their helpful criticisms and comments on earlier drafts of this chapter.
[1] Or possess (positive) 'moral worth' or 'value' (*moralischer Wert*) – I shall use these expressions interchangeably.
[2] Later, action 'from duty' is equated with action done for the sake of, or out of reverence for, the moral law: *G* IV 400, cf. *G* IV 390.

'philanthropist' and the 'gout sufferer' (*G* IV 397–9) – there is initially some more *direct* inclination towards performing an action that accords with morality, which is then stipulated away or otherwise rendered ineffective. We shall return to the details below. For the time being, let us just note that for Kant neither category contains actions that are morally good. As actions that coincide with what morality requires are on the face of it indistinguishable from truly moral acts, mere outward conformity with moral commands reveals nothing about moral value.[3]

It is not difficult to see why Kant thinks that dwelling on actions motivated by inclination does little to advance the argument of Section I. At this early stage he admittedly fails fully to state or defend these assumptions, but drawing on later sections of the book we can easily supply them on his behalf. Not implausibly, Kant holds the view that all human actions must be governed by laws. In fact, when we make use of our faculty of volition we act as a result of representing practical laws to ourselves as action-guiding (cf. *G* IV 412); and even if we fail to act rationally we succumb to the attractions of mere natural inclination and let our will be determined accordingly. Essentially the same point can be made by considering the will as a causal faculty. If Kant is right, causation is by definition law-like (cf., e.g., *G* IV 446). Actions are caused by the will; and this process obeys certain laws. If the will is not determined by the moral law it must be governed by another law, as a matter of fact: by a law of instrumental rationality that practical reason borrows from the workings of the world around us.

These suppositions are more controversial philosophically than Kant realized. Nevertheless, they help us to understand why actions that conform with duty without being determined by it are irrelevant to the analysis of duty in *Groundwork* I, which is meant to reveal the moral law.[4] Action that is directly or indirectly motivated by inclination may *coincide* with the moral law (of which, at this stage, we are still ignorant); but it is *determined* by a law of instrumental reasoning (with which we are familiar). The action is correctly described only with reference to the latter. It is not determined by the moral law; it has nothing to do with duty; coincidence with morality is

---

[3] For a particularly clear statement see *CpV* V 81: the moral quality of actions is grounded in their necessity from duty and from respect for the moral law, not from love or inclination towards that which they are meant to bring about.

[4] As mentioned in the opening paragraph, Kant changes the concept to be analysed at *G* IV 397. By virtue of what in the second *Critique* is called the 'paradox of method', Kant cannot derive the moral law by means of a direct analysis of goodness. The reason appears to be that any such investigation will only yield instrumental laws that specify how to realize a good end but never a law that is itself the condition of value (cf. *CpV* V 62 and V 8).

accidental. Moreover, such an action is willed just as a means to realizing the purpose suggested by inclination. It is worthless – it turns out to have been wrong – if it fails to bring about the intended effect. Consequently, no such action can be good in itself, independently of its effects (which was declared to be the defining characteristic of moral action in the first pages of the *Groundwork*). Moreover, even the objective value of inclination-based acts that do produce the end intended is conditional: it depends not only on achieving the end but also on the goodness of the agent's will, his funda-mental attitude, his maxim (*G* IV 393–4). That is why Kant assumes that moral action must be done for the sake of duty, i.e. determined by a moral law, to be unconditionally good. The law first selects the purpose to be pursued.

Note also that the judgement that a certain action accords with morality presupposes an implicit prior understanding of moral categories. Before the first official statement of the principle of morality at the end of Section I we *recognize* an action from inclination to be in conformity with moral com-mands only because we possess our common practical, everyday conception of morality; and actions governed by a law other than the moral law can do nothing to make this understanding more precise.[5] A clear and unambig-uous case of action that is in fact *determined* by – i.e. non-accidentally connected with – the moral law is needed for us to make any progress with the task of making this law explicit.

2 MORAL WORTH AND MORAL CONTENT: THE SHOPKEEPER AND THE PHILANTHROPIST

With this clarification in mind, let us return to Kant's famous examples. In *Groundwork* I, Kant wants to disclose the nature of duty, and ultimately its law. That is the reason why the celebrated case of the prudent merchant is 'set aside' (*G* IV 397). The shopkeeper's actions are uninformative because they reliably accord with duty if only he manages to take care of his professional interests. As by definition he is prudent, he does.[6] Kant thinks

---

[5] Of course, this is the argument that Kant later levels against the popular idea that moral philosophy should be founded on examples (see *G* IV 408).

[6] By contrast, Barbara Herman argues that the 'moral fault with the profit motive is that it is unreliable'. When 'it leads to dutiful actions, it does so for circumstantial reasons': see her seminal 'On the Value of Acting from the Motive of Duty' in *The Practice of Moral Judgment* (Harvard University Press, 1993), p. 3. In general terms that is true, but it is not the point of the present example. The shopkeeper's actions are *far too reliably* in accordance with duty to be informative; and it is precisely this general reliability that, though accidental, obscures the circumstantial nature of the shopkeeper's

it is obvious that the actions of this shopkeeper are not morally good. His customers are not treated honestly as a matter of moral principle. The sole purpose of the prudent shopkeeper's actions is his economic wellbeing; honest behaviour towards his customers as such is irrelevant. Moral concern does not determine his actions. As a consequence, the connection between his maxim and his honest behaviour, if de facto reliable, is ultimately still accidental because morality does not feature in it. Even if we did encounter a rare virtuous businessman who acts honestly on principle and out of due regard for his patrons, in our perception the regularity of his actions would still be prudential.[7] If asked to state a law that explains his decent behaviour we could only, like Kant, point to the familiar rules of prudential foresight. The prudent merchant's actions cannot reveal anything about the principle we are trying to identify, or about the attitude of those who let it guide their actions.[8]

The other examples concern actions frequently done from some more direct inclination: preserving one's life, helping those in need, and taking care of one's own wellbeing (G IV 398–9).[9] Of these three cases, the second – that of the 'philanthropist' – has attracted by far the most critical attention.[10] Kant insists that an effortless act of assistance occasioned by the innocent pleasure of a sympathetic soul lacks moral value, whereas the dour

---

morally correct behaviour. Looking at a prudent shopkeeper, we would never guess what is essential about a moral person's attitude. Herman is one of many sympathetic interpreters of Kant's account of acting from duty who underestimate the importance of maxims, as opposed to single acts.

[7] The example, though irrelevant to the progress of Section I, thus serves the purpose of illustrating the difference between the 'legality' and 'morality' of actions (see CpV V 70 ff.).

[8] For the most part, people behave morally, but that does not make them moral people. Kant rather doubts that they are (see, e.g. G IV 407). The shopkeeper is a case in question. At this point, the pessimism with which he regards the actual moral quality of people's attitudes is palpable. In the second Critique, Kant once again uses 'prudence' in a pessimistic and slightly pejorative sense, and links it with self-love (CpV V 35–6).

[9] There are important differences, though: Kant acknowledges that beneficence can also be motivated by higher-order concerns like 'vanity' and 'self-interest', but these are excluded because he wishes to focus on the 'sympathetic soul' (G IV 398). Taking care of one's happiness is considered morally relevant at first only 'indirectly', i.e. not commanded by duty as such, whereas a few lines further down Kant seems to presuppose a more morally charged conception of wellbeing (G IV 399). On these complications cf. my Kant's 'Groundwork of the Metaphysics of Morals': A Commentary (Cambridge University Press, 2007). Between them, the four examples (roughly) cover the divisions of strict and wide duties to the self and to others that are systematically established as a consequence of the Law-of-Nature Formulation of the categorical imperative in Section II (G IV 421–4).

[10] The prominence of this example is easily explained. Helping others is something that philosophers of almost all persuasions regard as central to morality, which is hardly true of taking care of one's own person. Moreover, even common moral consciousness needs some persuading that the action of an insensitive person acting from duty should be morally preferable to that of someone who is naturally disposed to be kind to others. For Kant, the prudent shopkeeper is *evidently* not a moral man; and he implicitly concedes that the same cannot be said of the 'philanthropist' (cf. G IV 397).

beneficence of an agent not thus favoured by nature or circumstance is genuinely morally good. When the mind of the man who used to take delight in helping others is 'overclouded' by a grief that 'extinguishes all sympathy with the fate of others' and 'no longer incited to it by any inclination, he nevertheless tears himself out of this deadly insensibility' and helps another 'simply from duty', then the action 'first has its genuine moral worth' (*G* IV 398).

At the very least, this prima facie curious verdict draws attention to an important feature of Kantian ethics: agents who act for the sake of duty are in charge of their actions in a way the sentimental philanthropist is not. The underlying reasons for Kant's judgements of moral value emerge when we examine the two different maxims that lead to the same beneficent act, i.e. the respective principles on which a sympathetic and a moral agent act. Recall that inclination, whether benign or destructive, does not automatically express itself in action. The agent must decide to act on it, i.e. he must endorse the end proposed by inclination by way of incorporating it into his maxim. This act is free in a dual Kantian sense: the agent is initially inclined but not necessitated to act as natural desire suggests (negative freedom); and because of a radical capacity to evaluate and revise maxims in the light of his very own rational considerations he is also free to do what ought to be done (positive freedom). When Kant's philanthropist acts on sympathetic inclination he endorses a subjective principle proposed by this amiable desire: to help his fellow human beings when he feels a compassionate urge to do so. His beneficence is therefore conditional on his motivational state, not on the need or merit of the beneficiary. Moral predicates do not feature in this maxim. It lacks, as Kant puts it, 'moral content'.[11] That is why his actions are vulnerable in a way that the beneficent acts of the insensitive but thoroughly moral person are not.[12]

Kant thus wishes to emphasize not so much that one might help those who do not deserve one's support (although no doubt one might).[13] Even a

---

[11] Actions have moral *worth*, maxims possess moral *content*. Kant does not use these expressions interchangeably, though they are of course related. Only actions that result from such maxims – from an unconditional commitment to performing acts that are commanded by morality, not from inclination but from duty (*G* IV 398) – are morally valuable.

[12] Cf. Kant's distinction between the sentimentalist 'philanthropist' and the true 'friend of humanity' in the late *Metaphysics of Morals*, *G* VI 472–3.

[13] As in Barbara Herman's well-known example of helping people carry heavy boxes at the back door of the Museum of Fine Arts late at night ('On the Value of Acting from the Motive of Duty', pp. 4–5). It is true, of course, that inclination cannot be as morally discriminating as one ought to be; and in this Herman is right. However, the crucial point Kant wishes to make is not so much that inclination is blind – which is true enough, though even reason can go astray owing to factual errors – but rather the commensurability and unreliability of *direct* inclination as opposed to long-term interest.

morally good person can err when presented with misleading evidence. Rather, he objects to a maxim that makes beneficence dependent on incentives that, as such, possess no inherent connection with morality. That the philanthropist's behaviour at times does and at other times does not coincide with the commands of morality is merely an expression of that. His sentiment is likeable, and those he helps are fortunate. As such, his behaviour is beyond reproach. But it does not possess the distinctive value that belongs only to moral action proper.

Kant's illustrations may strike us as odd, paradoxical or even repulsive. Yet it is important to bear in mind that they are there to play a well-defined role within the overall strategy of *Groundwork* I, which in turn serves the rather specific purpose of formulating, for the first time – if Kant is right – in the history of ethical thought, the supreme principle of morality. The first section is neither an exercise in moral psychology nor a treatise on virtue. It does not even concern particular good actions as such, if only because Kant thinks common moral consciousness is perfectly capable of judging moral value even without the aid of academic philosophy. Kant takes our judgement of individual acts and motives as his starting point. However, the discussion soon turns to maxims: the subjective principles behind actions, an agent's fundamental practical attitudes. That it is maxims, not acts, that capture Kant's interest is soon to be made official in the 'second proposition'. In short, Kant is not as such concerned about moral motivation but about the subjective principle that determines motivation, and ultimately the objective principle to which it ought to conform. In accordance with the project of analysing the concept of duty (*G* IV 397), which was said to contain that of the good will (moral worth or value), Kant first tries to find cases in which it is plausibly an agent's moral attitude that underlies an action that conforms with duty: a clear case of an action 'from duty'. He then pursues the question of what it is about this agent's attitude that makes his action not just likeable, welcome or useful but *morally* good. The latter three examples serve to demonstrate that the maxim of the morally good person makes him robustly independent of his inclinational state – in fact, that seems the most promising candidate for the missing 'first proposition'.[14] The distinctness and superiority of the moral realm is emphasized throughout. In Kant's four examples we constantly re-encounter the attributes of the good will, as set forth in the opening paragraphs of the book.

---

[14] Cf. my *Kant's 'Groundwork of the Metaphysics of Morals'*, pp. 39–40.

3 CUTTING KANT'S LOSSES: DUTY AS A 'BACKUP MOTIVE'?

The requirement that the maxim of the moral agent produce right actions non-contingently and independently of his motivational state may yet seem to allow for the possibility that dutiful action must be done for duty's sake if and only if there is no concurrent inclination that is sufficiently strong to motivate the dutiful deed. This idea seems to derive some support from the fact that Kant rarely discusses action from duty with concurrent inclination, and from his emphasis on cases in which the motive of duty has to clear away the most serious of obstructions. If so, which attitude is morally appropriate if there is no hostile inclination to be conquered and no obstacle to be overcome? Should we really let all our dutiful actions be determined by reason alone, even in these cases of lucky coincidence? May we not sometimes perform an act that is commanded *because* we are thus inclined?

The attractions of a less restrictive approach are obvious. It helps to keep some of the more sinister connotations of 'merely doing one's duty' at bay. If it is necessary to act for the sake of the moral law only comparatively rarely, when more ordinary motivation fails, maybe the spectre of the joyless austerity of the Kantian moral life can yet be dispelled. Modern moral philosophers like Michael Stocker assume that the role of the motive of duty must be restricted to such cases. They rebuke Kant for (as they see it) indiscriminately demanding action from duty even when more ordinary motives are sufficient to bring about the action in question.[15] This view has roots in an older tradition. Humeans and Aristotelians alike consider effortless moral action preferable to moral action that results from conscious self-restraint. Moreover, Kant scholars who reject the traditional rigorism of motivation frequently put forward the idea of duty as a mere 'backup motive' on Kant's behalf, or even as a reading of *Groundwork* I.[16] On this model, an action is either morally valuable, or at least permissible, if in the absence of friendly inclination the motive of duty *would have been sufficient* to produce the right act.[17]

---

[15] Cf. Michael Stocker's discussion of the 'The Schizophrenia of Modern Ethical Theories', *Journal of Philosophy* 73 (1976), 453–66.

[16] The classic account is Richard Henson's 'fitness report model', which he attributes to the late Kant of the *Metaphysics of Morals* ('What Kant Might Have Said: Moral Worth and the Overdetermination of Dutiful Action', *Philosophical Review* 88 (1979), 39–54).

[17] Alternatively, one might, like Allen Wood, entertain the idea that not all actions must have moral worth, but that moral worth is required only in cases of moral conflict, i.e. that there is nothing *morally* objectionable about acting on inclination as long as inclination coincides with duty, cf. *Kant's Ethical Thought* (Cambridge University Press, 1998), pp. 26–40.

The conception of duty as a backup that steps in when inclination fails is not altogether alien to Kant's thinking. He apparently toyed with it at the time he gave what we now read as his 'Lectures on Ethics': 'One can, for instance, be beneficent towards one's wife from love, but where the inclination has already departed it is done from obligation' (*Collins* XXVII 413).[18] However, one must always keep in mind that he gave these lectures well before he wrote the *Groundwork*. At that time, he had not yet conceived the idea that practical reason must be autonomous; there is no trace of respect or reverence for the law as the one legitimate moral incentive; and his theory of moral motivation was generally unstable.

In fact, we should not be surprised to find that the conception of duty as a backup motive is incompatible with Kant's mature moral theory of the 1780s and 90s. The proponents of the backup model owe us an answer to the question why, if the moral motive of respect for the law *would* have determined the agent's will in less favourable inclinational circumstances, de facto it was *not* the force that produced the dutiful action (which, ex hypothesi, was motivated by benign inclination). There are two possible replies. The most straightforward explanation is that the moral motive was ineffective because it was absent. But this is problematic because Kant not implausibly assumes that moral interest – respect for the law – is reliably generated by an appropriate moral judgement. Its absence would therefore suggest that the agent failed to appreciate the morally relevant features of the situation. Alternatively, let us assume that a strong moral motive was present but was consciously excluded by the agent from being the motivating force.[19] The agent also felt a strong inclination to do the act recognized as moral – e.g. to help a dear friend in need – and decided to act on it. His maxim would have to take the following shape:

Whenever I judge that I ought to help a person in need and at the same time sense a sympathetic inclination sufficient to produce the dutiful act I shall act from

---

[18] The Kaehler manuscript has 'it ought to be done from obligation' (*so soll man es thun aus Verbindlichkeit*: Immanuel Kant, *Vorlesung zur Moralphilosophie* (Werner Stark (ed.), De Gruyter, 2004), p. 350). See also 'Naturrecht Feyerabend', where the example is used in the spirit of the 'method of isolation' of the Groundwork: if love prevails in old age, when physical attraction is gone, it must rest on moral grounds (XXVII 1326). For a sympathetic discussion of Kant's ethical theory at the time see Manfred Kuehn's introduction to Stark's edition. Isolated passages such as these cannot be used to support attributing something like the 'fitness report model' to the Kant of the critical period.

[19] There seems to be a third option: when we act from inclination that coincides with duty respect, though present, is *weaker* than inclination and hence not effective. However, there is again the worry that the agent lacks moral appreciation of the situation; and it is difficult to see how a weak moral motive could suffice to conquer strong desires when circumstances oppose inclination to morality.

inclination. If, however, I fear that sympathetic inclination might be insufficiently strong I shall be beneficent from duty instead.

An agent committed to this maxim will just as reliably do the right thing as someone whose maxim possesses moral content in the more conventional sense of indiscriminately putting duty first and inclination second.[20]

It is not difficult to see why Kant must reject this kind of disjunctive maxim. As he constantly points out, we must distance ourselves from the influence of inclination, the proposed *object* of the will, in moral deliberation (e.g. *G* IV 400).[21] If so, it can hardly be right to re-admit the influence of inclination 'through the back door' when one proceeds to act on its results.[22] Why would someone choose to be motivated by inclination *because* it happens to coincide with morality? Why not simply act on moral grounds right away? To use a familiar phrase in a sense clearly not envisaged by its author: if you act on inclination *on condition* that it coincides with duty, i.e. if in a situation of moral urgency you do not merely ask yourself what you ought to do but also whether you are sufficiently inclined to do it, you entertain *one thought too many*.

4 THE *MODI OPERANDI* OF PRACTICAL REASON

We can take this analysis and defence of *Groundwork* I one step further still. So far, the difference between moral and non-moral interest has been mentioned only in passing. Let us examine these two types of incentive more closely. Action on moral grounds – for duty's sake, from respect for the moral law – is expressive of a direct interest in the *action* that reason commands. By contrast, action on non-moral grounds – from inclination – is determined by an interest in the *effect* that the agent intends to bring about with his action. This distinction is at work when following the 'third proposition'. Kant declares that (*G* IV 400):

only what is connected with my will merely as ground and never as effect, what does not serve my inclination but outweighs it or at least excludes it altogether from

[20] For present purposes, I shall ignore the question whether introspective knowledge of the respective nature and strength of our motives is available to us.
[21] See *Theory and Practice* VIII 278–9 and *CpV* V 80 for particularly clear statements of this point. At *CpV* V 118, Kant argues that concurrent inclination, while it makes moral action easier, does not suffice to make an action good because it is 'blind and servile' (*blind und knechtisch*).
[22] At *CpV* V 88, Kant consequently recommends that whatever attractions a moral life may have in store for us (i.e. its occasional agreement with inclination) can be used to counterbalance 'the allurements that vice does not fail to display on the opposite side' but must not have 'even the smallest part' in motivation.

calculations in making a choice – hence the mere law for itself – can be an object of respect and thus a command.

However, the most explicit account of the radical heterogeneity of action from duty and action from inclination is tucked away in two extensive footnotes in Sections II and III of the *Groundwork*. In the first, which occurs in the course of defining the different varieties of imperative in Section II at *G* IV 413–14, Kant first defines 'inclination' as 'the dependence of the faculty of desire upon sensations' and explains that 'this accordingly always indicates a *need*'. By contrast, 'the dependence of a contingently determinable will on principles of reason' is called 'interest'. He adds that as, by definition, interest is one of the forces at work in a will 'which is not of itself always in conformity with reason', it cannot be ascribed to a divine will. After these preliminaries, Kant turns to the mode of operation of the human will that is most akin to the actions of a perfectly rational will. He continues (*G* IV 413–14 fn):

> But even the human will can *take an interest* in something without therefore *acting from interest*. The first signifies *practical* interest in the action, the second *pathological* interest in the object of the action. The former indicates mere dependence of the will upon principles of reason by itself; the second, dependence upon principles of reason for the sake of inclination, namely where reason supplies only the practical rule as how to remedy the need of inclination. In the first case the action interests me; in the second, the object of the action (insofar as it is agreeable to me).

To conclude the note, Kant explicitly refers back to the results of Section I. In the case of an action from duty 'we must look not to interest in the object but merely to that in the action itself and its principle in reason (the law)' (*G* IV 414 fn.). Pure practical reason sparks an interest in activity as such, which in turn makes us pursue the object singled out as good. Empirical practical reason teaches us how to realize the interest in an object we happen to find agreeable (*angenehm*) to begin with.[23]

In the final section of the *Groundwork*, Kant returns to the distinction between 'acting from interest' and 'taking an interest in action' and addresses the delicate and philosophically elusive status of the latter mode of volition (*G* IV 449). Demarcating the 'extreme boundary' of practical philosophy, Kant adds his second clarificatory footnote on the topic of

---

[23] This distinction is rough. It glosses over the need for morality to draw on instrumental reason to help realize ends determined by reason, e.g. the happiness of others. Actions that we have to perform in the pursuit of our moral ends are a matter of 'indirect duty'. See my *Kant's 'Groundwork of the Metaphysics of Morals'*, App. D.

interest and action at *G* IV 459–60.[24] 'Interest' is now defined as 'that by which reason becomes practical, i.e. becomes a cause of determining the will' (*G* IV 459 fn.). In the sequel, he restates his distinction between the two fundamentally different modi operandi of practical reason in slightly different terms (*G* IV 459–60 fn.):

Reason takes an immediate interest in an action only when the universal validity of the maxim of the action is a sufficient determining ground of the will. Only such an interest is pure. But if it can determine the will only by means of another object of desire or on the presupposition of a special feeling of the subject, then reason takes only a mediate interest in the action, and since reason all by itself, without experience, can discover neither objects of the will nor a special feeling lying at its basis, this latter interest would be only empirical and not pure rational interest.

This radical distinction between action from duty and action from inclination, as introduced in Section I, thus re-appears throughout the *Groundwork*. All action involves both an object of volition and a law. As regards moral value, the decisive question is whether the formal or the material element takes precedence in the process of decision and subsequent execution of a 'dutiful' act, i.e. an act that, on the face of it, conforms or coincides with duty (*pflichtmäßig*). An agent is *either* interested in the realization of an object because he is interested in the action itself, which is directly commanded by the moral law; *or* because he is interested in acting in a certain manner for the sake of bringing about an object that appeals to him. In the former case his action is morally and unconditionally good; in the latter it is not. One might say that, unlike duty, inclination is by nature 'consequentialist'. Of course, by virtue of one's direct moral interest in an action one is also rationally committed to realizing a certain result to the best of one's abilities; but volition itself is the primary object, the desired effect or change that comes about in the world – if one is lucky and the world deigns to co-operate – is secondary. However, in acting from inclination the law that determines one's action is externally imposed by the object it is intended to produce.[25] Kant is systematically developing the theme of the incorruptible, sturdy and self-reliant nature of morality,

---

[24] In accordance with the project of Section III, the purpose of the second footnote is different from, and goes beyond, that of the first. Kant envisages a 'heteronomous' will that is incapable of taking an interest in actions and hence pure volition, i.e. the kind of will human beings possess according to the sceptical position attacked in this section.

[25] Herman puts this distinction somewhat differently when she says that an inclination such as sympathy 'can give an interest in an action that is (as it happens) right, it cannot give an interest in its being right' ('On the Value of Acting from the Motive of Duty', p. 5). The first kind of interest is mediate, the second immediate.

grounded solely in practical reason, as opposed to the fickle and unpredictable support actions that accord with duty may hope to receive from inclination.

5 CONSEQUENCES: ASYMMETRY AND 'OVERDETERMINATION'

Kant's dualistic conception of human volition has important philosophical consequences. We are finally in a position to see why, when, e.g. compassionate feeling and the duty of beneficence in effect coincide, there is no reason at all to prefer the motive of philanthropic inclination to a sense of duty. Suppose my action from duty is graced with success. I have been able to help a person in need. As compassion was directed at *the intended effect* of the act, i.e. the change to be brought about, my inclination is satisfied. For that, the fact that the person is no longer in distress is sufficient, even if my action was motivated by narrowly moral considerations. Inclination is interested in action only indirectly, on condition that it serves the desired purpose; and this condition is met.[26] By contrast, reason takes a direct interest in volition and its grounds. It is never content with action that was allowed to be determined by inclination, even if the effect happens to coincide with duty. Reason demands that the act be done for the sake of its very own law, that the coincidence of the action with the moral law be non-contingent. We are faced with a fundamental asymmetry. In morally relevant situations, action sparked by reason can at times satisfy inclination but action determined by inclination can never satisfy reason. The result is therefore the exact opposite of the view advocated by those who see duty as a backup motive, or those who wish to except subjectively easy moral acts from the requirement to be motivated by duty alone. We can 'eat our cake and have it' only if we act *from duty*.[27] When one is tempted to act on a friendly inclination and then realizes that a maxim of letting inclination determine one's acts is immoral, one can still act *from duty* without detriment – Kant's word would be *Abbruch* – to the very inclination in question. Inclination is indifferent as to whether the action is willed *directly*, for its inherent moral quality, or *indirectly*, as a mere

---

[26] However, it does seek to affect the maxim, which would guarantee satisfaction even contrary to the demands of morality.

[27] This also explains why duty can be more or less opposed to inclination, but not vice versa. An end's being realized – if it is realized, which after all does not solely depend on what we do – can be more or less contrary to one's inclination, whereas reason always feels equally slighted if a dutiful action is done for the sake of the effect, not the moral law.

means, as long as the intended effect is brought about. However, it is not at all the same to reason whether the action happens from inclination or from duty. The agent thus needs to choose between pure practical reason and inclination even if either action would have the same effects. In fact, this choice is a matter of principle: a choice of maxim, which inherently claims to be applicable in all cases of the same kind and does not distinguish between friendly and hostile inclination.

Furthermore, it is misleading to say that in the case of parallel duty and inclination an action is 'overdetermined'. Because of the heterogeneity of the two types of motivation, a trace of conflict always remains. Even if duty and inclination concur, the same act can result from two distinct acts of volition that are determined by different laws. It would be more accurate to say that, though empirically indistinguishable, these are actually two different actions. Note that those who think that actions from sympathy are ever morally sufficient – either because they are deemed to be morally good, or because they are considered morally adequate despite their lack of moral value – implicitly rely on a consequentialist criterion of action description. Consequentialism is an attractive model of action individuation because our knowledge of actions is *a posteriori*: we know them through their effects. But for very good reasons, in Section I Kant is moving away from the kind of moral theory that assesses particular acts (or even their motives).

Ultimately, Kantian ethics concerns the quality of an agent's moral character. It is important to emphasize that action is always a matter of principle. In Kant's moral psychology, inclination always has the first word (*Cp*VV 146) because it prompts us to act. The agent must make use of his powers of practical reason to react appropriately. This model is implicit in the four examples that illustrate the Law-of-Nature Formulation in Section II. In the first case, a man 'feels sick of life as the result of misfortune that has mounted to the point of despair'; but he 'is still so far in possession of his reason to ask himself whether taking his own life may not be contrary to his duty to himself' (*G* IV 421–2). In the second example, someone 'finds himself driven into borrowing money because of need' and he knows well that he will be unable to pay it back; 'but he sees too that he will get no loan unless he gives a firm promise to pay it back within a fixed time'. This person 'is inclined' to make such a promise, but he has still 'enough conscience' to ask himself whether the action is morally permissible (*G* IV 421–2).[28] The third and

---

[28] Interestingly, Kant is implying that some agents are so engrossed in their despair or sorrow that they fail to submit their maxims to the test of moral permissibility. He mentions the same kind of caveat in his discussion of the 'most hardened scoundrel' in Section III, who must be 'otherwise accustomed to

fourth examples, according to which we have a duty not to neglect our talents and a duty to help those in need, follow a similar pattern.

In all these cases, action on inclination would come about only if these agents freely endorsed a maxim to do so: a subjective principle that settles the question of what is to be done in the present situation and all others that are relevantly like it. This maxim is implicitly suggested by inclination when it makes its move; and it is precisely because it is rooted in inclination that it lacks moral content.[29] Morality requires that we adopt a maxim that does, even if the difference will only ever be apparent when duty and inclination come apart. When duty and inclination recommend the same act the right maxim will make sure that we act for the sake of the former, from reverence for the moral law. Again, Kant is not interested in motives as such, but in the attitudes human beings take towards their desires when they make themselves felt, and the principle(s) that then apply.

6 FINAL WORRIES

According to the above attempt to make Kant's motivational rigorism philosophically and ethically acceptable, whether a dutiful action possesses positive moral value depends on the agent's attitude towards the incentives available to him. Moral action must always be done for the sake of the law. Inclination, no matter how benign, must be ignored whenever the moral law speaks, but might still be satisfied by the consequences of an action from duty.[30] Obstacles to dutiful action are to be overcome when they occur; but there is no indication so far that acting contrary to strong inclination possesses any special moral cachet. On the contrary, it is surely easier for an agent to act from duty if inclination can expect to be satisfied as well. That is why on more than one occasion Kant indicates that care for one's

---

use reason' (*G* IV 454) to feel the wish to become a decent man. Agents who lack the capacity to deliberate because they are overwhelmed by passions or affects presumably lack direct responsibility for their actions. (Unfortunately, Kant does not indicate the precise boundaries of accountability.)

[29] This is the answer to Herman's question of how a motive could be present but not motivate/be ineffective ('On the Value of Acting from the Motive of Duty', p. 11). A maxim that puts duty above inclination thus works like a sieve or filter, which lets only specific motives through to determine volition. We can still be glad when concurrent inclination is satisfied.

[30] The thesis that our moral judgements must ignore inclination is compatible with an indirect duty to cultivate our sensuous nature as proposed in the *Metaphysics of Morals*, if only because friendly inclination makes it easier for us to act on rational insight. Harmonious co-existence of inclination and reason is the ideal, despite the fact that – see the third worry below – Kant considers action contrary to inclination to be particularly admirable, and useful in moral education.

own happiness is at least 'indirectly' morally relevant. Duty is best done from duty, but with a glad heart.[31]

Nonetheless, some worries remain. First, it is not obvious that Kant's dualism of motivation is morally adequate (let alone true). Even if we agree that the interest of pure practical reason (respect for the law) is primarily directed at volition or action while inclination is directed at states of affairs, why should the former be moral and the latter amoral? One might even harbour the suspicion that an interest in doing something is self-centred or egotistical in a way that an interest that something change or be done is not.[32] Kant's text sometimes invites this objection. Consider, for instance, the following passage from the review of heteronomous ethical theories at the end of Section II (*G* IV 441):

Thus, for example, I ought to try to further the happiness of others, not as if its existence were of any consequence to me [*nicht als wenn mir an deren Existenz was gelegen wäre*] (whether because of immediate inclination or because of some indirect agreeableness through reason), but simply because a maxim that excludes this cannot be included as a universal law in one and the same volition.

What would Kant's response be? The first thing to note is that, as a consequence, someone who acts for the sake of the law intends to further the happiness of others just like the person who simply takes delight in making others happy. It is not that the Kantian moralist is exclusively interested in acting on principle, whereas our 'philanthropist' is interested in other people's happiness. They both want to make other people happy, if for different reasons. In addition, and perhaps more importantly, the moralist's decision to *do* something – e.g. to make a friend happy – rests on a moral judgement to which the friend's need, one's own ability to help etc., will have contributed. Again, the moral agent is not just motivated by an abstract principle. The principle has enabled him to assess the situation, and draw the correct practical conclusion. Morality thus directly concerns actions, not just desirable states of affairs. Kant is saying that an amiable emotional response to the needs of others does not make us moral. We must

---

[31] In the second *Critique*, Kant argues that the consciousness of the powers of practical reason can lead to a certain detached contentment in a virtuous agent (*CpV* V 116–19); and as Christine Korsgaard and Marcia Baron have pointed out, it is only to be expected that an agent will display a positive emotional reaction when he perceives that a moral end is realized (see M. Baron, 'Acting from Duty' in Immanuel Kant, *Groundwork for the Metaphysics of Morals* (Allen Wood (trans.), Yale University Press, 2003), pp. 98–9). Of course, there is still no guarantee that developing a moral disposition will make the agent happy. Sacrifices may still be required – see the third worry below.

[32] Cf. M. Baron, 'Acting from Duty' for the related worry that the moral person 'has as his purpose simply his duty' (p. 96).

be able to *do* something about it. Moreover, we should recall one of the main points of Kant's own example: owing to the commensurability of all inclination, the philanthropist's willingness to help depends entirely on a subjective incentive that may or may not suffice to motivate the right act.[33] Reverence for the law is subject to none of these uncertainties. *If* such a motive can be had, it seems that we are better off with action from duty after all. Finally, recall that moral action was supposed to be immediately and unconditionally good; and that this is impossible if we act for the sake of the intended effect of our action.[34]

The second worry concerns the pervasiveness of morality. Does his theory of motivational rigorism commit Kant to the thesis that every single action must possess moral worth? Is there any legitimate role left for inclination to play in human practice? Or should our entire life be dominated by moral concerns? In reply, one might insist on the superiority of the life of reason and the autonomy of moral decisions. Yet while there may be some truth in this response, it is fortunately unnecessary to bite this particular bullet. Of course, actions are legitimate only on condition that they do not violate the commands of morality. It can never be permissible to act on a maxim that is completely devoid of moral content. It does not, however, follow that every single act could or should be exclusively determined by moral concerns. To begin with, Kant insists that there are morally permissible actions. It can thus be quite legitimate to act on prudential grounds and perhaps even on direct inclination when the moral law is silent. Less obviously, even actions initiated by moral judgement are rarely completely determined by moral concerns. A principle of pure practical reason may be able to settle the question whether you should visit a friend in hospital; but it has no answer in store for you if you are wondering whether to get her red or white roses, milk chocolate with 32 or 40 per cent cocoa content, or a book, and if a book which one (and so forth). Morality does not tell you whether to walk to the hospital, to cycle or to ask a colleague to give you lift. It does not determine the date and time of the visit. All these details are left to expediency and inclination to decide, and to your anticipation of the inclinations of your friend. Moral action will often be composite in this way. Pure practical reason shapes the lives of moral agents

---

[33] Cf. the famous example of the man who prefers spending the little money in his pocket on a ticket for the comedy to giving it to someone he usually helps with pleasure (*CpV* V 23).

[34] I am not certain whether these considerations can dispel the first worry altogether. For an extended discussion of these issues, cf. Philip Stratton-Lake, *Kant, Duty and Moral Worth* (London: Routledge, 2000).

and points them in a general direction, but it does not dominate it to the exclusion of everything else.

Thirdly, even if opposition by inclination is not required for an action to be morally good, and the cultivation of a harmonious (if unequal) relationship of reason and sensibility is recommended, Kant's examples seem to suggest that some 'genuine' or 'real' moral worth[35] attaches particularly to action from duty that is arduous, costly or subjectively difficult. Other passages also strongly suggest that there is something special about moral actions that do not just disregard inclination but either directly run counter to what one would like to do or have some negative long-term side effects. In *Groundwork* II Kant contends that 'the sublimity and inner dignity of the command in a duty is all the more manifest the fewer are the subjective causes in favour of it and the more there are against it' (*G* IV 425). Even more drastically, in the *Critique of Practical Reason* Kant argues that virtue 'reveals itself most splendidly in suffering' (*CpV* V 156); in his lectures on anthropology he apparently declares that there is not much merit in doing what is easy (*Anthropology* VII 148); and in a hand-written note, the good will is said to shine even more brightly 'on the black background of misfortune' (R 6968).

What is striking about these passages is that in most of them Kant uses the language of 'appearance' or 'revelation'. Difficult circumstances reveal the agent's true priorities. They prove that he puts morality first, how dear the moral law is to him even in the face of danger. He does not put a price on moral volition but rather gives morality the absolute weight it deserves. To use Kant's own terminology, the moral content is the *ratio essendi* of moral value, whereas moral action in testing personal circumstances is its *ratio cognoscendi*.

Over and above that, costly moral action does possess a special role in moral education. In the Doctrine of Method of the *Critique of Practical Reason* we read about a ten-year-old boy who is confronted with the example of a man who even when threatened with the death penalty by Henry VIII refuses to calumniate an innocent Anne Boleyn. This arouses the boy's admiration, and ultimately the fervent wish to be such a person – but not to be in that person's predicament (*CpV* V 155–6). Examples of this kind are particularly valuable not because it is morally desirable that one should have to sacrifice one's life, but rather because they remind us of one's

---

[35] For the first, cf. the second stage of the example of the philanthropist (*echter moralischer Wert*, *G* IV 398); for the second, the case of the person suffering from gout who does not give in to shallow hedonism (*eigentlicher moralischer Wert*, *G* IV 399).

autonomy and the dignity of the moral law.[36] Subjectively difficult actions
are therefore admirable in the sense that we *can* admire them, whereas the
very same moral action would not be revealed to be good even in a virtuous
person if supported by inclination. That is why extreme cases are so useful
in moral education and ethics alike. If so, it is neither necessary nor desirable
that one's moral strength be put to the test; but it is necessary that it should
prevail *if* it is put to the test. These claims are not uncontroversial philosophically, but they are neither completely outlandish or obviously misguided. The common understanding of moral matters may after all be on
Kant's side.

---

[36] Richard Henson calls this the 'fitness report model'; see 'What Kant Might Have Said', 45. In
addition, Kant seems to think that getting used to acting contrary to inclination fulfils a developmental purpose: we must get used to virtue, and 'know the enemy' (see *CpV* V 147).

CHAPTER 4

Making the law visible: the role of examples in Kant's ethics

Robert B. Louden

I INTRODUCTION: EXAMPLES IN PURE MORAL PHILOSOPHY

Nowhere is the stringency of Kant's *Groundwork of the Metaphysics of Morals* more evident than in his blunt statement that one could not 'give worse advice to morality than by wanting to derive (*entlehnen*)[1] it from examples' (*G* IV 408). Was the sage of Königsberg oblivious to the power of example? Was he indifferent to the adage that it is always 'personalities, not principles, that move the age'?[2] The outspokenness of the message becomes even more apparent when Kant applies it to some of the most fundamental commitments of his largely Christian eighteenth-century readership. 'Even the Holy One of the Gospel', he remarks pointedly, is unable to serve as a defensible norm in ethics (*G* IV 408). A recent popular bumper sticker to the contrary, the question is not 'What would Jesus do?'. Raising the religious ante still further, Kant next turns his sights on theists of all persuasions who look upon the deity as the ultimate criterion of moral norms: 'But where do we get the concept of God as the highest good?' (*G* IV 408–9). Even though Kant frequently claims to arrive at his own foundational moral principle simply by analysing 'the moral cognition of common

This essay borrows some points from my earlier articles, 'Go-Carts of Judgment: Exemplars in Kantian Moral Education', *Archiv für Geschichte der Philosophie* 74 (1992), 303–22; and 'Examples in Ethics' in *Routledge Encyclopedia of Philosophy* (Edward Craig (ed.), New York: Routledge, 1998), vol. III, pp. 487–90. I would also like to thank Jens Timmermann, Andreas Vieth, Norbert Mertens, and an anonymous reviewer for helpful advice; as well as the Alexander von Humboldt Foundation, for its support of an enjoyable research visit to Münster, Germany in June-July 2007, during which time a draft of this chapter was written.

[1] *Entlehen* also means 'to borrow'. In citing from Kant's *Groundwork*, I have made use of both Mary J. Gregor's translation, which is included in Immanuel Kant, *Practical Philosophy* (Mary J. Gregor (trans. and ed.), Cambridge University Press, 1996) and Allen W. Wood's more recent rendering (Immanuel Kant, *Groundwork for the Metaphysics of Morals* (Allen W. Wood (ed. and trans.), Yale University Press, 2002).

[2] Oscar Wilde in Richard Arlington (ed.), *The Portable Oscar Wilde* (New York: Viking, 1965), p. 658.

human reason (*die gemeine Menschenvernunft*)' (*G* IV 403; cf. IV 402),[3] the
so-called 'divine command theory of ethics', according to which our moral
duties are simply what God commands (subscribed to by a strong majority
of people in all times and places, and hence still today the planet's dominant
theory of normative ethics) is quickly rejected. Echoing Socrates' famous
dispute with Euthyphro,[4] Kant too argues that human beings ought not to
derive their moral norms from God. No one – not even Jesus or God – can
give morality to us.

Why does Kant make these radical claims? In the *Groundwork*, his major
objections to deriving moral principles from examples, while severely compressed, are both clear and compelling. First, whenever we judge an example
(be it person or event)[5] to be of moral value, we judge it so – sometimes
explicitly, but, more often, only implicitly – in virtue of a pre-existing
standard. To call x right or good (or pious, courageous, generous, etc.)
presupposes that we first have a general conception of right or good (or
pious, courageous, generous, etc.). This is what Kant means when he states
that 'every example (*jedes Beispiel*)' of morality 'must first be judged by
principles of morality' (*G* IV 408). This point too is Socratic,[6] and while
particularists of many persuasions continue to protest it,[7] their protests are
unpersuasive. In order to judge x to be right or good, we must first be in
possession of a general concept of rightness or goodness.

Kant's second objection to deriving morality from examples has roots in
Enlightenment culture, particularly in his own definition of Enlightenment.
At the beginning of his essay, *An Answer to the Question: What is
Enlightenment?*, for instance, he offers the following as a motto for the
Enlightenment: 'Have courage to make use of your *own* understanding!'
(VIII 35; cf. *CU* V 294, *Anthr.* VII 228). When applied to the ethical sphere,

---

[3] For further discussion, see '*Gemeine Menschenvernunft* and *Ta Endoxa*' in Robert B. Louden, *Morality and Moral Theory: a Reappraisal and Reaffirmation* (New York: Oxford University Press, 1992), pp. 116–20.

[4] 'Is the pious (*to hosion*) loved by the gods because it is pious, or is it pious because it is loved by the gods?' (Plato, *Euthyphro* 10a). See also the Preface to the First Edition of Kant's *Religion Within the Boundaries of Mere Reason*, where he proclaims that 'on its own behalf morality in no way (*keineswegs*) needs religion, ... but is rather self-sufficient by virtue of pure practical reason' (VI 3).

[5] In the following discussion, except where noted otherwise, I use the term 'example' broadly to refer both to exemplars (morally exceptional individuals) and to specific instances of morally praiseworthy conduct.

[6] 'Is the pious not the same and alike in every action, and the impious the opposite of all that is pious and like itself, and everything that is to be impious presents us with one form (*idea*) or appearance in so far as it is impious?' (Plato, *Euthyphro* 5d).

[7] The debate is not new, and goes back at least as far as Plato. For some recent contributions, see Brad Hooker and Margaret Olivia Little (eds.), *Moral Particularism* (Oxford: Clarendon Press, 2000), and Jonathan Dancy, *Ethics Without Principles* (Oxford: Clarendon Press, 2004).

the resultant advice is to make use of our own understanding in order to think about what is right and wrong, good and bad, rather than blindly follow others. This is Kant's point when he states tersely in the *Groundwork* that 'imitation [*Nachahmung*] has no place at all in ethics' (*G* IV 409).

A third, related argument against examples stems from Kant's views concerning the importance of autonomy in ethics. On Kant's view, autonomy or self-legislation – the capacity of rational beings to act in accordance with principles that they themselves create – is 'the supreme principle of morality' (*G* IV 440) as well as 'the ground of the dignity of human nature and of every rational nature' (*G* IV 436). If we allow any external sources – be they persons (again, even the Holy One of the Gospel or God himself) or things (e.g. the beauty and sublimity of nature, to which Kant himself was by no means blind)[8] – to determine our moral principles, we run the risk of forfeiting our autonomy. Instead of correctly grasping the fact that the ground of morality lies in our own practical reason, we may begin to assume falsely that it lies in external, heteronomous sources.

A fourth Kantian objection to grounding morality in examples is briefly hinted at toward the end of the famous paragraph in *Groundwork* IV 408–9, but elaborated on at greater length elsewhere. Because moral norms are categorical and involve concepts of necessity and universality, they cannot be grounded in experience. Rather, 'necessity and strict universality', as he notes in the Introduction to the *Critique of Pure Reason*, are 'sure signs [*sichere Kennzeichen*] of an *a priori* cognition' (*CrV* B 4; cf. *Collins* XXVII 333).

This is essentially Kant's point in the *Groundwork* when he states that the 'true original' of morality 'lies in reason' rather than in experience (*G* IV 409); or, as he puts it at the beginning of the next paragraph, there exists 'a genuine supreme principle of morality' that 'must rest independently of all experience' (*G* IV 409).

Finally, a fifth objection to grounding morality in examples stems from Kant's methodological dispute with the popular philosophers (*Popularphilosophen*) of the time.[9] As we have seen, Kant holds that moral norms, because they involve necessity and universality, cannot be derived

---

[8] For instance, in *The Metaphysics of Morals* Kant refers to 'the indescribable beauty of plants', arguing that a propensity to wantonly destroy what is beautiful in nature is a violation of moral duty (*MdS* VI 443).

[9] The most significant representative of this school of thought was Christian Garve (1742–98), a prolific translator and author who was a major contributor to German Enlightenment culture. Garve's translations of Adam Ferguson (*Institutes of Moral Philosophy*), Edmund Burke (*Philosophical Inquiry into the Origin of Our Ideas of the Sublime and the Beautiful*), and Adam Smith (*The Wealth of Nations*) were instrumental in introducing German readers to British moral

from experience. This conviction in turn convinces him 'of the utmost necessity to work out for once a pure moral philosophy, completely cleansed of everything that may be only empirical' (*G* IV 389). However, the popular philosophers of Kant's day (and this strategy continues to find support in many circles at present) tried to ground their ethical theories in experience, and were thus opposed to the very idea of a pure moral philosophy. In Kant's words, popular philosophy 'goes no further than it can get through groping [*durch Tappen*] by means of examples', and is thus unable to arrive at a metaphysics of morals, 'which no longer lets itself be held back by anything empirical' (*G* IV 412). The title of Section II of the *Groundwork* is 'Transition [*Übergang*] from Popular Moral Philosophy to Metaphysics of Morals' (*G* IV 406), and Kant's arguments against deriving morality from

philosophy and aesthetics. He also produced translations and commentaries of Aristotle's *Politics* and (at the suggestion of Frederick the Great) Cicero's *De Officiis*. His own works (none of which, alas, has been translated into English) include *Über die Verbindung der Moral mit der Politik* (Korn, 1788), *Über verschiedene Gegenstände aus der Moral, Literatur und dem gesellschaftlichen Leben*, 5 vols. (Korn, 1792), *Über Gesellschaft und Einsamkeit*, 2 vols. (Korn, 1797–1800), *Einige Betrachtungen über die allgemeinen Grundsätze der Sittenlehre* (Korn, 1798), and *Übersicht der vornehmsten Principien der Sittenlehre, von dem Zeitalter des Aristoteles an bis auf unsre Zeiten* (Korn, 1798). (This last book is dedicated to Kant, and concludes with a forty-three page discussion of the alleged inadequacies of his moral system.) Garve also published one of the first reviews of Kant's *Critique of Pure Reason*, complaining in his opening sentence that the *Critique* 'often strains the attention of its readers to the point of exhaustion'. (An English translation is available in Brigitte Sassen (ed. and trans.), *Kant's Early Critics: the Empiricist Critique of the Theoretical Philosophy* (Cambridge University Press, 2000), pp. 53–8. The review was first published anonymously in *Zugabe zu den Göttingischen Anzeigen von gelehrten Sachen* 1 (1782), 40–8.) Stung by Garve's criticisms, Kant, according to Johann Georg Hamann, set out in 1784 to produce a 'counter-critique [*Antikritik*] – though the title is not yet determined – against Garve's Cicero as an indirect answer to his review [of the first *Critique*]' (Hamann to Johann George Scheffner, February 18, 1784; in Johann Georg Hamann, *Briefwechsel* (Arthur Henkel (ed.), Frankfurt: Insel, 1965), V129; cf. Manfred Kuehn, *Kant: a Biography* (Cambridge University Press, 2001), p. 278; Jens Timmermann, *Kant's Groundwork of the Metaphysics of Morals: a Commentary* (Cambridge University Press, 2007), p. xxvii). The result (though the final product does not match Hamann's description), published in 1785, was the *Groundwork of the Metaphysics of Morals*. For Garve, morality was not at all a matter of pure reason, and the concept of a specifically practical reason was foreign to him. For instance, in his concluding critique of Kant's ethics in *Übersicht der vornehmsten Principien der Sittenlehre*, he writes: 'In the Kantian philosophy I hear talk for the first time of a *double* reason, a theoretical and a practical, and I experience neither the essence nor the ground of this distinction' (p. 342). Garve's own stance in ethics was one that stressed common experience over abstract reasoning; historical examples over principles. In the last sentence of *Übersicht* he summarizes his criticisms of Kant's categorical imperative as follows: 'what I *ought to do*: this I am usually taught very accurately by consideration of my special circumstances and relationships, and it would become difficult for me and by itself impossible to infer what I ought to do from the universal relations of human beings to one another' (p. 383). For discussion of the *Popularphilosophen*, see Lewis White Beck, *Early German Philosophy: Kant and his Predecessors* (Harvard University Press, 1969), pp. 319–24. For more information on Garve, see Fania Oz-Salzberger's entry on Garve in the *Encyclopedia of the Enlightenment* (New York: Oxford University Press, 2003), vol. 2, pp. 101–2. See also Part I (VIII 278–89) of *On the Common Saying: That may be Correct in Theory, but it is of No Use in Practice* (VIII 273–313), where Kant responds to several of Garve's criticisms of his ethics.

examples are themselves part of this larger project of defending the need for, and showing the way to, a metaphysics of morals.

However, one should not infer from what has been said thus far that Kant's position on the role of examples in ethics is entirely negative. But unfortunately, in the *Groundwork*, his estimation of their positive role is even more compressed than is his criticism of their weaknesses. For example, after stating his *Aufklärung* conviction that imitation has no place in morality, he notes: 'Examples serve only for encouragement [*Aufmunterung*], that is, they put beyond doubt the feasibility [*Tunlichkeit*] of what the law commands' (*G* IV 409).[10] His point here is that when we are confronted by a truly virtuous person, this helps to convince us that what morality demands is humanly possible (cf. *CpV* V 158, *MdS* VI 480). Still, the primary lesson to be learned from moral exemplars is one of encouragement, not imitation. As he states in *Collins* (XXVII 334):

An example is not for imitation, but it is certainly for emulation [*Nachfolge*]. The ground of the action must not be derived from the example, but rather from the rule. But if others have shown that such an act is possible, we must emulate their example, and also exert ourselves to perform such moral actions, and not let others surpass us in that respect.

A second (and even terser) argument in defence of examples in ethics presented in the *Groundwork* is located in the same sentence quoted in the previous paragraph (*G* IV 409). Examples also 'make visible [*machen ... anschaulich* – the second word also means 'clear', 'vivid', 'concrete', 'perceptible', 'intuitive'] what the practical rule expresses more generally' (*G* IV 409; cf. *CpV* V 77). A sharp and vivid example brings the moral point home for human beings in a way that the abstractions of theories, principles and rules often cannot. Again though, the example itself does not ground or justify the principle – quite the contrary. Rather, the right kind of example helps human beings to see what is at stake in the principle. Examples help make the moral law visible to human beings.

However, this is certainly not the whole story about the role of examples in ethics. Kant's *Groundwork* has a tightly focused and limited aim. As he

---

[10] 'Beyond doubt' may seem too strong, given Kant's well-known insistence on the inscrutability of our moral status: we don't know with certainty who is morally good and who is not. At *G* IV 407, for instance, he asserts: 'In fact, it is absolutely impossible by means of experience to make out with complete certainty a single case in which the maxim of an action otherwise in conformity with duty rested simply on moral grounds and on the representation of one's duty' (cf. *MdS* VI 392, *Religion* VI 51). But what is placed beyond doubt is the feasibility or possibility of virtue for human beings – not its certain attainment.

writes toward the end of the Preface: 'the present groundwork is ... nothing more than the search for and establishment of the *supreme principle of morality*, which constitutes by itself a business that in its purpose is complete and to be kept apart from every other moral investigation' (*G* IV 392). Once this specific goal of finding and justifying the supreme principle of morality has been reached, additional investigations – e.g. how do we apply the principle to the contingencies of human life? – can then be undertaken. And when Kant undertakes this latter task, he has much more to say about the role of examples in ethics.

2 EXAMPLES IN THE MORAL LIFE OF HUMAN BEINGS

Given Kant's specific and limited aim in the *Groundwork*, it is easy to see why he devotes so little discussion to the role of examples in ethics. Because he is trying to justify a moral principle that 'must hold, not only for human beings, but for all *rational beings as such* [*alle vernünftigen Wesen überhaupt*]' (*G* IV 408), and because he believes that this principle also must hold 'not merely under contingent conditions and with exceptions but with *absolute necessity*' (*G* IV 408), it is clear both that any references to specific persons and actions drawn from human life will be too weak to justify the principle and that such examples will fail to offer the right kind of moral guidance.

However, when Kant turns to what he variously calls 'practical anthropology' (*G* IV 388), 'moral anthropology' (*MdS* VI 217) and 'the second part of morals' (*Moral Mrongovius II* XXIX 599), his remarks about the place of examples in ethics are much more extensive. For here he is concerned with 'the subjective conditions in human nature that hinder people or help them in *carrying out* the laws of a metaphysics of morals' (*MdS* VI 217).[11] In other words, the question now becomes: what are the specific features of human nature that make it difficult and/or easy for human beings to act morally?

Moral education. One morally relevant fact about human nature concerns our biological and cognitive development. We are not born as autonomous moral agents; rather, we develop our moral reasoning capacities slowly over a number of years. Young children do not yet possess the ability to reason autonomously about moral matters; and, at least at the beginning, they do learn best by imitation. Hence, their ability to reason autonomously about

---

[11] For discussion of this second part of Kant's ethics, see Robert B. Louden, *Kant's Impure Ethics: From Rational Beings to Human Beings* (New York: Oxford University Press, 2000); and 'The Second Part of Morals' in Brian Jacobs and Patrick Kain (eds.), *Essays on Kant's Anthropology* (New York: Cambridge University Press, 2003), pp. 60–84.

ethics can only be fostered effectively through exposure to concrete examples. Parents and moral educators need to take these developmental factors into account. For instance, in a section called 'Ethical Didactics' in the *Metaphysics of Morals*, Kant writes (*MdS* VI 479):

The *experimental* (technical) means for cultivating virtue is *good* example on the part of the teacher (his exemplary conduct) and *cautionary* example in others, since, for a still undeveloped human being, imitation is the first determination of his will to accept maxims that he afterwards makes for himself.

Similarly, in the *Methodenlehre* section of the second *Critique*, which is concerned with 'the way in which one can provide the laws of pure practical reason with *access* to the human mind and *influence* on its maxims' (*CpV* V 151) – in other words, with how to make moral principles efficacious in human life – Kant also refers several times to the need for concrete examples when discussing ethics with young people. Near the beginning of his discussion, for instance, he states that 'it certainly cannot be denied, that in order to bring ... a mind that is still uncultivated (*ungebildet*) ... onto the track of the morally good in the first place, some preparatory guidance is needed' (*CpV* V 152).

However, in both the *Critique of Practical Reason* and in the *Metaphysics of Morals*, he warns that this strategy of teaching ethics by example, while humanly necessary, carries a danger: 'not the conduct of other human beings, but rather the law must serve as our incentive [*Triebfeder*]' (*MdS* VI 480; cf. *CpV* V 152). Exposure to moral exemplars should help set the child on the right moral track, but after a while the pupil must come to understand the norms by which these exemplars themselves are judged.

As we have seen, in the *Metaphysics of Morals* Kant stresses the role of teachers themselves as moral exemplars – not an easy assignment for any teacher. However, in the second *Critique*, he advocates a different strategy, one that involves searching through 'the biographies of ancient and modern times': 'I do not know why educators of the young ... have not, after first laying the foundation in a purely moral catechism, searched through the biographies of ancient and modern times in order to have at hand illustrations [*Belege*] of the duties presented' (*CpV* V 154). Here, the goal is to help the student 'feel the progress of his power of judgement' (*CpV* V 154) by discussing different cases with him and helping him to gradually grasp the underlying principles by means of which the cases are properly appraised. By drawing examples taken from real life rather than from fiction or the teacher's own imagination, Kant seems to reveal a preference for examples that are less 'cooked' – less theory-laden. And what real-life exemplars does he have in mind? Anne Boleyn, 'an innocent but powerless person' is briefly singled out in the *Critique of Practical Reason* (*CpV* V 155); while in the *Metaphysics of Morals* Curtius and Seneca are referred to as heroes whose deaths perhaps constituted morally permissible exceptions to the prohibition against suicide – as was the carrying into battle of a fast-acting poison by 'a great king who died recently' (*MdS* VI 423; cf. *Anthr.* VII 258 – Kant refers here to Frederick the Great), so that if and when he was captured by enemy troops, he could not be forced to agree to conditions that would prove harmful to his subjects.[12]

In his *Lectures on Pedagogy*, the major theme of which is *moral* education, Kant also refers several times to the importance of examples in discussing ethics with children. For instance, at one point he advises parents not to place any value in fancy clothes, so that their children will do likewise: 'for here as everywhere example is all-powerful and reinforces or destroys good teaching' (IX 486).[13] And later he advises that 'in order to ground a moral character in children, ... one must teach them the duties that they have to fulfil as much as possible by examples [*so viel als möglich durch Beispiele*]' (IX 488).

However, none of these passages concerning the necessity of teaching ethics to children by example contradicts the infamous anti-example paragraph in the *Groundwork*. For his point in the latter work is primarily *logical*, and concerns the impossibility of grounding an allegedly universal and necessary moral principle in empirical cases. His point in the former texts is *biological* and *psychological* (or what Kant would call 'anthropological'), and concerns morally relevant facts of human nature. Because of the specific ways in which human cognitive development occurs, examples are necessary in their moral education.

Limitations of human reason. Even after human beings have reached adulthood and developmental maturity, there remain hindrances in human nature that make it difficult for them to act from moral principle. One of most fundamental challenges is the fact that the developmentally

---

[12] The examples from *MdS* come up in one of the many 'Casuistical Questions' sections that Kant intentionally weaves into his presentation 'in a *fragmentary* way, not systematically' (*MdS* VI 411). His goal here is to engage readers with complex moral scenarios 'that call upon judgement to decide how a maxim is to be applied in particular cases' (*MdS* VI 411), and it is clear that he thinks adults as well as children will benefit from, and take enjoyment in, opportunities to exercise their practical judgement skills. At the same time, as I show later, Kant also warns elsewhere that overreliance on examples tends to weaken human beings' natural capacity for judgement.

[13] I have recently prepared a new English translation of this text, which is included in Immanuel Kant, *Anthropology, History, and Education* (Günter Zöller and Robert B. Louden (eds.), Cambridge University Press, 2007).

mature human mind is still a finite intelligence rather than an infinite intelligence. The adult human mind is equipped only with 'a discursive, image-dependent understanding' (*CU* V 408): in order to think abstractly, we need images. The finitude of the human condition thus poses a *permanent* challenge to the task of grasping ideas of pure reason such as *a priori* moral norms or the concept of a morally perfect will.

Kant's basic response to this challenge of human finitude is to articulate various strategies for representing moral concepts analogically and symbolically through images. As he remarks in *Religion Within the Boundaries of Mere Reason*, 'for the human being the invisible needs to be represented through something visible (sensible)' (*Religion* VI 192). In an important footnote in this same work, he elaborates as follows (*Religion* VI 64–5 fn.):

It is admittedly a limitation [*eine Beschränktheit*] of human reason, and one which is ever inseparable from it, that we can conceive of no considerable moral worth in the actions of a personal being without representing that person, or his manifestation, in human guise. This is not to assert that such worth is in itself [κατ' ἀλήθειαν] so conditioned, but merely that we must always resort to some analogy with natural being in order to make supersensible qualities comprehensible [*faßlich*] to ourselves.

This particular passage is complicated by the fact that the larger context of Kant's discussion concerns Jesus as the archetype (*Urbild*) of the perfectly good will. And as we noted at the beginning of our discussion, on his view even the Holy One of the Gospel must first be compared to a standard of moral perfection – one created by our own reason – before we are able to recognize him as a moral exemplar (cf. *G* IV 408). However, the two passages are consistent with one another. His point at *Groundwork* IV 408 is simply that any example, be it person or event, held to be morally good presupposes a standard by which it is judged morally good. At *Religion* 64–5 fn. and other supporting texts to be discussed in this section, his point is that the adult human mind needs concrete images in order to fully understand moral goodness. Due to our nature and because of the way our minds function, we need personal exemplars and tangible examples, not just principles. As he remarks later in *Religion*, there exists 'a natural need of all human beings to demand for the highest concepts and grounds of reason something that *the senses can hold onto*, some confirmation from experience' (*Religion* VI 109).

An additional complication in *Religion* 64–5 fn. concerns Kant's difficult doctrine of schematism. In resorting to some analogy with natural being in order to make supersensible qualities comprehensible to ourselves, we are engaging in a 'schematism of analogy' – adopting a concept to the spatial-temporal conditions of human experience by means of another object (in this case, Jesus), which in turn is a symbol for the original concept. However, in the *Critique of Practical Reason* Kant asserts that 'no schema on behalf of its [i.e. the moral law's] application *in concreto* is possible' (*CpV* V 69). No schema is possible for the categorical imperative, while a schema – or at least a 'schematism of analogy', one that differs from a 'schematism of objective determination' in that it does not extend our knowledge but only helps us to make sense out of highly abstract concepts – is possible in the case of the perfectly good will. Has Kant contradicted himself here? Why is it possible to provide a schema for the concept of a morally perfect will, but impossible to provide a schema for the moral law? Both are concepts of pure reason, and if a schema is possible for one, then why not for the other?

I am not aware of a satisfactory Kantian solution to this conundrum,[14] but I am also not sure if one is necessary. For in the second *Critique*, after announcing that the moral law cannot be schematized, Kant offers a figurative substitution for the schematization of the moral law, which he calls 'the typic of pure practical judgement' (*CpV* V 67; cf. V 69–70). And at bottom, the typification of the moral law achieves the same results as the schematization of the morally perfect will. For in both cases, human beings, in order to better grasp abstract moral concepts, represent these concepts symbolically to themselves by making analogies to 'something that the senses can hold onto'.

Before moving on, it is important to underscore Kant's basic point that the finitude of the human condition implies a life-long need for concrete moral examples and personal exemplars. With his second argument in defence of examples, we are no longer talking about a strategy of moral education that is to be applied only to children and that can be dispensed with once they reach adulthood. Adult human beings do have stronger powers of reflection and abstraction than do children. But even adults remain saddled with 'a discursive image-dependent understanding', and thus they will always need examples in order to make the law visible to themselves.

Hope and inspiration. Kant's third major argument in defence of examples in ethics is primarily psychological. The existence and availability of

---

[14] One reader has suggested that Kant's considered view is simply that while we cannot hope for a schematization of the moral law in which that law becomes an object of experience, we can still seek a sensible analogy for a pure concept of reason (in this case, the morally good will). Perhaps. But as I go on to argue, a neat interpretive solution to the puzzle is not necessary for my purposes.

examples of moral goodness, be they persons or their deeds, give us hope and inspiration that what morality demands is achievable by human beings. Here as elsewhere, his argument in defence of the necessity of examples is based on certain facts about human nature. Examples provide us with palpable evidence that morality is humanly possible – that the actual carrying-out of morality's demands is not a pipe-dream but something achievable by real people like us.

Human beings need hope: without it, our lives become static; we lack goals and are unable to move under our own direction. In *Anthropology from a Pragmatic Point of View*, Kant notes that 'overwhelming sadness (which is alleviated by no hope)' is an emotional state 'that threatens life' (VII 254); and he repeatedly insisted that the question 'What may I hope?' was one of three or (in later formulations) four fundamental questions that philosophy was obligated to address.[15] Kant's best-known work within the philosophy of hope involves the attempt to show that the concepts of God and immortality are necessary presuppositions for a human moral life (albeit presuppositions that cannot be objectively proven). But his argument that examples in ethics serve to give human beings needed hope and inspiration constitutes an additional but underexplored contribution to the philosophy of hope – a more mundane and this-worldly contribution that is free of controversial religious assumptions.

Versions of this third argument appear in each of Kant's central writings on ethics. In the *Groundwork*, for instance, he states that examples 'put beyond doubt [*außer Zweifel*] the feasibility [*Tunlichkeit*] of what the law demands' (G IV 409); in the second *Critique* he discusses the specific example of someone who sacrifices his own life for his country, noting that 'we find our soul strengthened and elevated by such an example when we can convince ourselves, in it, that human nature is capable [*fähig*] of so great an elevation above every incentive that nature can oppose to it' (*CpV* V 158); and in the *Metaphysics of Morals* he states that the exemplary conduct of the teacher should serve as 'proof of the feasibility of that which is in

---

[15] For a new English translation of this text, see Immanuel Kant, *Anthropology from a Pragmatic Point of View*, Cambridge Texts in the History of Philosophy (Robert B. Louden (ed. and trans.), Cambridge University Press, 2006). Kant poses three questions in the *Critique of Pure Reason* (A 805/B 833) and in the *Menschenkunde* anthropology transcription (XXV 1198): What can I know? What should I do? What may I hope? A fourth question (What is the human being?), to which the first three all relate, is added later in the *Jäsche Logic* (IX 25), letter to Stäudlin of 4 May 1793 (XI 429), and *Metaphysik Pölitz* (XXVIII 533–4). For further discussion of Kant's philosophy of hope, see 'Hope after Horror', in Robert B. Louden, *The World We Want: How and Why the Ideals of the Enlightenment Still Elude Us* (New York: Oxford University Press, 2007), pp. 213–23.

accordance with duty [*Beweis der Tunlichkeit des Pflichtmäßigen*]' (*MdS* VI 480).

The strong language of 'proof' (*Beweis*) in the last quotation deserves comment, for in certain respects it is very unKantian. As we have seen, one of Kant's central objections against trying to derive morality from examples is that empirical examples can never constitute proof of universal and necessary propositions. In the *Collins* moral philosophy lectures, for instance, he speaks directly to this issue, using the same German word '*Beweis*', but now stating that an example can never serve as proof of an *a priori* proposition (XXVII 333):

> What is apodeictically *a priori* needs no example, for there I perceive the necessity *a priori*. Mathematical propositions, for instance, need no examples; for the example serves not as proof, but as an illustration [*das Beispiel dient nicht zum Beweise, sondern zur Illustration*] … All cognitions of morality and religion can be set forth apodeictically, *a priori*, through reason. We perceive *a priori* the necessity of behaving so and not otherwise; so no examples are needed [*nötig*] in matters of religion and morality.

From a *logical* point of view, examples are not necessary in ethics: moral principles, since they are *a priori* concepts involving necessity and universality, cannot be proved by means of empirical examples, and this is one of the main reasons why a pure moral philosophy needs to be 'fully cleansed of everything that might in any way be empirical and belong to anthropology' (*G* IV 389). But from an *anthropological* point of view, examples are necessary in ethics. Given our subjective nature, we do need examples. Human beings cannot function without hope, and examples help to convince us of the feasibility of moral demands. Thus, in the *Metaphysics of Morals*, when Kant asserts that examples serve as proof, 'proof' is intended in a more informal, anthropological sense; while in *Collins* (and elsewhere), when he asserts that examples cannot serve as proof, 'proof' is meant in a formal, logical sense. Alternatively stated, examples can serve as proof that it is possible for human beings to act in accord with duty, but they cannot be used to prove or justify an *a priori* moral principle.

There is also an important flipside to Kant's argument that examples in ethics give us hope and inspiration. If no plausible examples can be found, then we have an excuse that morality is impossible: what it demands is not feasible for human beings, for no examples can be found of people who have lived up to its demands. As he states in *Collins*: 'Human beings like, in general, to have examples, and if none exists, they are happy to excuse themselves, on the ground that everybody lives that way' (XXVII 334). If no cogent examples can be found of persons who have lived up to morality's demands, then we are liable to avoid morality on the ground that it is simply beyond our capacities.

Kant's hope and inspiration argument in defence of examples may appear to overlap a bit with the earlier-discussed limitations of human reason argument, for in both cases we do find support for the claim that concrete examples are necessary for human morality. But there is a key difference. The limitations of human reason argument is primarily *epistemological*. Here, Kant's main point is that human beings, due to their discursive intellects, need to think analogically and metaphorically. The hope and inspiration argument is more *psychological*. Here, Kant's central point is that human beings are creatures who cannot function without hope, and that examples fulfil this function in the sphere of ethics. Examples serve to give human beings hope that what the moral law demands is feasible.

Emulation. Finally, Kant has a fourth major argument in defence of examples in ethics, which we may call the *emulation argument*. When human beings are presented with a viable moral example, they have something specific to emulate. Examples of moral goodness give us a concrete goal to aim at; a tangible ideal on which to model our own behaviour and character. In *Collins*, for instance, Kant states: 'Examples serve us for encouragement and emulation [*zur Aufmunterung und zur Nachfolge*], but must not be used as a model [*Muster*]. If I see a thing *in concreto*, I recognize it all the more clearly' (XXVII 333).

Here already we see a complication in Kant's emulation argument. We are urged to emulate examples, but we are also told not to use them as a model. We should strive to be like them, but we must not simply imitate or copy them. But how does one emulate something without imitating it? This complication is referred to again on the next page of the *Collins* lecture (XXVII 334):

An example [*ein Beispiel*][16] is not for imitating [*Nachahmung*], though it is certainly for emulation [*Nachfolge*]. The ground of the action must be derived, not from the example, but from the rule; yet if others have shown that such an act is possible, we

---

[16] In Paul Menzer's important edition of Kant's lectures on ethics, *Eine Vorlesung Kants über Ethik* (Berlin: Pan Verlag Rolf Heise, 1924), which is based on the Brauer, Kutzner and Mrongovius manuscripts, the word '*Exempel*' occurs here rather than '*Beispiel*' (p. 138), while the rest of the quoted passage is virtually identical with the above passage from *Collins*. In a footnote in *The Metaphysics of Morals*, Kant tries to differentiate between *Beispiel* and *Exempel*. The two words, he asserts, 'do not have the same meaning' (*MdS* VI 479 fn). *Exempel*, he claims, is properly used in the sense of 'taking something [or someone] as an *example* [*Exempel*]': whereas *Beispiel* is correctly used in the sense of 'to bring forward an instance [*Beispiel*] to clarify an expression' (*MdS* VI 479 fn.). Unfortunately, Kant

must emulate their example [*ihrem Beispiel nachfolgen*] and not let others surpass us in that respect.

We are guilty of imitating or copying an example in Kant's sense if we simply mimic it without reflecting on *why* it is a good example in the first place. It is wrong to copy or imitate examples in this manner, because when we do so we are not thinking things through for ourselves. We have failed to grasp that the true standard of moral assessment lies within our own autonomous reason. In the *Anthropology* he notes: 'The *imitator* [*Nachahmer*] (in moral matters) is without character; for character consists precisely in originality in the way of thinking. He who has character derives his conduct from a source that he has opened by himself' (VII 293). The same thought occurs in the *Groundwork*: 'Imitation [*Nachahmung*] has no place at all in matters of morality', and even though examples serve many humanly necessary and important functions in ethics, 'they can never justify setting aside their true original, which lies in reason' (*G* IV 409).

Kant also seeks to differentiate emulation (or imitation in the good sense) from mere copying (or imitation in the bad sense) by reminding readers that ultimately it is not any actual person or event that we should try to emulate, but rather an ideal of reason created by rational agents; an ideal which the person or event merely represents or makes visible to us. As he writes in *The Metaphysics of Morals*: 'it is not comparison with any other human being whatsoever (as he is), but with the *idea* (of humanity), as he ought to be, and so with the law, which must serve as the constant standard of the teacher's instruction' (*MdS* VI 480). Comparing ourselves to other people is always to be avoided,[17] because it can only lead to two bad outcomes: envy, in cases where we decide that they actually are better than us; or ridicule, in cases where we conclude that we are in fact better than them. As Kant states in his *Lectures on Pedagogy* (IX 491):

When the human being values his worth according to others, he seeks either to raise himself above others or to diminish the value of the other one. The latter, however, is envy [*Neid*]. One then always tries to impute a wrong to the other one ... The inappropriate spirit of emulation [*Geist der Ämulation*] merely stirs up envy. The case in which emulation could be of some use would be to convince someone

rarely follows his own advice regarding how to use these two terms, even in *MdS*, where the advice is presented. For example, at *MdS* VI 479 he refers to '*das gute Beispiel* of the teacher himself', whereas he should have referred to '*das gute Exempel* of the teacher himself'.

[17] For further discussion of this important point, see Allen W. Wood, *Kant's Ethical Thought* (Cambridge University Press, 1999), pp. 133–7; and Jeanine Grenberg, *Kant and the Ethics of Humility: a Story of Dependence, Corruption, and Virtue* (Cambridge University Press, 2005). For an appreciative critique of Grenberg, see Robert B. Louden, 'Kantian Moral Humility: Between Aristotle and Paul', *Philosophy and Phenomenological Research* 75 (2007), 632–9.

of the feasibility of a thing; for example, if I demand of a child that a certain lesson be learned and show the child that others can do it.

Ultimately, we should seek to compare ourselves only to the moral law itself, never to other people. Similarly, in the final analysis it is the moral law that we should seek to emulate, not other people or their actions. The latter merely help to make the former visible to the human eye.

The emulation argument may appear to overlap with the previously-discussed hope and inspiration argument, in the sense that both of them involve the general claim that reflection on actual examples can help us to achieve what moral principles demand of us. (Indeed, at the end of the passage just cited from *Pedagogy* IX 491, Kant himself, in saying that emulation is useful when it convinces us of the feasibility of a thing, blends the two arguments together. Cf. *G* IV 409.) But there is a fundamental difference. The emulation argument functions as a strategy for moral improvement: we should strive to equal and surpass the achievements and qualities of moral exemplars, and when presented with actual examples of moral goodness, we can see which aspects of our character and conduct need improvement. The hope and inspiration argument, on the other hand, functions more as a grounding for possibility. When we are presented with real exemplars and plausible examples, we become convinced that what morality demands is humanly feasible.

Once we step back from the *Groundwork's* tightly-focused aim of locating and justifying a supreme principle of morality that holds for all rational beings and redirect our attention to the more terrestrial task of finding out how human beings can become morally better, we see that Kant in fact offers four distinct arguments in defence of the necessity and importance of examples in the moral life of human beings. First, examples play a necessary role in the moral education of young people, for the immature human mind is not yet able to apply abstract moral principles effectively. Secondly, moral examples remain epistemologically necessary even for adult human beings. Human beings are saddled with a 'discursive, image dependent under-standing', and because of this they need to represent abstract moral concepts symbolically and analogically. Thirdly, examples provide us with hope and inspiration that what morality demands is humanly feasible. And fourthly, examples give us something concrete on which we can focus our own efforts – a mark to emulate and perhaps even to surpass.

3 WHY EXAMPLES ARE NOT ENOUGH

We have seen that on Kant's view examples perform necessary and impor-tant functions throughout the moral life of all human beings – they are essential not only for children but for adults as well. And they perform these functions due to certain basic facts of human nature. It is because of our all-too-human biological, psychological and epistemological make-up that we need examples in ethics. If we were non-human rational beings with a different biology, psychology and epistemology (and Kant did think that such creatures existed),[18] then his arguments in defence of examples would not apply to us at all.

But it remains the case that examples alone are insufficient for human morality. When Kant asserts in the *Groundwork* that morality cannot be legitimately derived from examples, he is on the one hand referring to moral principles that in his view hold 'not merely for human beings, but for all *rational beings as such*' (*G* IV 408; cf. IV 389). However, at the same time he is urging his human readers (and as far as we know, this is the only kind of reader he has yet had) not to fall into the trap of supposing that examples alone are enough in ethics. Any feasible human morality requires both general principles and concrete examples. Both components are necessary within our moral outlook; neither on its own is sufficient.

In order to gain a more balanced perspective on Kant's final assessment of the place of examples within human morality, let us therefore return briefly to some of the points raised in the Introduction concerning Kant's objections to assigning examples a foundational role in pure moral philosophy. We will then conclude by adding to this list of objections an additional Kantian criticism of examples in ethics which is not raised in the *Groundwork*.

Examples presuppose standards. First, any moral example, e.g. of right conduct or good character, presupposes a general standard by means of which it is judged to be right or good. This is a fundamental point that Kant defends not only in the *Groundwork* (IV 408) and *Collins* (XXVII 333), but also in the *Critique of Pure Reason* (A 315/B 372).

Think for yourself. Secondly, any critical approach to morality requires that we think for ourselves about the criteria of moral rightness and goodness. If we allow others to do our moral thinking for us by blindly following their example, we are cowards: we lack the courage to use our own understanding, and we have violated the motto of enlightenment. This is why Kant states repeatedly that 'imitation has no place at all in matters of

---

[18] For example, toward the end of the first *Critique* Kant notes that he has 'a strong belief (on the correctness of which I would wager many advantages in life) that there are also inhabitants of other worlds' (*CrV* A 825/B 854). For additional references and further discussion, see Louden, *Kant's Impure Ethics*, pp. 188 fn. 30, 212 fn. 89, 224 fn. 10, 13, 229 fn. 9.

morality' (*G* IV 409; cf. *Collins* XXVII 334, *MdS* VI 480, *Anthr.* VII 293). As he notes in the *Anthropology* (VII 229; cf. *Aufklärung* VIII 35, *CU* V 294):

The most important revolution from within the human being is 'his exit from his self-incurred immaturity'. Before this revolution he let others think for him and merely imitated others or allowed them to guide him by leading-strings. Now he ventures to advance, though still shakily, with his own feet.

Autonomy. Thirdly, if we rely too much on examples we run the risk of forfeiting our autonomy. The true source of morality lies within our own reason and not in any external, heteronomous sources, regardless of whether these sources be persons – even the Holy One of the Gospel or God himself – or actions. Even in the moral education of children, where examples are particularly important due to the inability of young people to think conceptually, Kant urges that moral education be an education *toward autonomy.* Students must come to see that the true norm of their conduct lies in their own reason, not in other people's behaviour. For instance, in his discussion of moral culture in the *Lectures on Pedagogy*, Kant states: 'everything is spoiled if one tries to ground this culture on examples [*Exempel*] ... One must see to it that the pupil acts from his own maxims ... He must at all times comprehend the ground of the action and its derivation from the concepts of duty' (IX 475). Similarly, in the 'Fragment of a Moral Catechism' (essentially, an imaginary conversation between teacher and student) that Kant presents toward the end of *The Metaphysics of Morals*, the teacher at one point reminds his pupil that (*MdS* VI 481):

as to how you should set about sharing in happiness and also becoming at least not unworthy of it, the rule and instruction in this lies in your *reason* alone. This amounts to saying that you need not learn this rule for your conduct from experience or from other people's instruction. Your own reason teaches you and directly commands you what you have to do.

Moral norms are a priori. Fourthly, genuine moral principles involve necessity and universality, and thus cannot be grounded in experience. Empirical examples alone are insufficient to justify *a priori* concepts and propositions. As Kant states in the second *Critique*: 'It is an outright contradiction to want to extract necessity from an empirical proposition (*ex pumice aquam*) and to give a judgement, along with necessity, true universality' (*CpV* V 12).

Groping in the dark. Finally, the methodology of popular philosophy, which seeks to ground ethics in examples, is defective and unable to arrive at a metaphysics of morals. But it is only within a metaphysics of morals that moral principles, as *a priori* propositions, can receive their necessary support. In order to reach the destination of a metaphysics of morals, a better philosophical method is needed, one that does not place more philosophical weight on examples than they are able to carry. 'Groping by means of examples' (*G* IV 412) cannot take us where we need to go.

Finally, Kant has an important additional argument against examples which he does not discuss in the *Groundwork*.

Overreliance on examples weakens judgement. Related to the autonomy argument is a more specific warning: overreliance on examples weakens our own native power of judgement. 'Examples [*Beispiele*]', Kant proclaims in a famous passage from the first *Critique*, 'are the go-cart [*Gängelwagen*] of the power of judgement, which he who lacks the natural talent for judgement can never do without' (*CrV* A 134/B 174). Concrete examples help us to learn how to exercise our judgement, just as a go-cart (a two-wheeled cart that was formerly used to teach children to walk by giving them support, the way training wheels are used on bicycles) provides support for children when they are first beginning to walk. But overreliance on examples in turn weakens our own ability to make independent judgements. As Kant remarks in the first *Critique* (*CrV* A 134/B 173; cf. *Aufklärung* VIII 36):

as far as the correctness and precision of the insight of the understanding is concerned, examples more usually do it some damage, since they only seldom adequately fulfil the condition of the rule (as *casus in terminis*) and beyond this they often weaken the effort of the understanding to gain sufficient insight into rules in the universal and independently of the particular circumstances of experience, and thus in the end accustom us to use those rules more like formulas than like principles.

Similarly, overreliance on go-carts may hinder a child's own natural ability to walk. In the *Lectures on Pedagogy*, Kant notes: 'It is customary to employ *leading strings* and *go-carts* in order to teach children how to walk. But it is striking that one should want to teach children how to walk, as if any human being could not have walked for lack of instruction' (IX 461).

Kant's Rousseauian conviction[19] that teachers and parents should not interfere with the organic development of natural human capacities lies behind this particular argument against examples. Examples can become crutches: if we rely too much on them, our own cognitive muscles may weaken and atrophy to the point where we are unable to think critically and

---

[19] 'Emile shall have no head-pads, no go-carts, no leading-strings; or at least as soon as he can put one foot before another he shall only be supported along pavements, and he shall be taken quickly across them' (Rousseau, *Émile* (Barbara Foxley (trans.), London: Dent, 1911; reprinted New York: Dutton, 1974), p. 42; cf. pp. 11–12 and 35–6).

independently about the principles by means of which the examples are judged. Overreliance on examples – as well as on go-carts – must be avoided (IX 466):

The first and foremost rule here is that all tools be dispensed with as far as possible. Thus leading-strings and go-carts should be done without right from the beginning, and the child should be allowed to crawl about on the ground until it learns to walk by itself, for then it will walk all the more steadily. For tools only ruin natural skill.

In conclusion, examples are necessary and important in the moral life of all human beings, but they are not sufficient. Examples help to make the moral law visible for human beings; without them, we are unable to see the law clearly. But examples do not make the moral law. We, as self-legislating rational beings, make this law. We are its co-authors, and we give it to ourselves by means of our own reflection and deliberation (cf. *G* IV 431).

CHAPTER 5

The moral law as causal law

Robert N. Johnson

A well-known gap exists in Kant's argument that the categorical imperative is the fundamental principle of morality. The gap is between the claim that rational agents act only on maxims that could serve as universal laws and the more substantial requirement contained in the categorical imperative.[1] There does not appear to be any obvious route from the seemingly trivial requirement to conform to universally valid laws to the controversial and substantive requirement of acting only on maxims that one can at the same time will that all other rational agents act on.[2] Kant apparently assumed that we conform our wills to universally valid laws only if we act on maxims that we can will to be universal laws, but many have pointed out he gives no defence of this assumption. In what follows, I focus on a preliminary step to connecting the two claims, the step that connects rational agency to conformity to universally valid laws. Why must the will of a rational agent, insofar as he is rational, be such that it is universally valid in any sense? My hope is that by first considering this question, some light can be shed on the nature of the remaining argument for the categorical imperative.

Many readers assume that for Kant, a rational agent must conform to universally valid laws because rational agency is *rational*, and rationality requires this sort of universal validity. For instance, this view appears to be implicit in Onora O'Neill's claim that 'the interest of a Kantian universality

I want to thank Stephen Darwall, Thomas E. Hill, Jr, Matthew McGrath, Andrew Melnyk, Mark Schroeder, Jens Timmermann, Alexander von Schönborn and an anonymous referee for helpful comments and discussions of the ideas in this chapter.

[1] Henry E. Allison, 'On a Presumed Gap in the Derivation of the Categorical Imperative', *Philosophical Topics* 19(1) (1991), 1–15; Bruce Aune, *Kant's Theory of Morals* (Princeton University Press, 1979), pp. 28–31; Thomas E. Hill, 'Kant's Argument for the Rationality of Moral Conduct', *Pacific Philosophical Quarterly* 66 (1985), 3–23, also in P. Guyer (ed.), *Kant's Groundwork of the Metaphysics of Morals: Critical Essays* (Rowman & Littlefield, 1998); Samuel Kerstein, *Kant's Search for the Supreme Principle of Morality* (Cambridge University Press, 2002); Christine Korsgaard, 'Kant's Formula of Humanity' in her *Creating the Kingdom of Ends* (Cambridge University Press, 1998), pp. 106–32; Allen Wood, *Kant's Ethical Thought* (Cambridge University Press, 1999), p. 81.

[2] See Hill, 'Kant's Argument for the Rationality of Moral Conduct', 268.

test is that it aims to ground an ethical theory on notions of consistency and rationality rather than upon considerations of desire and preference.'[3] This understanding of Kant's view as grounding universalization in rationality, in turn, draws objections from, for instance, particularists who believe that rationality is compatible with non-universalization.[4] But, as I contend below, the requirement that rational agents must conform their wills to universally valid laws is not based on the fact that rational agency is *rational*, but on the fact that it is *agency*. Indeed, the argument leading to the first formulation of the categorical imperative relies on the idea of rational willing as a kind of causation in order to show this. The moral law is a unique causal law, and it is in virtue of this fact that the moral law requires one's will to be universally valid.

My plan is as follows. I start by discussing the rationale behind thinking that conformity to universally valid laws is a requirement of rationality, where I conclude that it is at least an open question what grounds the 'universal' in the formula of universal law of nature. I then explain the role that conformity to universally valid causal laws plays in Kant's project of seeking out and justifying the supreme principle of morality. I follow this with a discussion of some burdens this leaves for Kantians who favour the first formulation of the categorical imperative as a criterion or test of right action. I end by claiming – admittedly without much argument – that while reason does not provide the universalization requirement in the categorical imperative, it does provide a spontaneity requirement. Whatever the moral law is, it must be the law of spontaneous self-governed agency, because our agency is the agency of rational beings, and reason is a spontaneous faculty. This is, of course, just the familiar message of Kant's ethics, that the moral law is the law of an autonomous will. Thus, the innovation I introduce to understanding the argument for the first formulation in what follows is that the universality required by the moral law originates in the causality of the will, while the spontaneity of the will comes from the rational origin of that causality.

A preliminary methodological point is worth making. The argument of the *Groundwork* is, by anyone's standards, exceedingly difficult to extract from the text. That is because, as is plain, the argument is very compressed and the writing is not particularly elegant. So it is often not obvious how to

---

[3] Onora O'Neill, 'Consistency in Action' in Paul Guyer, *Kant's Groundwork of the Metaphysics of Morals: Critical Essays*, pp. 103–31, at p. 127; see also Hill, 'Kant's Argument for the Rationality of Moral Conduct'.

[4] See, e.g. Jonathan Dancy, *Moral Reasons* (Oxford: Blackwell, 1993), p. 83.

move from one claim Kant makes to another. As a result, there are a variety of different, but reasonable, ways of putting together these claims into an argument. In what follows, I piece together a variety of texts in a way that makes philosophical sense overall, but I make no claim that this is the only defensible way of doing so. My main aim is to offer an argumentative structure that I believe makes sense out of what Kant says, and although I do claim that my reading raises problems for the defence of the first formulation of the categorical imperative, it does so by solving other problems.

I RATIONALITY AND UNIVERSALITY

A rational agent, insofar as she is a rational agent, acts on maxims that conform to principles to which all other similarly situated rational agents conform. Unfortunately, it is perfectly consistent with acknowledging that other similarly situated agents would be rational to adopt her principle that, nevertheless, a rational agent could not will that other agents adopt it. She need not be able to will this, and may well will that others do not adopt her principle, though she acknowledges that they could adopt it. That this does not follow leaves a gap in the argument establishing the first formulation of the categorical imperative. Possessing only the fact that rational agents conform their wills to what would apply universally in this sense, we cannot conclude that they must be able to will that everyone adopt their maxim. But why must a rational agent's volitional principle be universal in any sense?

It seems that many of Kant's readers think that it is in virtue of their rationality that it must be universally acceptable, willable, or whatever. Henry Allison, who regards this as only the 'first step' in a Kantian argument for universalizability, nicely summarizes this way of reconstructing the connection between rationality and universality:

In claiming that one's reason for acting in a certain way is 'good' in the sense of justifying reason, one is, implicitly at least, assuming its appropriateness for all rational beings ... Since ... to regard one's reason for acting in a certain way as good is to assume its legitimacy for all rational beings in similar circumstances, it would seem, so the argument goes, that rational agents cannot reject the universalizability test without, at the same time, denying their rationality.[5]

The idea is that it would be irrational to hold that one's reasons justify one's action and yet deny that it would be appropriate for all other rational beings

[5] Allison, *Kant's Theory of Freedom*, pp. 204–5.

in similar circumstances to act on those reasons as well. So rational agents must hold that the principle of their wills is appropriate for any rational agent to adopt. One passage from the *Groundwork* that might be thought to support this reconstruction tying universal validity to rationality is this (*G* IV 420–1):[6]

> When I think of a *categorical* imperative I know at once what it contains. For, since the imperative contains, beyond the law, only the necessity that the maxim be in conformity with this law, while the law contains no condition to which it would be limited, nothing is left with which the maxim of action is to conform but the universality of law as such.

Rational agents, at least insofar as they are rational agents, conform to categorical as well as hypothetical imperatives, or so is the message of the *Groundwork*. And while you can have no idea what taking the means to your ends will require of you until you have some end in mind, you do not require an end in order to know what a categorical imperative requires of you, and so you know 'immediately'. Categorical imperatives tell us to conform our maxims to practical laws without any such 'condition'. But, the proposed reconstruction of this argument goes, practical laws (as Kant explains in the footnote associated with the term 'maxim') are objectively valid. And objectively valid laws are 'valid for every rational being'. Therefore, rational agents act on universally valid laws (*G* IV 421 fn.). We might say that the proposed connection between rational agency and universality is through objectivity: rationality brings with it objectivity (in justification) and objectivity brings with it universal validity.

However, Kant himself does not say that rational agents must act on universally valid principles *because they are rational*. It may well be, of course, that their rationality demands this. But it may also be that rational agents are bound to universalize because being an *agent* of a certain sort demands it. There is no indication in the above passage from Kant which of these is so. However, as I will argue below, I believe the answer has in fact already been given in the discussion leading up to it. That discussion is best understood as claiming that it is because rational agents are causes that they must operate in a universally valid way. I return to explain why I think this prior discussion should be understood in this way below. Before I do, I want to say a few more things about the connection between rationality and universality.

---

[6] See, e.g. Wood's gloss on this passage in Wood, *Kant's Ethical Thought*, pp. 78–82.

Another route connecting rational agency to universal laws is through consistency rather than objectivity:

(1) Rationality requires consistency.

(2) Consistency requires conforming to universally valid laws.

From (1) and (2) it does indeed follow that rational agency requires conforming to universally valid laws in virtue of its being *rational*. It would be inconsistent, and hence irrational, to regard a principle as justifying your doing some action, but deny that it would justify similarly situated agents. Of course, rationality in this sense also requires conforming to the laws of non-contradiction, excluded middle and other laws of logic. It would, for instance, be contradictory, and hence also irrational, to adopt a self-contradictory principle. Rational agency thus brings these laws of reason that are valid for every rational being to bear on actions.

The difficulty with extracting universal validity out of rationality in this way is that it puts the moral law on a par with logical laws. But if the moral law is on a par with logical laws, it is difficult to see how it is supposed to be a law of *practical* rather than *theoretical* reason. The analysis of the concept of a rational being yields the conclusion that rational beings conform to logic. So if the conformity with universal laws contained in the categorical imperative is on a par with the laws of logic, it would seem the categorical imperative is a law of *thought*. But while rationality requires thought be one way rather than another, the puzzle is how to use this fact to explain how rationality requires action to be one way rather than another. More precisely, a straightforward application of logical laws to action would seem only to yield principles it would be impossible not to fulfil such as 'For every action, either do it or don't do it' or 'For every action, don't both do it and fail to do it'. Since the logical laws are the laws of what is logically possible, they have nothing to say about what one ought to do.

R. M. Hare, who took himself to be at least in part a follower of Kant, got conformity to universal laws out of rationality through the notion of *supervenience*.[7] Rational agents (oversimplifying) treat like cases alike. And to treat like cases alike is to do such things as the following: if I judge I ought to ø in C_1, then for every C_n that is like C_1, I should judge I ought to ø in C_n. If I am in circumstances that are exactly like other circumstances I was in and judged I ought to perform some action, then I should not judge anything other than that I ought to perform that action in the present circumstances. But to judge that in all C_n that are like C_1 I ought to ø is just to judge that I

---

[7] R. M. Hare, *The Language of Morals* (New York: Oxford University Press, 1991), p. 70.

ought to conform to a universally valid law. In essence, reason requires us to be *non-arbitrary* in our judgements about what we ought to do.

Hare's supervenience requirement is, however, in one sense weaker and in another sense stronger than Kant's. It is weaker in the sense that all that it requires is that, for all rational agents, if one judges x is F, then one must judge anything else that is like x is also F, and that, as Hare himself admitted, does not rule out a Nazi morality.[8] Indeed, human beings, even idealized ones, will differ in their ends, and given this, supervenience will not yield universally valid prescriptions.[9] Rationality may require supervenience, but supervenience does not provide laws valid for every rational agent. Hare's supervenience requirement is in another sense, however, stronger than Kant's, since for Hare universalization requires us to take each person's interests into account equally. But, quite famously, Kant's universalization does not do so, since the impact of an action on people's interests does not play a foundational role as it does for Hare.

Perhaps Kant thought that rational agents conform their wills to universally valid laws because he thought that rationality brings universality. But there is room to doubt that this is the source of the universalization requirement. Consider a very general point about the idea that a law or rule is 'valid of' or 'applies to' someone. Take some set of persons S and some law L that governs the actions of a person x who is in S. Knowing that L governs those who are in S requires knowing both L and the property F in virtue of which that L applies to those who are in S. That is, L applies to x who is in S because all Ss are F. Thus, answering the question 'Does L apply to x?' requires us to know what the F is in virtue of which L applies, and the content of the set of laws that govern persons with that property.

For instance, suppose I want to know whether the rule 'Be thrifty' applies to a given group of people. I will have an answer once I discover that the members of the group are Boy Scouts and that all Boy Scouts are adherents of the Scouting Laws. It is in virtue of being an adherent to the Scouting Laws that the law 'Be thrifty' governs Bobby, a given Boy Scout. Naturally, not every person who is actually a Boy Scout is also an adherent of the Scouting Laws, but let's suppose 'Boy Scout' is like 'rational agent' in the sense that someone who is a Boy Scout conforms to that rule, insofar as he is acting as a Boy Scout, or perhaps a Boy Scout who violated that rule is not in some sense being a *real* Boy Scout.

---

[8] R. M. Hare, *Freedom and Reason* (Oxford University Press, 1963), p. 192.
[9] See David Sobel, 'Do the Desires of Rational Agents Converge?', *Analysis* 59 (1999), pp. 137–47, for a treatment of this question, in connection with the views of Michael Smith.

Suppose now that Bobby is also a member of T, another set of persons, and because of this is not only an F but, in virtue of his membership in T, also a G. It then becomes a live question in virtue of which property L applies to Bobby, F or G. Suppose Bobby is both in the Boy Scouts and is a member of a martial arts group, say, Tae Kwon Do. Members of Tae Kwon Do are adherents of the Tae Kwon Do goals. We can ask in virtue of which membership the rule to be thrifty applies to Bobby. Is it in virtue of being a member of the Boy Scouts or Tae Kwon Do that Bobby must be thrifty? And, of course, there are three possibilities: he must be thrifty either because he is a Boy Scout, an adherent of Tae Kwon Do, or both.

Likewise, if there are laws or rules that apply to every rational agent, they will apply in virtue of the fact that every rational agent is rational, or is an agent, or both. More precisely, the rules that apply to rational agents will be such that their nature and content will be determined in part because of their rationality and in part because of their being agents. We could, for instance, imagine rational beings that are not agents, beings that do not bring about events in the world.[10] Whatever rules or laws apply to them would be distinctly different from those applying to rational beings who are also agents, and, moreover, whose agency operates through their rationality. So it is an open question whether the categorical imperative, as the supreme law of rational agency, requires universalizable maxims in virtue of the rationality of rational agents, their agency, or both.

It doesn't follow from this, of course, that Kant didn't, in the end, think as Allison or Hare does about these matters. The foregoing only shows that it is not obvious that this is so, or at least whether Kant thought in these ways about universalization. Thus, it is worth exploring an alternative proposal. In summary, my alternative is this: if reason is a cause, then at minimum it must act as a cause. And to act as a cause is to conform to universal law, or so acting as a cause is on Kant's view.

2 ROLE OF THE IDEA OF CAUSATION IN IDENTIFYING AND JUSTIFYING THE CATEGORICAL IMPERATIVE

The first paragraphs of Section III of the *Groundwork* show Kant arguing that conformity to universal law by rational agents is because they are causes, not because they are rational. There he asserts these two claims (*G* IV 446):

---

[10] Kant himself imagines such beings at *Religion* VI 26 fn.

(a) 'Will is a kind of causality of living beings insofar as they are rational'
(b) 'The concept of causality brings with it that of laws in accordance with which, by something we call a cause, something else, namely an effect, must be posited.'

(a) and (b) imply that it is in virtue of being a cause that a free rational agent must conform to universally valid laws. Thus, causation, not rationality, brings with it the idea of universally valid laws. Rational agents are causes and so are thereby bound by universal laws. And, indeed, Kant draws just this conclusion (*G* IV 446):

(c) 'So freedom, although it is not a property of the will in accordance with natural laws, is not for that reason lawless but must instead be a causality in accordance with immutable laws but of a special kind.'

They must be of a 'special kind' because no *natural* causal law can direct the workings of a free will; the causality of a rational agent must be non-natural, a causality of which rational agents, simply in virtue of their being rational agents, are the sources. Thus, the claim that an agent is a cause, together with the contention that causes do their work in conformity with universally valid laws, delivers the conclusion that rational agents, because they are agents, do their work in conformity with universal laws. The additional step that nature cannot be the source of the law according to which the causation of a rational agent is exercised allows us to conclude that this law is one and the same as the law of an autonomous will. Kant goes on to explain that whether rational beings such as ourselves *are* free causes in this sense is a 'third cognition', making the claim that we as free rational agents are bound by universal laws a synthetic claim (*G* IV 447).

Notice an important consequence of thinking of universalization as the upshot of causation rather than rationality. Every rational agent, Kant states, must act under the Idea of freedom. To act under the Idea of freedom is to act under the idea that one is a cause of a special kind, a 'first cause' of one's actions, but nonetheless a cause. If causation brings with it universal law, then in order to act under the idea that one is a (first) cause, one must act under the idea that one's actions are the upshot of one's will *in an essentially repeatable way*. It cannot be that one bears, in virtue of one's causality, a *sui generis*, one-off relation to one's action, or at least one cannot act under the idea that one bears such a relation. That is, acting under the Idea of freedom commits rational agents to acting under the idea that the law under which their volition falls is a causal law covering every other rational agent's causality. Rational agents are thus committed to this, not because they are rational, but because the alternative is that they would not be a self-originating cause of their actions.

Kant makes repeated references to the moral law as 'a law of causality through freedom' throughout his ethical works, and elsewhere in the *Groundwork*.[11] I want to discuss one of these references to which I referred above, the argument in *Groundwork* II leading up to the statement of the first formulation of the categorical imperative. That argument concerns how imperatives are possible. The line of reasoning hinges on the idea that willing is a kind of causation. This is why Kant held it to be analytic that whoever wills an end also wills (insofar as he is a rational agent) the necessary means to that end (*G* IV 417):

> In the volition of an object as my effect, my causality as acting cause, that is, the use of means, is already thought, and the imperative extracts the concept of actions necessary to this end merely from the concept of a volition of this end.

This idea introduces a feature of causation on Kant's view. Very roughly, if x is the cause of y, then if there is some z that is a cause of y, then either x is the cause of z or x = z. Thus, if one is to be the cause of an end, one must be the cause of whatever are the necessary means to that end. So in thinking of oneself as a cause of an end, one is *thereby* thinking of oneself as a cause of the means by which that end is to be brought about. We derive this law according to which our causality as rational agents operates – the law of willing the means to the ends that we will – from simply the idea of being the cause of an end.

By contrast, proving that rational agency demands conformity to the categorical imperative is not as easy. We cannot derive the law according to which our causality as rational agents operates in willing *moral* actions analytically from the idea that we aim to be the cause of some end to which the action is a means. Instead, the idea of ourselves as a cause is connected 'immediately with the concept of the will of a rational being as something that is not contained in it' (*G* IV 420 fn.). The idea of the law according to which a rational agent is the cause of actions that are *moral* actions is not 'contained in' the very idea of an agent who (contingently) wills some end, since it is not supposed to be the fact that we will be a cause of such an end that is the ground or reason for our willing the action. We will the action for its own sake, not for the sake of the end it brings about or realizes. Nevertheless, this law is 'immediately' (*a priori*) connected with rational agency. This entire line of reasoning moving toward a statement of the fundamental principle of morality thus relies on the idea that, whatever

---

[11] See, e.g. *CpV* V 47; also V 42–58, V 103–5, *passim*.

role rationality ultimately plays, it will also be the nature of causality that constrains what the fundamental principle of morality turns out to be.

Again, a key move in the line of reasoning in *Groundwork* I identifying the categorical imperative as the fundamental principle of morality relies on viewing the issue as having to do with the nature of causality in rational agency. That move is the argument for the premise that duty is conformity to universal law as such. This argument appeals to the nature of the motive of a good will, respect for duty. Respect, Kant argues, cannot be taken up toward something that gets a grip on us by way of the effects of our actions. This is because the object of respect must satisfy a kind of uniqueness condition: for any effect of our action, that effect (*G* IV 401):

could have been also brought about by other causes, so that there would have been no need, for this, of the will of a rational being, in which, however, the highest and unconditional good alone can be found.

Respect is thus elicited only by something *unique*, in particular, a unique *cause*, while anything that is caused by a will of that sort could have been caused by something other than it. If true, this claim has the consequence that respect can focus only on the 'activity of the will' itself, insofar as it is an activity of a cause, and not on *what* the will causes or the outcomes of agency (*G* IV 400). Respect for duty thus involves conceiving of the special way in which practical reason operates as a cause. In particular, it represents the causation of practical reason as unique. And in turn, that, Kant states, is 'the representation of the law in itself, *which can of course occur only in a rational being*, insofar as it and not the hoped for effect is the determining ground of the will' (*G* IV 401). The 'it' in the last clause is the representation of the law. Why it can 'of course' occur only in a rational being is explained later in the *Groundwork* II: only a being with reason can derive actions from laws. But if I am right, it is in representing practical reason as a cause that we thereby are representing a law, but a unique one that can only be found in a rational will.

In *Groundwork* II, Kant spells out more fully the line of argument from agency to universalization, although the reasoning here, well known as it is, is also quite compressed. The operation of a rational will is itself, he argues, the source of the requirement of conformity to universal laws. He sets up the discussion by stating that, in seeking out the content of the moral law (*G* IV 412):

we must follow and present distinctly the practical faculty of reason, from its general rules of determination to the point where the concept of duty arises from it.

This line of reasoning would make most sense if Kant believes that a correct understanding of reason insofar as it is a cause will itself reveal the universalization requirement. The discussion that follows turns to the will's 'general rules of determination', that is, the rules according to which it brings about action (read: causal laws). The determination of the will is, he states, according to *representations of laws* and not merely, as with everything else in nature, according to laws of nature. His first claim is thus (*G* IV 412):

Everything in nature works in accordance with laws. Only a rational being has the capacity to act *in accordance with the representation* of laws, that is, in accordance with principles, or has a *will*.

If rational beings alone had the capacity to entertain representations, then of course *a fortiori* only rational beings would have the capacity to act in accordance with their representations of laws. But having the capacity for representation is too broad a feature to explain what it is to be a rational agent, and, anyway, animals also have the capacity to entertain representations. One might suppose, instead, that Kant's idea is that other beings, while capable of entertaining representations, might (so far as his statement supposes) still lack the capacity to represent *laws*. And so one might justifiably think that Kant's view is that beings that cannot represent *laws* are not rational agents, that to have a will requires being able to represent laws.

Now one might think this because one supposes that the representation of anything requires the representation of laws. But this would be a mistake. Suppose, for instance, that y is a painting by an abstract expressionist. And suppose x is the sketchbook of an art student who is studying the painting by reproducing it in her sketchbook. x is thus a drawing of y. In being a drawing of y, x could be a representation of y. Yet y contains nothing in it that is lawfully related to anything else. Then x represents y, but, if it is faithful, neither x nor y contains any lawful relations within them. A representation thus need not contain anything in it that is lawfully related to anything else. One might assume that the possibility of representation itself requires some organizing principles within the thing represented. But why? There are paintings, for instance, that have no elements and *ipso facto* no organizing principles of those elements – for instance, a red canvas. And our imagined artist could represent those paintings, too.

There could be creatures that represented the world as if some sort of abstract expressionist created it – completely without any regular relations between any elements of the representation – but nevertheless moved about that world in a regular, law-like way through means that do not involve representations of that world. If that is how things are for other agents, then perhaps only rational beings represent the world as operating according to laws. Then, again *a fortiori*, it would follow that only rational beings would have a capacity to act in accordance with such representations. However, this doesn't seem to be what Kant is getting at. It doesn't seem to be simply for lack of thoughts about the lawful operation of the world that non-rational agents lack a rational will. One could, for instance, imagine a creature who could represent the world as operating according to laws, in fact could represent itself as connected through laws to the operations of that world, and yet not have these representations lead to any action, to any willings, at all. Its representations of the lawfully related elements of the world might be causally isolated from that world.

Whether or not lawfulness is in fact a necessary condition of the possibility of being represented, Kant himself of course might have, for some reason or other, thought that it was. But, even if he did, it does not seem that the reason he held that only a rational being can act according to its representations of laws has to do with such a belief. It has instead to do with the fact that only such a being can *act* on the basis of representations, only such a being's causal power operates on the basis of representations, rather than simply on the laws of nature themselves. And this is in turn because only such a being possesses the rational faculty required, both in terms of representing and in terms of making things happen on the basis of those representations. In fact, this explains what Kant says next (*G* IV 412):

Since *reason* is required for the derivation of actions from laws, the will is nothing other than practical reason.

This statement should not be misunderstood of course. Kant is not here making the disastrous mistake some commentators have attributed to him, that since the will is practical reason, we cannot will irrationally, hence we cannot will immorally, hence we are not responsible for immorality.[12] We can indeed will immorally according to his view. In so doing, we are simply failing to conform our wills to principles that, insofar as we are fully rational agents, we will that we adopt and act on. Indeed, the will is a faculty that must employ reason to bring about action. Thus, only a rational being can act according to the representation of laws precisely because acting according to such representations requires reason to 'derive' an action from the law.

---

[12] See, e.g. Robert Paul Wolff's *The Autonomy of Reason* (New York: Harper and Row, 1973), p. 211.

Kant here says that reason is required to derive an action from a law itself, not the *representation* of a law. This is important. One might assume that Kant is saying something akin to what has puzzled Aristotle's readers for millennia, namely, that the conclusion of a practical syllogism is an *action*.[13] That is, one might assume that Kant is representing practical reasoning in a way that is completely parallel to the way that many have thought that Aristotle represented it, with the major premise being the agent's representation of some law of action, the minor premise being the agent's representation of her particular situation (say, a perception) as covered by the law, with the action being the outcome of reason's putting these two things together. Reason's work does not appear to be of this sort, if we take Kant at his word in this passage. Reason derives actions from laws, where we are to understand that this is all conceived of as occurring within the realm of reasoning, rather than partially within that realm and partially in the realm of actions and events. The idea is that rational beings represent laws, laws represented as connecting their actions to the world through these laws, and in so doing they derive representations of their actions from these laws. Thus, practical reasoning occurs all within representations. Because it takes reasoning to derive anything from anything, it takes reason to derive an action from a law: in other words, to reason about how actions are lawfully related to the world.

For instance, given my aim to drink the water in the glass on the table and the belief that picking up the glass is a necessary means to drinking it, it takes reason to derive the representation 'Pick up the glass' from the representation of the law 'Take the necessary means to your ends'. Having derived this conclusion, however, I still must bring it about that I pick up the glass. Nevertheless, the correct explanation for my picking it up, should I do so, will have to include the fact that I formed the intention to pick it up by way of deriving it from this principle of instrumental rationality – a representation of a law.

Now consider in general how the representation of a law would be involved in the determination of the will. How, for instance, could a belief whose content concerns a law lead us to decide on a course of action? One obvious way in which it could do so is this: the law is a natural causal law and concerns how we are through our acts to cause some end that we have adopted. In that case, believing that a given causal law holds will lead us to act. Believing the law 'Touching fire causes burning sensations' will lead me, under circumstances in which I am aware of being in the presence of fire, to

---

[13] Aristotle's *Nicomachean Ethics* (2nd edn, T. Irwin (trans.), Indianapolis/Cambridge: Hackett, 1999), 1147a27.

decide not to touch it, since *ceteris paribus* I am averse to burns. Believing the causal law 'Eating candy produces pleasure' will lead me, under circumstances in which I am aware of being in the presence of candy, to decide to eat the candy, since *ceteris paribus* I desire such pleasure. I say *ceteris paribus*, because of course there are other background conditions that must be met for me to decide any of these things.

So the representation of a law can determine the will when reason has derived an action from that law and there is a background end that is produced by or realized in that action as represented by the resulting derivation from that law. In the cases we have just considered, the laws may seem only to include psychophysical causal laws, laws connecting material events and sensations. Practical reason's job would, in this circumstance, seem to be purely cognitive and theoretical: reason simply locates and represents the relevant natural causal law connecting our actions to the fulfilment of our desires. However, Kant is not talking about the representation of *any* law as capable of determining the will, but clearly only those laws that are connected in the right way to the agent herself.

Return now to the (presumed) law of rational agency: 'Take the necessary means to your ends'. Much, if not all, of the time, 'take' and 'means' are causings and 'ends' are effects. Oversimplifying, the principle of the hypothetical imperative mostly amounts to 'insofar as you are a rational agent, cause the causes of your (aimed at) effects'. Since you aim to cause the effect, it is analytic that you cause the causes of those effects, by way of the principle noted above, that to conceive of x as the cause of y is to think that if there is some z that causes y, then either x causes z or x=z. However, even though 'take' and 'means' are both causal terms, in fact they are radically different kinds of causes. 'Means' can be thought of as causes that operate according to natural causal laws, but the idea of 'taking' those means is the idea of being a *first* cause, of being the origin of the causal chain referred to as the means that will result in an end. So, it turns out that one very surprising feature of Kant's conception of rational agency is this: *in every bit of rational agency*, we are acting according to our representations of *two* entirely different sorts of law, the laws governing the means, or phenomenal causation, and the law governing the exercise of our rational agency, a law of intelligible causation.

It is these sorts of considerations, along with the passages that support them, that seem to me to make a very strong case for the view that the moral law is a special sort of causal law. The moral law is the law according to which the causality of a rational will operates. And it must be universal because the very idea of a causal law requires universal validity.

3 PROBLEMS

One reason for thinking that Kant took the moral law to be a law of causality was that he discussed some of the difficulties this posed for his view. In the second *Critique*, he states that Hume was 'quite correct in declaring the concept of cause to be deceptive and a false illusion' given he 'took objects of experience as things in themselves' (*CpV*V 53). By contrast, he thought that since his transcendental idealism holds that the objects of experience are 'only appearances':

I was able not only to prove the objective reality of the concept of cause with respect to objects of experience but also to *deduce* it as an a priori concept because of the necessity of the connection that it brings with it

leaving him an embarrassing question, namely:

How is it with the application of this category of causality ... to things that are not objects of possible experience but lie beyond its boundaries?

That is, Kant's line of argument, both in the *Groundwork* and in the second *Critique*, requires us to apply the concept of causation to rational beings. Indeed, 'in the concept of a will ... the concept of causality is already contained, and thus in the concept of a pure will there is contained the concept of a causality with freedom' (*CpV* V 55). But the exercise of free rational agency is not a possible object of experience, indeed *precisely because* it is free and hence not governed by natural causal laws. Since it is not a possible object of experience, there seems to be no justification for applying the concept of causation to any rational being.

   Kant's solution to this potentially devastating problem was to claim that our purpose in applying the concept of causation to rational agents is a *practical* not a *theoretical* one. I take this to mean that because we are reasoning our way to conclusions about what we ought to do, and not to conclusions about what we are, we are justified in applying the concept of causality to *noumena* such as rational wills. In so reasoning, given the fact that thoughts about 'what we ought *to do*' are at bottom thoughts about 'what we ought to *cause*', we have to make use of the concept of causation. We are 'authorized' to apply the concept in this case (*CpV* V 56):

by virtue of the pure, not empirical origin of the concept of cause, inasmuch as I consider myself authorized to make no other use of it than with regard to the moral law which determines its reality, that is, only a practical use.

That is, since the moral law presents itself to us as a law of causing an action whether there is any prior desire in us to do so or not, it is a law of causing an action whether there is any prior natural cause in us that will have this action as its effect. And since it is a law of causing an action whether there is any prior natural cause in us that will have this action as an upshot, it is a law of a free causation. This 'fact of reason' 'determines the reality' of our wills as free causes but only for practical purposes.

Thus, it seems very much as if Kant's argument is that since he has shown that the concept of causation is justifiably applied to appearances, it now can be applied to things as they are in themselves *for practical purposes*. There are further problems that Kant does not discuss. For one thing, causation, insofar as it is a concept the analysis of which yields conformity to universal laws, is a *schematized*, not a pure, category. Unschematized, the concept is merely the logical connection 'if-then', logical antecedent and consequent, with no temporal dimension. It is its schematization that makes it possible for us to make phenomenal causal judgements that imply that events are lawfully related (*CrV* A146–7/B185–7). But if it were to apply to noumena, causation could not possibly be a schematized category, and so could not possibly yield the notion of conformity to universal law. Causal judgements about agents do not merely apply a concept that is only theoretically justified for use in the world of appearances; they apply a concept that *is itself* partly empirical. Indeed, it is just this fact that allows Kant to draw, by appeal to the concept of causation, the conclusion that, because rational agents are causes, they are bound by universal laws.

In Kant's defence, however, the first *Critique* argues that we can at least think of causation in two ways, as *natural* causation or as *free* causation, and it is the latter '*transcendental* idea of *freedom* on which the practical concept of freedom is grounded'. The faculty of free causation in us is (*CrV* A533/ B561):

the faculty of beginning a state *from itself*, the causality of which does not in turn stand under another cause determining it in time in accordance with the law of nature ... a spontaneity, which could start to act from itself.

What is needed is some way of getting from this idea of spontaneity, of a being's 'beginning a state from itself' to the idea of conformity to universal law, *without* appealing to the concept of 'the connection of a state with a preceding one in the world of sense upon which that state follows according to a rule', that is, without appealing to the concept of natural causation. The problem is that free causality does not, as he puts it, 'stand under any conditions of sensibility and is not itself appearance' (*CrV* A 539/B 567).

Kant appears to think he has gained the notion of conformity to universal law in this way: when we think about the world governed by natural causation and hence universal natural laws, we are thinking about everything that has happened, is happening, or will happen. But when we consider the idea that reason might be a spontaneous cause of something in the world, 'we find a rule and order that is entirely other than the natural order', the order, not of what happens, but what *ought* to happen (*CrV* A 550/B 578). Since it is still an order of 'happenings' it is still a causal order. The 'non-natural' laws of free causation govern this alternative 'non-natural' causal order. While this thought goes some way toward helping us to understand why and how Kant thought that causation can be rightfully deployed in practical matters, it still leaves unexplained why this non-natural free causation should be ordered lawfully, given it seems that it is the concept of natural causation that carries with it the idea of universally valid laws.

Perhaps there is some further idea that will render Kant's views internally consistent on this point, though I fail to see what it is. A final issue nevertheless remains. Any defence of the formula of universal law will have to rely on a conception of causation according to which a causal relation between particular events implies that there is some universally valid law governing the types of events that are so related. But it is by no means uncontroversial that the concept of causation implies such law-governed relations. There could be counterfactual accounts, for instance, that comport well with the idea that there is some sort of metaphysical connection or 'glue' between causally related events, just the sort of metaphysical glue that regularity theories deny. And while the existence of laws may well in turn be required to explain these connections, whether it does or not depends, not upon the analysis of the concept of causation, but the metaphysical structure the universe. What this means for Kantians who would like to defend the universal law of nature formulation of the categorical imperative is that, if I am right, they will not only have to plug the gap between conformity to universal law and the canonical statement of that formulation; they will also have to defend the idea that causation implies the existence of universal laws governing the causal relata.

4 THE ROLE OF REASON IN RATIONAL AGENCY

If conformity to universal laws is a requirement of agency rather than rationality, what is left for the 'rational' in rational agency to do? I want to end on a few thoughts about this. What is distinctive about the laws of *rational* as opposed to other sorts of law-governed causality? As I see it, Kant's thought was that reason brings spontaneity, not universality, to the moral law. Whatever the universally valid law is according to which the will is a cause, it is the law of a spontaneous 'first' cause. In part, I believe he thought this because of the way in which reason operates, or at least as we understand or sense how reason operates (*CpV* V 48, V 101). When reasoning, either theoretically or practically, we do so with some sense of our reason as operating with a kind of spontaneity. This spontaneity, moreover, is not apparent when, for instance, we observe people or (if possible) ourselves reasoning. Hence, Kant states that (*CrV* A 547/B 575):

in the case of lifeless nature and nature having merely animal life, we find no ground for thinking of any faculty which is other than sensibly conditioned. Yet the human being, who is otherwise acquainted with the whole of nature solely through sense, knows [*erkennt*] himself also through pure apperception, and indeed in actions and inner determinations which cannot be accounted at all among impressions of sense.

Kant thought that we somehow 'know' through 'pure apperception' that we are spontaneous origins of actions. I put 'know' in scare quotes because counting this as knowledge runs counter to Kant's official line that knowledge extends no further than the objects of possible experience, and he is here denying that we can know about this spontaneity through some sort of empirical introspection. That this apperception is 'pure' implies that it is not an empirical awareness of oneself. So Kant believes we are in some special sense conscious of ourselves and how our reasoning operates, but not through empirical introspection. Kant adds 'and indeed in actions'. It is not merely the spontaneity of reason in theoretical reasoning, in reasoning from belief to belief, of which we are (somehow) cognizant; we are also aware of the spontaneity of reason in practical reasoning, in reasoning from imperatives to action.

Apperception is supposed to be some kind of consciousness of oneself of the sort contained in connecting 'I think' to all of our representations. Although I myself am unable to make completely clear what it is that Kant is thinking of with the idea of 'pure apperception', I have some idea of what he is getting at. With regard to our experiences of the world, it is difficult to imagine that someone could be unsure of whose experiences he was having. Of course, it is trivially true that my experiences are mine. And some schizophrenics feel that their thoughts aren't really theirs or that they are not the authors of their thoughts, that their thoughts in fact belong to someone else who is beaming them into their consciousness. But in some sense beyond the bare analytic truth, yet which is consistent with psychotic phenomena, we are aware that our experiences are necessarily ours. Likewise, it is difficult to imagine someone who could be unsure of whose volitions he was having. Again, in some sense beyond the related bare analytic truism, but consistent with the phenomena associated with some kinds of psychoses, we are aware that our volitions are necessarily ours.

Now, turning to the awareness of the spontaneity of our reason: what Kant himself says (again in *Groundwork* III) is this (*G* IV 448):

> In [a rational agent] we think of a reason that is practical, that is, has causality with respect to its objects. Now, one cannot possibly think of a reason that would consciously receive direction from any other quarter with respect to its judgements, since the subject would then attribute the determination of his judgement not to his reason but to an impulse. Reason must regard itself as the author of its principles independently of alien influences.

The idea expressed in this passage, I take it, is roughly this: it is impossible to imagine someone who could be unsure whether his reason operated spontaneously through a given bit of reasoning that he engaged in. A person is apparently necessarily aware of the spontaneity of the operation of his reasoning. There is some plausibility to this: consider reasoning through a maths or a logic problem. It is not that we have an *experience* or *feeling* of our own reason spontaneously moving from thought to thought, nor do we *believe* our reasoning faculty's movements from premise to conclusion or through steps of addition is spontaneous. Indeed, we may believe quite the reverse, that this sense of our reason as operating spontaneously is an illusion. Nevertheless, in such activities, we do seem to be operating under some conception of our own reason as not 'made to' reach conclusions from outside of itself, as moving freely from premise to conclusion. Reason is making itself move through premise to conclusion, from figures to sums, and so on. That, at any rate, seems to be a datum, if not of experience, then of an overall conception under which we reason.[14]

Likewise, we have a sense of our reason's spontaneity provided by apperception of the operation of practical reason as a cause. Given Kant's own arguments regarding natural necessity, no natural laws govern this causality. Yet there can be no causality without laws. So our apperception of the spontaneity of reason is left with a vacant place where a law should stand. 'Pure practical reason', Kant boldly states in the second *Critique*, 'fills

---

[14] Thanks to my colleague Alexander von Shönborn for pointing out this passage. His helpful paper covers Kant's views on intelligible causation: 'Kant and the Absolute', *Southwestern Journal of Philosophy* 7 (1976), 145–52.

this vacant place with a determinate law of causality in an intelligible world (with freedom), namely the moral law' (*CpV* V 49). If our reason is a spontaneous cause, or at least if we have to operate under that conception of ourselves, then the law according to which our causality as agents operates is the law of a spontaneous causality. And, of course, the law of a spontaneous cause can only be a law of which that cause is itself the author. So whatever else reason brings to rational agency, it brings the 'auto' part of the idea of autonomy, the idea that this universal law according to which it must operate originates in the cause itself.

CHAPTER 6

Dignity and the formula of humanity

Oliver Sensen

I INTRODUCTION

It is central to Kant's moral philosophy that one should always treat other human beings with respect.[1] He articulates this requirement in his formula of humanity as an end-in-itself, which he calls the supreme limiting condition of one's freedom: '*So act that you use humanity, whether in your own person or in the person of any other, always at the same time as an end, never merely as a means.*' (*G* IV 429, cf. IV 430 ff.) However, the exact reason why one should respect others remains a matter of debate. The standard view in the Kant literature is that one should respect others because of an absolute inner worth or value[2] all human beings possess. The absolute value is often called 'dignity',[3] and dignity is said to be the reason why one should respect others.[4] The debate focuses on the question whether human beings have this value or dignity in virtue of a pre-moral capacity they have (such as freedom or the capacity to set ends),[5] or because of a morally good will.[6]

I would like to thank audiences at the APA in San Francisco, the Eastern Study Group of the NAKS in New York, the Universities of Cambridge, Tulane, Washington St Louis, and the ZetKIK in Siegen for helpful challenges.
[1] Kant famously credits Rousseau for his appreciation of the importance of respecting all human beings, cf. 'Bemerkungen zu den Beobachtungen über das Gefühl des Schönen und Erhabenen' XX 44.
[2] In the following I shall use 'worth' and 'value' interchangeably as Kant only used one word: '*Werth*'.
[3] Cf., e.g. H. J. Paton, *The Categorical Imperative* (Hutchinson, 1947), p. 189; G. Löhrer, *Menschliche Würde* (Alber, 1995), pp. 34–44; A. Wood, *Kant's Ethical Thought* (Cambridge University Press, 1999), p. 115; Dieter Schönecker and Allen Wood, *Kant's 'Grundlegung zur Metaphysik der Sitten.' Ein einführender Kommentar* (Schöningh, 2003), p. 142.
[4] Cf., e.g. Paton, The *Categorical Imperative*, p. 171; D. Ross, *Kant's Ethical Theory* (Clarendon Press, 1954), pp. 52–4; Löhrer, *Menschliche Würde*, p. 124, and pp. 34–6; and A. Wood, 'Kant on Duties Regarding Nonrational Nature I', *Aristotelian Society Supplement* 72 (1998), 189–210.
[5] Cf. Paul Guyer, *Kant on Freedom, Law, and Happiness* (Cambridge University Press, 2000), ch. 4; Christine Korsgaard, *Creating the Kingdom of Ends* (Cambridge University Press, 1996), ch. 4; Wood, *Kant's Ethical Thought*, ch. 4.
[6] Cf. Paton, The *Categorical Imperative*, p. 168; Ross, *Kant's Ethical Theory*, p. 51; Richard Dean, *The Value of Humanity in Kant's Moral Theory* (Clarendon Press, 2006), chs. 1–5; Samuel Kerstein, 'Deriving the Formula of Humanity' in C. Horn and D. Schönecker (eds.), *Kant's Groundwork of the Metaphysics of Morals: New Interpretations* (de Gruyter, 2006), pp. 200–21.

Against the standard view I shall argue that Kant does not ground the requirement to respect others on any value at all. Rather, one should respect others because it is commanded by the categorical imperative.[7] While this claim is not novel,[8] what is new is my argument that the formula of humanity passage (*G* IV 427–9) supports this claim.

In order to argue for the above claims I shall first give the reasons why I do not follow the standard reading. In Section 2 I shall suggest that prominent arguments to establish an absolute value all human beings possess prior to being moral do not succeed. While Kant does tie an absolute worth to a morally good will, this worth is not the reason why one should respect others. In Section 3 I shall present my alternative reading of the derivation and justification of the formula of humanity. I shall argue that ends-in-themselves are the ground of the categorical imperative in virtue of freedom[9] – a conclusion that anticipates Kant's justification of the imperative in the third section of the *Groundwork*. One should respect others because it is implied by the requirement of the categorical imperative to universalize one's maxim. In Section 4 I shall address Kant's conception of human dignity in *Groundwork* IV 434–6. Since people often interpret Kant as using 'dignity' as a name for a non-relational absolute value property all human beings possess, and since I am arguing that Kant does not have such a conception of value, I will need to show that his usage of 'dignity' reflects that fact as well.

In short, my aim in this chapter is to give a reading of the formula of humanity and dignity that can do without a value as a foundation. In Section 2 I shall shift the burden of proof to the defenders of the standard reading; Sections 3 and 4 present my positive reading of the terms.

2 THE STANDARD READING

In the *Groundwork*, Kant seems to be saying that all human beings as such have an absolute worth (cf. *G* IV 428), and that only a morally good will can have an absolute worth (cf. *G* IV 393). Accordingly, much of the

---

[7] Here and throughout the rest of the chapter with 'categorical imperative' I shall refer to the universal law formula: 'act only in accordance with that maxim through which you can at the same time will that it become a universal law' (*G* IV 421).

[8] Cf., e.g. Julius Ebbinghaus, 'Die Formeln des Kategorischen Imperativs und die Ableitung inhaltlich bestimmter Pflichten', in his *Gesammelte Schriften* (Bouvier, 1988), vol. II, p. 216; Onora O'Neill, *Constructions of Reason* (Cambridge University Press, 1989), ch. 7; and Roger Sullivan, *Immanuel Kant's Moral Theory* (Cambridge University Press, 1989), pp. 193–5. Paul Guyer argues along similar lines that the categorical imperative is implied by the formula of humanity, cf. his *Kant* (Routledge, 2006), p. 194.

[9] Throughout this chapter I shall only be concerned with freedom of the will. Whenever I use 'freedom' I shall mean it in this sense.

contemporary literature on the formula of humanity attempts to determine which of the two views justifies the requirement to respect others. In this section I shall argue that in fact Kant uses neither teaching for that end. First, I shall suggest that prominent arguments to establish an absolute value of all human beings fail. Secondly, I shall argue that the absolute worth of a morally good will is neither a property all human beings possess, nor is it the reason why one should respect others.

The derivation of the formula of humanity is commonly interpreted along the following lines:[10] Kant says that every action needs an end (cf. *MdS* VI 385). Accordingly, it is alleged, morally worthy actions, in which the agent follows the categorical imperative for its own sake, also need an end. This end cannot be an end that the agent sets for himself based upon his inclinations, as such ends are relative; for relative ends could only ground hypothetical imperatives ('do x if you are inclined to y'), but not a categorical one. Therefore, the end of moral actions must be a self-existing one (cf. *G* IV 437). In a further step, it is argued that this end-in-itself is humanity.

On textual grounds, this common reading does not seem correct. The passage in the *Doctrine of Virtue* that is commonly cited in support of it does not refer to ends that are the ground of the categorical imperative, but to ones that *follow* from the imperative: 'Hence in ethics the *concept of duty* will lead to ends ... we *ought* to set ourselves, grounding them in accordance with moral principles.' (*MdS* VI 382). These ends that one ought to pursue are one's own perfection and other people's happiness (cf. *MdS* VI 385 ff.). In the *Groundwork* Kant says that every maxim (which one may set for oneself) has an end, and that the formula of humanity specifies what the categorical imperative says 'in respect' of ends (*G* IV 436, cf. IV 431), without invoking there the idea of a ground of the imperative.

Apart from these textual difficulties with the standard view, Kant does not seem to give an argument that *all* human beings have an absolute worth. I shall now briefly[11] consider the three most prominent ones ascribed to him in the literature, and suggest that they do not succeed internally. I do not claim to show that these arguments could never work, but my points aim to shift the burden of proof to the defender of these arguments. According to the first one, human beings have an absolute worth because they are the

[10] For the following see Paton, *The Categorical Imperative*, p. 167; Korsgaard, *Creating the Kingdom of Ends*, p. 109; Dean, The *Value of Humanity in Kant's Moral Theory*, pp. 110–12.

[11] For further discussion see my 'Kants Begriff der Menschenwürde' in F.-J. Bormann and C. Schröer (eds.), *Abwägende Vernunft* (de Gruyter, 2004), pp. 227–31.

unconditional condition of the value of things.[12] The argument starts with the view that the value of things is always conditioned. For instance, a knife only has value if one values it as a means for something else (e.g. cutting bread). What makes a thing valuable as a means is that it is the object of one's choice; in choosing, human beings are said to confer value on the thing. Now, human beings can confer this value, it is said, only if they themselves have an absolute value. The argument is said to be contained in the derivation of the formula of humanity in the way explained above: every action needs an end; moral actions cannot be grounded in relative ends; humanity is an end-in-itself in being the unconditioned condition of the goodness of things.

However, even if one grants the starting point that the value of things is always conditioned, the argument is not convincing. For the value of things is considered to be a relational property, while the value of human beings is said to be non-relational or intrinsic.[13] Yet a relational property need not be conditioned by the same property non-relationally: if something is only funny if it is funny to human beings, for instance, it does not follow that human beings must be funny in themselves. Similarly, if one construes the value of things as a relational property, 'a knife has value' means something like 'a knife is useful for'. If a knife is only useful if it is useful for human beings, it does not follow that human beings have an absolute value. The value of a knife can be explained by its utility for human beings, whether or not they have any value 'in themselves'.[14]

As a response to my objection one could argue for the weaker claim that every human being *has to regard* himself as having absolute value (instead of actually having it). This is a second argument that is often read into the derivation of the formula of humanity.[15] It refers to Kant's seeming claim that everyone has to regard himself as being an end-in-itself, and that therefore it would be an objective principle that everyone is an end-in-itself (cf. *G* IV 428 ff.). The problem is that it is not clear why one should respect others. Knowing that everyone values himself is perfectly compatible

---

[12] See Korsgaard, *Creating the Kingdom of Ends*, pp. 122, 240 ff.; Löhrer, *Menschliche Würde*, pp. 269–98; Wood, *Kant's Ethical Thought*, p. 130. I will confine myself to the main lines of the argument.

[13] Korsgaard, *Creating the Kingdom of Ends*, p. 257.

[14] The argument is not changed essentially if one claims that a thing has to be held to be good *for all*. In addition, several scholars argue that this move is not Kant's; cf. Kerstein, 'Deriving the Formula of Humanity', pp. 206–10; and Jens Timmermann, 'Value Without Regress: Kant's "Formula of Humanity" Revisited', *European Journal of Philosophy* 14 (2006), 73–80.

[15] To the following cf. C. Korsgaard, *The Sources of Normativity* (Cambridge University Press, 1996), pp. 122, 124 ff., 132, 250; cf. also Paton, The *Categorical Imperative*, p. 176; Gerald Prauss, *Kant über Freiheit als Autonomie* (Klostermann, 1983), pp. 126–46.

with a Hobbesian war of all against all.[16] In order to work the argument would have to establish that human beings have to regard each other as valuable.

One attempt to deliver that conclusion is the third argument I want to consider. In the derivation of the formula of humanity, Kant refers to the third section of the *Groundwork* to justify the claim that everyone has to regard himself as an end-in-himself. Since he also says that everyone has to regard himself and others as part of a world as it is in itself, might he not think that everyone is valuable in virtue of being part of such an order? After all, he does say that the world in itself is the ground of appearances, and that the way one is in oneself is one's 'proper self' (*G* IV 457 ff., IV 461).[17] However, it does not seem to follow from this that human beings have an absolute worth in virtue of being part of a world as it is in itself. For instance, a chair as it appears has its ground in the world as it is in itself. From this it does not follow that the chair (or its ground) has an absolute value. The relative superiority of the world as it is in itself does not by itself entail a moral claim. One still would need a further argument to show that human beings have an absolute value. Accordingly, Kant talks about the 'proper self' in the context of explaining why one should take an interest in the moral law: 'the law interests because it is valid for us as human beings, since it arose from our will as intelligence and so from our proper self' (*G* IV 461). If there is a conflict between one's inclinations and what morality demands, one should be moral, because morality originates from one's proper self. In other words, the agent should give preference to morality; for, in acting morally, one is not determined by external forces, but free. Kant does not give a further argument that a world as it is in itself has absolute value.

These difficulties in finding an argument for the absolute value of *all* human beings strengthen the other strand of the standard reading. According to this strand, one should respect others because they (possibly[18]) have a morally good will. This reading is suggested by the wider context of Kant's thought. At the beginning of the *Groundwork* Kant famously states that only a morally good will can be said to be unconditionally and absolutely good. And he reiterates that in saying that the absolute worth

[16] Cf. Raymond Geuss, 'Morality and Identity' in Korsgaard, *Sources of Normativity*, p. 198; and A. Gibbard, 'Morality as Consistency in Living: Korsgaard's Kantian Lectures', *Ethics* 110 (1999), 140–64 at 163.

[17] See especially Schönecker and Wood, *Kant's 'Grundlegung zur Metaphysik der Sitten.'*, pp. 142–7, 195–202; D. Schönecker, *Kant: Grundlegung III. Die Deduktion des kategorischen Imperativs* (Alber, 1999), pp. 387–9.

[18] Cf. *G* IV 437; and Friedo Ricken, 'Homo noumenon und homo phaenomenon' in O. Höffe (ed.), *Grundlegung zur Metaphysik der Sitten. Ein Kooperativer Kommentar* (Klostermann, 1989), pp. 234–52 at p. 246.

of a human being is something one can give only oneself in being morally good.[19]

However, it does not follow that this value is the reason why one should respect others. For it remains unclear what exactly is meant by 'absolute worth', and whether it can ground such a requirement. What exactly is this value ontologically, and how can it be known? Does one mean that a good will has a non-natural, non-relational value property adhering to it? One could argue that this value is known through the feeling of respect.[20] However, Kant's ethics would then rely on a moral sense rather than pure reason, and he rejects that approach (cf. *G* IV 426; *MdS* VI 400). More importantly, Kant repeatedly claims that the respect one feels for others is properly speaking a respect for the moral law of which the other gives us an example, not respect for an absolute value property inherent in another.[21] Most importantly, Kant explicitly denies that the morally demanded respect for others is a feeling: to have a feeling cannot be commanded (cf. *G* IV 399). Rather Kant conceives of the demanded respect for others as a maxim one should have (cf. *MdS* VI 449, cf. VI 468 ff.).

However, the main reservation I have against this view is that it treats value as if it were a non-relational property and foundational. Kant never elucidates absolute worth in this way. For instance, he writes: 'That will is *absolutely good* that cannot be evil, hence whose maxim, if made into a universal law, can never conflict with itself.' (*G* IV 437). In passages like these where Kant specifies when something is absolutely good, he never says that something is good because of a non-relational value property it possesses. The logical form 'X has absolute value' does not commit Kant to an ontological claim of the form 'X has a non-relational value property'. Rather, something is absolutely good if it follows the categorical imperative for its own sake. Ontologically, there is only a will and the categorical imperative. I therefore agree with scholars who say that what Kant means by 'absolute worth' is simply a *prescription* of what one should do, or a description of what a fully rational being would do.[22] To say 'a good will is absolutely good' is then a shorthand for saying 'one should value following the categorical imperative for its own sake independently of what one is

---

[19] See especially *CU* V 433, cf. V 208ff., but also, e.g. *G* IV 439, IV 449 ff., IV 454; *CpV* V 110 ff., V 147 ff.

[20] Cf. Wood, *Kant's Ethical Thought*, pp. 141 ff., 147–9; and Dean, *The Value of Humanity in Kant's Moral Theory*, ch. 7.

[21] Cf. *G* IV 401 fn.; *CpV* V 76 ff., V 87; and *MdS* VI 467 ff.

[22] Cf. Ross, *Kant's Ethical Theory*, p. 50; Thomas Hill, 'Treating Criminals as Ends in Themselves', *Annual Review of Law and Ethics* 11 (2003), 17–36 at 19; Thomas Hill, *Dignity and Practical Reason in Kant's Moral Philosophy* (Cornell University Press, 1992), p. 48; and Richard Dean, 'Cummiskey's Kantian Consequentialism', *Utilitas* 12 (2000), 25–40 at 34.

inclined to'. This suggestion will form an important part of my argument in sections 3 and 4 of this chapter.

Finally, the standard reading seems to me misguided because, in Kant's presentation, absolute value does not serve as the justification for rights in the sense of entitlements; rather, it is the categorical imperative that does so. One can claim a right in reminding the agent of his duty: 'the *moral imperative* ... is a proposition commanding duty, from which ... the concept of a right, can afterwards be explained.' (*MdS* VI 239).

3 THE ALTERNATIVE READING
(*GROUNDWORK* IV 427–9)

In the previous section I cast doubt on the view that Kant justifies the requirement to respect others on the basis of an absolute value of human beings. In this section I shall present an interpretation of the *Groundwork* passage in which Kant presents the formula of humanity (*G* IV 427–9). I shall argue that, on a close reading of that passage, the following picture emerges: Kant introduces the formula of humanity in order to bring the categorical imperative closer to intuition. Every action and every maxim has an end, and in respect of ends the imperative says that one should treat the subject of all ends, a rational being, always as an end-in-itself. I shall argue that 'end-in-itself' is foremost a descriptive term. Human beings are ends-in-themselves in virtue of freedom, that is they are not determined, or not the means to another's end, but in themselves an end. By itself this is not a normative claim. One *should* treat others as ends-in-themselves because of the universalization requirement of the categorical imperative. The imperative requires that one not act on maxims that could not be adopted by others (cf. *G* IV 421). This, Kant says, is the same as respecting them as ends-in-themselves. The significance of my interpretation is therefore that it construes the categorical imperative and the formula of humanity without referring to an absolute value as their foundation.

To understand the passage in which Kant first states the formula of humanity, one has to start as early as *G* IV 425, right after the law of nature formula: 'act as if the maxim of your action were to become by your will a *universal law of nature*' (*G* IV 421, second-order emphasis deleted). Kant concludes the discussion of this formula by emphasizing that he has not yet justified the categorical imperative. So far, he has only argued for a conditional: if there is moral duty, it can only be expressed in a categorical imperative. 'But we have not yet advanced so far as to prove a priori that there really is such an imperative, ... and that the observance of this law is duty' (*G* IV 425). Kant warns again that one cannot answer these questions in referring to a special property of human nature, as morality should be valid for all rational beings; and he reiterates the question that has not yet been answered: 'is it a necessary law *for all rational beings* always to appraise their actions in accordance with such maxims as they themselves could will to serve as a universal law?' (*G* IV 426).

Kant continues in light of this question. He says that if there is such a law, 'it must already be connected (completely *a priori*) with the concept of the will of a rational being as such' (*G* IV 426). (Unfolding these *a priori* connections is what Kant means by 'metaphysics', cf. *MdS* VI 216.) Because Kant explains the concept of a will in the next paragraph, one might think that he wants to give a justification of the categorical imperative within the derivation of the formula of humanity. However, in Section 2 I suggested that there is no such justification at this point. Rather, Kant is still dealing with the question of whether the categorical imperative is a necessary law for all. In saying that the law is connected to the concept of a will, Kant anticipates his conclusions of the third section of the *Groundwork*. There, he argues that freedom is connected to the concept of a will, and that freedom is the ground of the imperative. The categorical imperative is directly given with freedom; Kant does not invoke a value of freedom. As the causality of nature has its law, so the causality of freedom has a law: 'a free will and a will under the moral law are one and the same' (*G* IV 447).[23] In *G* IV 426, Kant does not yet talk about the requirement to respect others.

On a close reading, Kant's specification of the concept of a will in the next paragraph (*G* IV 427) does not contain anything new. Ends serve to determine the will. If those ends follow from reason (like the ends that are also duties – one's own perfection and the happiness of others) they are objective and the same for every rational being. Ends that one adopts because of an inclination could not ground the categorical imperative; for these ends are relative to one's faculty of desire, and therefore cannot ground a *universal* moral law. This has been the tenet throughout the *Groundwork*.

The crucial passage comes in the next paragraph. Kant says (*G* IV 428):

But suppose there were something the *existence of which in itself* has an absolute worth, something which as *an end in itself* could be a ground of determinate laws; then in it, and in it alone, would lie the ground of a possible categorical imperative, that is, of a practical law.

---

[23] This view has not changed in the *Critique of Practical Reason*. There Kant confirms: 'Thus freedom and unconditional practical law reciprocally imply each other' (*CpV* V 29), and he calls freedom the '*ratio essendi*' of the moral law (*CpV* V 5 fn.).

Since in the next sentence Kant asserts that human beings are ends-in-themselves, this passage can easily be read as saying that human beings have an absolute worth that justifies the categorical imperative and the requirement to respect others. Yet, a different picture emerges if one looks more closely at how Kant uses 'end-in-itself' (and 'absolute worth'). I shall argue that it is *freedom* in virtue of which something is an end-in-itself. Freedom is then the ground of the categorical imperative. This is the same justification as Kant gives in the third section of the *Groundwork*. There is no further justification in the passage in which Kant presents the formula of humanity.

To understand this passage, one therefore has to clarify his usage of 'end-in-itself'. What does Kant mean by an 'end-in-itself [*Zweck-an-sich*]'? The expression clearly has a normative component. A human being (as an end-in-himself) 'must in all his actions ... always be regarded *at the same time as an end*' or 'may not be used merely as a means' (*G* IV 428). As such these specifications merely state how one should treat something that is an end-in-itself; they state the normative connotations. However, they do not clarify in virtue of which feature something is an end-in-itself: what is the descriptive component of 'end-in-itself'? And what is the justification for the normative connotations?

Adding that an end-in-itself has 'an absolute worth' does not clarify anything. For, as I suggested in Section 2, 'absolute worth' is merely a shorthand for the prescription of what one should value independently of one's inclinations. Nothing Kant says here contradicts that account. Therefore, to say that an end-in-itself has absolute worth is merely to reformulate the normative component of 'end-in-itself' – that is, that one should value human beings independently of whether one wants to.[24] The key to understanding the descriptive aspect of 'end-in-itself' must be found elsewhere.

In order to find the descriptive component of the concept of 'end-in-itself' one has to go beyond the *Groundwork*. Throughout his published writings Kant uses the phrase 'end-in-itself' only twenty-six times.[25] Where he does specify it, he equates it with 'final end' (see Kant's essay on *Theory and Practice* VIII 279 fn.; *CU* V 429). What he means by speaking about a

---

[24] This is the same for the second time Kant talks about absolute worth. He says that human beings should not be treated as mere means, 'since without it nothing of *absolute worth* would be found anywhere' (*G* IV 428), i.e. without the requirement to respect others, there would be nothing one should value for its own sake. If there is nothing that should be valued this way, there would not be a categorical imperative. This passage makes sense if the requirement to respect others is the same requirement as the categorical imperative (see below).

[25] In his published writings he uses the exact phrase only twenty-two times: see *G* IV 428–31, IV 433–5, IV 438; *CpV* V 87, V 110, V 131; *MdS* VI 345, VI 423, VI 435; and *Religion* VI 13. Four times he uses the

final end depends on the context. In an Aristotelian sense he calls happiness the final end of one's (pre-moral) strivings (*Religion* VI 6 fn.). He talks about the highest good as the final moral end (*Theory and Practice* VIII 279 fn.); and he talks about freedom as the final end of nature (*CU* V 448 ff.). For the *Groundwork*, in which Kant says that an end-in-itself is the ground of morality, the first two candidates for 'final end' cannot be meant. Kant repeatedly says that happiness cannot be the ground of morality, and the highest good *follows* from morality (*Theory and Practice* VIII 279). This suggests that, in the *Groundwork*, something is an end-in-itself in the sense of final end of nature.

Kant talks about 'final end of nature' in the *Critique of Judgement*. There, Kant argues at length that, in order to unify one's cognitions about the natural world, one is justified in regarding the world as if it has a final end (cf. *CU* V 425–34). While one does not have certainty of the truth of the proposition, reason necessarily conceives of nature this way. It is a regulative, not a constitutive principle (cf. *CU* V 396, V 403 ff.). The final end of nature is rational beings, i.e. beings that have free will, in virtue of which they are 'under the moral law' (*CU* V 448 ff., cf. V 436). The descriptive element in virtue of which human beings are final ends of nature or ends-in-themselves is freedom and the capacity for morality (cf. *CU* V 448 fn.).

In other words, without freedom one would be a mere plaything of nature, or the means to someone else's end. It is only in virtue of freedom that one is not merely a means to another's end, but in itself an end.[26] What is important to note is that this claim by itself only amounts to a descriptive sense of 'end-in-itself' and 'freedom', without making a moral claim. It says only that in being free, one is not causally determined by an outside ground. Again Kant does not invoke a value property. Rather, all normative requirements follow from the categorical imperative, which is itself given with freedom. It is therefore one and the same claim, when Kant (in the derivation of the formula of humanity) says that an end-in-itself is the ground of the categorical imperative, and when he (in the third section of the *Groundwork*) says that freedom is that ground.

The paragraph in which Kant first states the formula of humanity now appears in a new light. The question Kant started out with was whether the formula of natural law is a necessary or objective law for all rational beings (*G* IV 426). Kant had said that such a law must spring *a priori* from the

plural (*G* IV 433, IV 462; *Cp*V V 87; *CU* V 429). In addition, he thrice talks about something being 'in itself an end [*an sich selbst Zweck*]': *G* IV 391, IV 428; and *On the Common Saying: 'This May Be True in Theory, But It Does Not Apply in Practice'*, VIII 289.

26 See Feyerabend's notes on Kant's 'Naturrecht' lectures, XXVII 1322.

concept of a will (presumably because only *a priori* reasoning can yield necessity, cf. *CrV* B 3 ff.). Kant now describes this process in a way that anticipates his answer in the third section of the *Groundwork* (*G* IV 428 ff.):

> If, then, there is to be … a categorical imperative, it must be one such that, from the representation of what is necessarily an end for everyone because it is an *end in itself*, it constitutes an *objective* principle of the will and thus can serve as a universal practical law. The ground of this principle is: *rational nature exists as an end in itself.*

If the categorical imperative is to be a necessary and objective principle it must spring from what is a necessary feature of everyone's will. The necessary feature is that rational nature exists as an end-in-itself. I have argued that this amounts to saying: 'A rational nature is free.'[27] Everyone is free, and freedom is the ground of the categorical imperative. Therefore the categorical imperative is a necessary law for all, i.e. an objective principle. Kant goes on to qualify the statement that everyone is free in direct reference to the third section of the *Groundwork* (*G* IV 428 ff.):

> The human being necessarily represents his own existence in this way; so far it is thus a *subjective* principle of human actions. But every other rational being also represents his existence in this way consequent on just the same rational ground that also holds for me; … thus it is at the same time an *objective* principle from which, as a supreme practical ground, it must be possible to derive all laws of the will.

Everyone has to regard himself as being free. As freedom is the ground of the imperative, it is therefore a subjective principle of everyone. But one also has reason to attribute freedom to every other rational being. In the footnote Kant explicitly refers to the third section of the *Groundwork* for a justification of this claim. There, he argues that everyone has to regard himself and others as being free in virtue of having reason (cf. *G* IV 447 ff.). 'It', that is the categorical imperative,[28] is therefore an objective principle. Kant's answer to the original question at *G* IV 426 therefore is: the imperative is a necessary law for all rational beings, because it springs from a rational will in virtue of freedom which all share.

Accordingly, Kant's claim in the context of the formula of humanity, that an end-in-itself is the ground of the categorical imperative, merely anticipates the conclusions he reaches elsewhere about the justification of the imperative. However, this means that the derivation of the formula of humanity is not explained at *G* IV 427–9. He states (*G* IV 429):

---

[27] For Kant's usage of 'rational nature' see Timmermann, 'Value Without Regress', p. 71.
[28] Schönecker and Wood, *Kant's 'Grundlegung zur Metaphysik der Sitten'*, p. 145, fn. 70.

The practical imperative will therefore be the following: *So act that you use human-ity, whether in your own person or in the person of any other, always at the same time as an end, never merely as a means.*

Kant has not yet explained why one should respect others. To put it differently: so far, I have argued that the expression 'end-in-itself' has a descriptive and a normative component. The descriptive component is freedom; the normative component is that one should treat beings with freedom never merely as a means, but always at the same time as ends-in-themselves (i.e. as being free). The reason for that requirement has not yet been spelled out. So far I have only argued for the negative claim (in Section 2) that it is not an absolute worth human beings possess.

At *Groundwork* IV 427–9 Kant does not spell out the justification for the requirement to respect others. However, he states it clearly in the summary of the derivation he gives a few pages later. Kant's answer is that one should respect others because it is demanded by the categorical imperative. The formula of humanity is 'at bottom the same' (*G* IV 437) as the formula of universal law. That is, the requirement to respect others is implied by the requirement to universalize one's maxims. The reason Kant gives is this (*G* IV 438):

to say that in the use of means to any end I am to limit my maxim to the condition of its universal validity as a law for every subject [formula of universal law] is tantamount to saying that the subject of ends, that is, the rational being itself, must be made the basis of all maxims of actions, never merely as a means but as the supreme limiting condition in the use of all means, that is, always at the same time as an end [formula of humanity].

In other words, in the requirement to universalize one's maxim for every subject, one is thereby required to respect those over whom one universalizes.

Kant states this point more explicitly in the *Critique of Practical Reason*. The formula of universal law requires that no rational being be subject to a maxim that could not arise from its own will. This is the same as requiring that one treat another always as an end-in-itself (*CpV* V 87):

by virtue of the … moral law … every will … is restricted to the condition of agreement with the *autonomy* of the rational being, that is to say, such a being is not to be subjected to any purpose that is not possible in accordance with the law that could arise from the will of the affected subject himself; hence this subject is to be used never merely as a means but as at the same time an end.

Both formulas express the same requirement, but the formula of humanity focuses on the affected subject, while the formula of universal law focuses on the will of the agent: the agent should test whether his maxim can be universalized, which – if looked at from the perspective of the recipient of one's actions[29] – means that one should reject a maxim that could not spring from the will of the affected. The reason why one should respect others is therefore that it is commanded by the categorical imperative.

However, this view raises new questions: why does the imperative not demand respect for non-rational beings (e.g. non-rational animals)? If, as I have argued, the imperative does not rest on a value of rational natures, is the requirement to respect other rational beings arbitrary? Is Kant a species- ist? In the *Groundwork* Kant is as brief about the status of non-rational beings as he is elsewhere.[30] Kant says: 'Beings the existence of which rests not on our will but on nature, if they are beings without reason, still have only a relative worth, as means, and are therefore called *things*' (G IV 428). The idea seems to be that non-rational beings do not possess freedom, and are therefore mere playthings of nature (cf. *CU* V 426). But why does this lack of freedom give things the *normative* status as means? Why do human beings not have a direct duty to respect them?

The key point in answering these questions seems to me to be a matter of burden of proof.[31] Kant rejects the view that there is a value property 'out there' (in heaven or earth) on which one can then base the requirement to respect either humans or non-rational beings: 'we see philosophy put in fact in a precarious position, which is to be firm even though there is nothing in heaven or on earth from which it depends or on which it is based' (G IV 425). If there is no value property that could justify the requirement to respect non-rational things, then the burden of proof is on the defender of such requirements. Kant does not arbitrarily give human beings a status that he should also attribute to non-rational beings; rather, the only requirement that he can find is that one should universalize one's maxims and thereby respect others, which as such only extends to beings who are able to act on maxims. Kant then uses this requirement to extend respect as far as he can to non-rational beings. One has an indirect duty to respect animals because cruelty to them would jeopardize the maxims needed for being morally good (cf. *MdS* VI 442–4). The question is what effect cruel behaviour has on the agent himself, rather than whether one respects an existing value property.

---

[29] Cf. O'Neill, *Constructions of Reason*, pp. 141–4.
[30] Cf., e.g. *MdS* VI 442–4; *Collins* XXVII 458–60; R 7305 XIX 307.
[31] Cf. Onora O'Neill, 'Kant on Duties Regarding Nonrational Nature II', *Aristotelian Society Supplement* 72 (1998), 211–28 at 222.

To conclude, the formula of humanity is introduced to bring the categorical imperative 'closer to intuition'. Every action and maxim has 'an end, and in this respect the imperative says that a rational being … must in every maxim serve as the limiting condition of all merely relative and arbitrary ends' (*G* IV 436). The formula of humanity does not introduce a new claim, it merely expresses the same moral requirement in a more accessible way. Kant makes explicit the reason why one should respect others only in the summary of the formula of humanity (*G* IV 437 ff.).

4 DIGNITY (*GROUNDWORK* IV 434–6)

At first sight my interpretation of the formula of humanity might seem to be at odds with Kant's account of human dignity. I have argued that Kant does not ground the requirement to respect others on an absolute value property. However, one might object that Kant explicitly defines such an absolute value of human beings as dignity later in the *Groundwork* – for how else is one to read his expressions: 'inner worth, that is, dignity' (*G* IV 435) and 'dignity, that is, an unconditional, incomparable worth' (*G* IV 436)? The objection loses force if one keeps in mind what Kant means by 'absolute worth'. If I am right that for Kant 'absolute worth' is not a non-relational value property all human beings possess, but rather a prescription of what one should value, then defining 'dignity' as 'absolute worth' would be no objection to my interpretation of the formula of humanity. 'X has dignity' would be another way of saying 'X should be valued unconditionally'.

However, Kant's conception of dignity is more complicated than this. I shall argue that it is neither a name for a non-relational value property, nor is it simply a prescription to value something. Instead, Kant's conception of dignity is indebted to Cicero and the Roman conception of *dignitas*, according to which dignity is an elevated position or rank.[32] The Roman *dignitas* is a complicated notion that has further connotations, e.g. worthiness, duties and privileges. Many of these are reflected in present-day usage, as when one speaks of a 'dignitary' or behaving with dignity. However, the additional connotations are not essential to *dignitas*.[33] The essential component is that dignity expresses a *relation*, an elevated standing

---

[32] For a fuller defence of the following cf. my 'Kant's Conception of Human Dignity', *Kant-Studien* (forthcoming).

[33] For Cicero's conception of *dignitas* cf. the *Oxford Latin Dictionary* (P. G. W. Glare (ed.), Oxford University Press, 1996); and V. Pöschl, 'Der Begriff der Würde im antiken Rom und später', in *Sitzungsberichte der Heidelberger Akademie der Wissenschaften. Philosophisch-historische Klasse* (Carl Winter, 1969), vol. III, pp. 7–67.

of something over something else. Cicero applied this notion to *all* human beings: all human beings are said to be elevated over the rest of nature in virtue of having a certain capacity (reason). Only in a further step does having reason logically yield a normative requirement, a duty to behave in a certain way.[34] Kant knew and approved of the Stoic conception of dignity,[35] and he adhered to it himself. Throughout his writings Kant specifies 'dignity' as sublimity [*Erhabenheit*] or the elevation of something over something else.[36] Ontologically 'dignity' refers to a relational property of being elevated, not to a non-relational value property. 'X has dignity' is another way of saying that 'X is elevated over Y' or 'X is higher than Y'. In particular, Kant specifies sublimity as the highest form of elevation,[37] so that to say 'X has dignity' is to say 'X is raised above all else'. What it is raised above, and why, depends on the context in which Kant uses 'dignity'. For instance, Kant uses expressions like the 'dignity of a monarch'[38] to refer to the elevated position a king has in the state; when he talks about the 'dignity of humanity [*Würde der Menschheit*]'[39] he is expressing the view that human beings are special in nature in virtue of being free (i.e. in a pre-moral sense elevated over the rest of nature). When he talks about the dignity connected to morality[40] he is saying that morality is raised above all else in that only moral dictates should be followed unconditionally.

The latter use is prominent in the main *Groundwork* passage that deals with dignity (*G* IV 434–6). The first thing to note is that this passage does not at all have the importance one would expect if 'dignity' were the name for an absolute value property. In that case one would expect Kant to talk about dignity at a point where he wants to justify the requirement to respect others. Rather, the passage on dignity is an addendum to the formula of autonomy: 'act only *so that the will could regard itself as at the same time giving universal law through its maxim*' (*G* IV 434).[41] Kant raises the question

---

[34] Cf. Cicero, *De Officiis*, book I, § 105–107; and my 'Kants Begriff der Menschenwürde', pp. 221–4.

[35] See *Religion* VI 57 fn. Klaus Reich argues that Kant's *Groundwork* was (in part) a direct response to Cicero's *De Officiis*; cf. K. Reich, 'Kant and Greek Ethics II', *Mind* 48 (1939), 446–63.

[36] Cf. 'Observations on the Feeling of the Beautiful and Sublime' II 212, 215, 241; *G* IV 425, 440; *CpV* V 71; *MdS* VI 435; *Logic* IX 30. Sometimes Kant expresses this as something being below someone's dignity, e.g. in: *CrV* III 419; *CpV* V 327; *Religion* VI 113; *MdS* VI 327; *Lectures on Pedagogy* IX 489.

[37] Kant characterizes sublimity or *Erhabenheit* as that which is absolutely great or great without comparison, cf. *CU* V 248.

[38] *The Conflict of the Faculties* VII 19.

[39] For instance, in *G* IV 439, IV 440; *CU* V 273; *Religion* VI 80, VI 183; *MdS* VI 420, VI 429, VI 436, VI 449, VI 459, VI 462; *Lectures on Pedagogy* IX 488, IX 489.

[40] Cf. *G* IV 440; *CpV* V 147; *MdS* VI 464, VI 483.

[41] For a fuller treatment of the reason why in this passage dignity is not an absolute value property, see my 'Kant's Treatment of Human Dignity in the *Groundwork*', in V. Rohden *et al.* (eds.), *Recht und Frieden in der Philosophie Kants* (de Gruyter, 2008), vol. III, pp. 391–401.

of why a morally good being abides by this formula. His answer (in brief) is because morality has an elevated worth (i.e. only moral dictates are categorical).

The passage begins (*G* IV 434):

The practical necessity of acting in accordance with this principle [the formula of autonomy], that is, duty, does not rest at all on … inclinations …. Reason accordingly … does so … from the idea of the *dignity* of a rational being, who obeys no law other than that which he himself at the same time gives.

The question Kant addresses in the main passage on dignity is accordingly a question about moral motivation in the widest sense. The end of the quotation makes clear that Kant has the dignity of a morally good being in mind. A morally good being does not abide by the formula of autonomy because of an inclination, but from the idea of the dignity of being morally good.[42]

Kant goes on to elucidate dignity as elevation: 'what on the other hand is raised above all price' (*G* IV 434) has a dignity. He makes clear that it is morality that is raised above price, and that '[h]ence morality, and humanity insofar as it is capable of morality, is that which alone has dignity' (*G* IV 435). If this were a statement that morality and humanity have an absolute value, this sentence would be problematic. There could be conflicts between the requirements to value above all else both humanity and a good will.[43] If, however, Kant understands dignity to be an elevated position and not a value, then the statement makes sense: morality is elevated over merely relative values, humanity is elevated over the rest of nature in virtue of being capable of morality. I therefore do not read his claim that morality has an 'inner worth, that is, *dignity*' (*G* IV 435) as a definition of 'dignity' as inner worth, but to emphasize 'inner'[44] (and later 'incomparable', cf. *G* IV 436). Morality has an inner and incomparable worth, i.e. an *elevated* worth or an elevated position in terms of worth. This reading is equally possible, and it is supported both by the context of the passage, and by Kant's wider use of 'dignity'.[45]

The same holds for the second passage in which Kant seems to define dignity as absolute worth. Kant says that the moral law determines all

---

[42] This is a common theme throughout Kant's writings, cf. e.g. *MdS* VI 483, VI 459; *CpV* V 152; *Religion* VI 183; *The Conflict of the Faculties* VII 58.

[43] Cf. Kerstein, 'Deriving the Formula of Humanity', pp. 216–20.

[44] Kant uses 'inner' to express the negative claim that something is not merely relative, cf. Löhrer, *Menschliche Würde*, p. 35.

[45] See again my 'Kant's Conception of Human Dignity', *Kant-Studien* (forthcoming).

worth, and that therefore the law-giving that determines all worth must have a dignity and an unconditional worth. I have argued in Section 2 that this is not a valid argument for establishing that all human beings have an unconditional worth. In fact, this passage confirms the opposite: 'nothing can have a worth other than that which the law determines for it' (*G* IV 435 ff.[46]): there is no value (of human beings or otherwise) that grounds the moral law. It is the other way around. What the passage says is that the moral law determines all worth, and that therefore the process of giving law, i.e. actually being morally good, must have the unconditional or elevated worth of morality and its elevated position (dignity). Kant can therefore conclude the main passage on dignity in the *Groundwork* by saying that autonomy, i.e. the process of giving universal law (or being morally good), is the ground of the realized dignity of rational nature (*G* IV 436).

Rather than justifying a value of human beings that can ground the requirement to respect them, the main passage on dignity repeats familiar claims from the *Groundwork*. One should not follow the categorical imperative out of inclination, but because of the unconditional worth of morality (i.e. moral dictates are categorical). Kant uses 'dignity' to express the elevated position morality has in terms of worth. The main passage on dignity in the *Groundwork* is therefore compatible with my interpretation of Kant's view as to why one should respect others.

5 CONCLUSION

In this chapter I have argued that, on a close reading of Kant's text, the standard view of Kant's justification for the requirement to respect others does not stand up. Kant grounds the requirement to respect others not on an absolute value property all human beings possess, but on the categorical imperative. Concepts like 'worth', 'end-in-itself' and 'dignity' are secondary concepts for Kant. None of them is foundational. None of them is used to *justify* moral requirements. My reading therefore makes sense of the structure of the *Groundwork*, the fact that Kant does not rely on these concepts when he says he justifies the categorical imperative – as the standard view would lead one to expect. Moreover, and more importantly, my reading prevents Kant's requirement of respect for others from being saddled with the high metaphysical demands of a non-relational value property, demands imposed by the standard reading of Kant.

---

[46] Cf. *CpV* V 63 ff.: 'the concept of good and evil must not be determined before the moral law ... but only (as was done here) after it and by means of it'.

CHAPTER 7

Kant's kingdom of ends: metaphysical, not political

Katrin Flikschuh

The concept of every rational being as one who must regard himself as making universal law through all the maxims of his will, so as to appraise himself and his actions from this point of view, leads to a closely connected and very fruitful concept, namely that *of a kingdom of ends*. (*G* IV 433)

The law of reciprocal coercion necessarily in accord with the freedom of everyone under the principle of universal freedom is, as it were, the *construction* of that concept, that is, the presentation of it in pure intuition *a priori*, by analogy with presenting the possibility of bodies moving freely under the law of the *equality of action and reaction*. (*MdS* VI 232)

I INTRODUCTION

Much recent writing on Kant's 'kingdom of ends' gives it a semi-political interpretation, representing it as the normative ideal of a democratic order of mutually legislating citizens of equal moral standing. Implicit parallels are drawn between Kant's account of agents as each legislating the moral law to themselves and John Rawls' ideal of a well-ordered society in which a community of co-legislators reach reasonable agreement on shareable principles of justice. Related liberal values are introduced in the course of textual exposition, yielding richly normative interpretations of what Kant himself says is 'only an ideal' (*G* IV 433). One finds the subtle alignment of Kantian moral autonomy, conceived as the free subjection of *Willkür* under *Wille*, with liberal personal autonomy understood in terms of individuals' competence to judge for themselves what the good life consists in for them. The kingdom of ends is specified as that ideal of a morally co-operative political legislation among equals, the principal end of which is the mutual fostering

Many thanks to Otfried Höffe, Camillia Kong, Jens Timmermann and Lea Ypi for helpful comments on earlier drafts of this chapter. Particular thanks to Sorin Baiasu for extremely valuable written comments on an early draft.

of the successful pursuit of the personal autonomy of each. Andrews Reath argues in this vein that 'Kant believes that autonomy is exercised by enacting principles that could serve as law for a community of agents, each of whom possesses the same legislative capacity as oneself [such that] the laws enacted by such an agent must be able to gain the agreement of all members of this community of ends'.[1] Christine Korsgaard similarly holds that, 'I must make your ends and reasons mine, and I must choose mine in such a way that they can be yours. Generalised to the Kingdom of Ends, my own ends must be the possible objects of universal legislation, subject to the vote of all. And this is how I realise my autonomy.'[2]

A principal motivation behind readings such as these is a concern to demonstrate the continued practical relevance of Kant's moral philosophy and in so doing to contest its traditional reception as an 'empty formalism'.[3] The categorical imperative, its third variant included, is not to be read as a 'metaphysical abstraction' but is to be understood as an action-guiding normative principle that applies to our social world as we know it. This defence concedes much to Kant's critics from the start. It assumes that *unless* supplemented by an anthropologically oriented specification of its moral content the categorical imperative *would* be empty and non-action guiding. Underlying this concession is a deeper suspicion of substantive metaphysical argument and a related concern to preserve Kant from association with it: Kant's analysis of duty as a concept of pure practical reason is not to be thought of as uncritically committed to supersensible entities or ideas. Ironically, the endeavour to rescue Kant from the 'mere formalism' charge by incorporating specifically human normative assumptions into the analysis of the categorical imperative is a consequence of the perceived need to attribute such formalism to him in order to avoid burdening him with a substantive metaphysical position.

Such normatively oriented curtailment of Kant's *metaphysics* of morals is regrettable. Kant clearly takes himself to be engaged in substantive metaphysical argument of some kind in *Groundwork* II, the difficulties

---

[1] Andrews Reath, 'Legislating for a Realm of Ends: the Social Dimension of Autonomy' in his *Agency and Autonomy* (Oxford University Press, 2006), pp. 173–96, at p. 173.

[2] Christine Korsgaard, 'Creating the Kingdom of Ends: Reciprocity and Responsibility in Personal Relations' in her *Creating the Kingdom of Ends* (Cambridge University Press, 1996), pp. 188–224, at p. 193. For a more cautious reading of the kingdom of ends formula as an unattainable ideal, see Barbara Herman, 'A Cosmopolitan Kingdom of Ends' in B. Herman, C. Korsgaard and A. Reath (eds.), *Reclaiming the History of Ethics: Essays in Honour of John Rawls* (Cambridge University Press, 1997), pp. 187–214.

[3] This practically oriented approach is due to John Rawls' influential interpretation of the *Groundwork* in his *Lectures on the History of Moral Philosophy* (Harvard University Press, 2000), pp. 143–214.

surrounding the specification of the exact nature of this endeavour notwith-standing.[4] He also clearly regards metaphysical inquiry as of supreme practical importance, contending that while our ordinary consciousness of duty unfailingly tells us what we ought to do in any given situation, philosophical confusion concerning the proper grounds of morality encour-ages the conflation of moral with non-moral considerations, especially with the search for happiness, leading to disappointment over morality's failure to deliver such happiness and, eventually, to a 'hatred of reason' (*G* IV 395). It is such hatred of reason born of misconceptions regarding the proper grounds and ends of morality which Kant seeks to counteract when he embarks upon an inquiry into its supreme principle.

Apart from misrepresenting its status as metaphysical ideal, the depiction of the kingdom of ends as a normative blueprint for a moral political order threatens to distort the basic orientation of Kant's philosophy of Right. In many respects what Kant calls the 'construction' of the concept of Right in the *Doctrine of Right* (*MdS* VI 232) is the opposite of the idea of the kingdom of ends as a *spontaneous* ethical order that guides each individual will's self-legislated conformity of subjective maxims with universal law. The estab-lishment of the *Rechtsstaat* is not a function of the autonomous willing of a plurality of co-legislating agents. The external coercibility of agents' out-ward conformity of action with universal law forms the political counter-part, in the *Doctrine of Right*, to the ethics of autonomous willing in the *Groundwork*.[5] The aim of the following analysis of the kingdom of ends argument in *Groundwork* II is therefore twofold. I want primarily to make a case for a metaphysical interpretation of the kingdom of ends formulation as part of Kant's analysis of the categorical imperative in *Groundwork* II (sections 3 and 4). But I also want briefly to contrast the idea of a spon-taneous *ethical* order with the constructed, more limited endeavour of Kant's *Rechtsstaat*, suggesting that we have good reason not to confuse a juridical order with an ethical one (section 5). Before turning to either task, I should say a little more about what I mean by Kant's substantive practical metaphysics (section 2).

---

[4] The status of Kant's practical metaphysics has been the subject of perennial philosophical disagree-ment. See Ludwig Siep, 'Wozu eine Metaphysik der Sitten?' in Otfried Höffe (ed.), *Grundlegung zur Metaphysik der Sitten. Ein kooperativer Kommentar* (Berlin: Klostermann, 1989); Allen Wood, 'The Final Form of Kant's Practical Philosophy' in Mark Timmons (ed.), *Kant's Metaphysics of Morals: Interpretative Essays* (Oxford University Press, 2002), pp. 1–22.

[5] Bernd Ludwig, 'Whence Public Right? The Role of Theoretical and Practical Reasoning in Kant's *Doctrine of Right*' in Timmons, *Kant's Metaphysics of Morals*, pp. 159–85.

2 SUBSTANTIVE PRACTICAL METAPHYSICS:
SOME VERY BRIEF REMARKS

The suggestion that Kant's is a substantive practical metaphysics will worry those who take metaphysical commitments of that kind to conflict with the idea of a critical philosophy. That Kant regards metaphysical inquiry as indispensable to the moral inquiry of the *Groundwork* is beyond question: 'pure philosophy (that is, metaphysics) must come first, and without it there can be no moral philosophy at all' (*G* IV 390). At the same time, the first critique's forceful rejection of rationalist speculative metaphysics reverberates in the admonishment that the search is for 'a completely isolated metaphysic of morals, mixed with no anthropology, no theology, no physics or hyper-physics, still less with occult qualities (which might be called hypophysical)' (*G* IV 410). This is a tall metaphysical order, seemingly of a wholly negative kind. It is frequently concluded that Kant fails in this strangely negative metaphysical endeavour – perhaps predictably so – and that the resulting 'emptiness' of the proposed 'formalism' compels him to introduce anthropologically specific normative assumptions which unavoidably relativize the analysis of purportedly pure practical reason to the specifically human context.[6]

Yet although he rules out speculative aspirations, Kant's proposal that 'all moral concepts have their seat and origin in reason completely *a priori*' (*G* IV 411) remains continuous with the first critique's contention that metaphysics is inescapable for human reason (*CrV* A vii), which problematically extends itself beyond the conditions of sensible knowledge. To locate all moral concepts in reason *a priori* is to locate them, in one sense, beyond that which is sensibly given or sensibly knowable. To the extent to which Kant acknowledges the coherence of such an 'extension' beyond sensible conditions he remains sympathetic to the rationalist metaphysical impulse. Yet unlike the latter, Kant does not think of reason as affording cognitive access to independently existing true ideas or supersensible entities. Rather, human reason is constrained to operate with moral *concepts* (such as the concept of a good will or the concept of a rational being) that have no sensible intuitions corresponding to them and that are not amenable to empirical inquiry – concepts to which we nonetheless assign substantive content (cf. *CrV* B 98, B 384). When in the *Groundwork* Kant proposes to 'derive our principles from the general concept of a rational

---

[6] Thus Thomas Pogge in 'The Categorical Imperative' in Höffe *Grundlegung zur Metaphysik der Sitten*, pp. 172–93.

being as such' (*G* IV 412), his starting point is neither anthropology, nor theology or hyper-physics, but a *non-empirical concept* of practical reason which he claims we employ in everyday moral discourse. We implicitly presuppose non-sensible ideas in our moral assumptions about and inter-actions with one another. It is in connection with Kant's analysis of this everyday, non-empirical concept of a rational being that *Groundwork* II introduces, as we shall see, a number of substantive metaphysical proposi-tions regarding the nature and ends of the rational willing of such a being without which the inquiry could not proceed. The decisive contrast between speculative metaphysics and Kant's practical approach lies not in the latter's formalism in contrast to the former's substantive assertions, but in Kant's acknowledgement of the theoretical non-vindicability of his substantive metaphysical presuppositions: by the end of the inquiry in *Groundwork* III it has become clear that although, in so far as we act morally, we necessarily *think* ourselves members of a possible intelligible order, we must yet acknowledge that we have no way of proving the independent reality of this practically necessary, metaphysically substantive self-conception. When in the following I refer to Kant's substantive prac-tical metaphysics, I have in mind the non-empirical substantive content which he claims we must assign our practical concepts in the course of philosophical inquiry into them whilst yet acknowledging the non-provability of the concept-independent existence of the entities and powers thus posited.[7]

3 THE PLACE OF THE KINGDOM OF ENDS FORMULA IN *GROUNDWORK* II

Apart from recent politically oriented interpretations, the kingdom of ends formulation remains the perhaps least discussed among Kant's three variants of the categorical imperative's basic formulation, the formula of universal law, which exhorts us to 'act only on that maxim through which you can at the same time will that it should become a universal law' (*G* IV 421).[8] There is some uncertainty as to how far it is even appropriate to speak

---

[7] I offer a more extended defence of Kant's practical metaphysics in Katrin Flikschuh, 'Kant's Indemonstrable Postulate of Right: A Response to Paul Guyer', *Kantian Review* 12 (2007), 1–39.

[8] The precise number of formulae of the categorical imperative, and of the relations between them, remains subject to debate. In his influential edition of the *Groundwork*, H. J. Paton identified the 'formula of a law of nature' (FULN) as well as the 'formula of autonomy' (FA), as additional to the formulae of universal law (FUL), of humanity as an end-in-itself (FHE), and of the kingdom of ends (FKE). Most others have focused their interpretative attention on the relation between FUL,

of the kingdom of ends formula (FKE) as a distinct, action-guiding variant of the categorical imperative. In contrast to the law of nature formula (FULN) as well as that of humanity as an end-in-itself (FHE), FKE 'is not initially stated as a single second-order practical principle'.[9] Whereas FULN tells us to 'act as if the maxim of your action were to become by your will a universal law of nature' (G IV 421), and FHE demands that we 'act in such a way that you always treat humanity, whether in your own person or in the person of any other, never simply as a means, but always at the same time as an end' (G IV 429), FKE represents 'a systematic union of different rational beings under common laws' conceived 'in accordance with the above principles' (G IV 433). In his summary of the three variants of the basic formulation, Kant says of FKE that it yields the 'complete determination of maxims' (G IV 436) in accordance with FULN as the form and FHE as the content of universal law. One thus arrives at FKE through the conjunction of the preceding two variants of the basic formulation, and although the 'formal principle' for FKE is finally stated in the last few pages of *Groundwork* II – 'so act as if your maxims had to serve at the same time as universal law (for all rational beings)' (G IV 438) – it is not immediately clear what precisely FKE, thus articulated, adds to FULN and FKE taken individually.

The structural similarity of the 'complete determination' characterization of FKE to the threefold division of categories in the first *Critique* is pointed out by Kant himself (G IV 436). In *CrV* Kant remarks in relation to the table of categories that 'the third category in each class always arises from the combination of the second category with the first'. He goes on to warn that (*CrV* B110–11):

it must not be supposed, however, that the third category is merely a derivative, and not a primary, concept of the pure understanding. For the combination of the first and second concepts, in order that the third may be produced, requires a special act of the understanding, which is not identical with that which is exercised in the case of the first and the second.

We should similarly assume the non-derivative status of FKE: the *combination* of FULN and FHE into FKE does not simply follow as a corollary of

FHE and FKE as the three most important formulae. See, e.g. Onora O'Neill, 'Universal Law and Ends-in-themselves' in *Constructions of Reason* (Cambridge University Press, 1989), pp. 126–44; Arthur Melnick, 'Kant's Formulations of the Categorical Imperative', *Kant-Studien* 93 (2002), 291–308. More recently, Jens Timmermann has argued that FUL constitutes the 'basic formulation' of the categorical imperative, with FULN, FHE and FKE being the three variants of the basic formulation designed to bring the basic formula 'closer to intuition' (Jens Timmermann (ed.), *Grundlegung zur Metaphysik der Sitten* (Vandenhoek & Ruprecht, 2004), pp. 117–18 and 134). I here follow Timmermann's suggestion.
[9] O'Neill, 'Universal Law and Ends-in-themselves', p. 127.

FULN and FHE but requires a 'special act of [practical] understanding'. Since the proposed reading nonetheless depends on acknowledging FULN and FHE as jointly necessary conditions of FKE, I begin with a brief outline of the arguments for FUL as the basic formulation of the categorical imperative and of FULN and FHE as the first two variants respectively derived from FUL.

The principal object of analysis in *Groundwork* II is the idea of unconditional duty as a concept of pure practical reason that is distinct from everything that is empirical. While the negative strategy of abstraction from all sensible conditions is a necessary aspect of the transition from ordinary moral knowledge into practical metaphysics, abstraction alone is not sufficient. Kant departs from the non-empirical practical concept of a rational being in general, and *Groundwork* II quickly introduces a practically substantive conception of the will of such a being as possessing a distinctive power (*G* IV 412):

Everything in nature works in accordance with laws. Only a rational being has the power to act in accordance with *the representation of laws*, that is, in accordance with principles, or has a will.

The proposition that everything in nature works in accordance with laws and that only the will of a rational being has the power to act in accordance with the *representation* of laws introduces the idea of the will as categorically distinct from the rest of nature. Implicit in Kant's characterization of the will as a rational power (*Vermögen*) is its ability self-consciously either to act from laws or to fail so to act: the relevant laws must be acknowledged by the will as required for the action in question. This conception of the will as a 'power' is reminiscent of the lengthy discussion in the third antinomy of the first *Critique*, where the theoretical possibility of the rational will as a *causality* distinct from the rest of nature is first entertained: 'there is in man a power of self-determination, independently of any coercion through sensuous impulses' (*CrV* A 534/B 562). By a power of self-determination Kant there has in mind something akin to the Aristotelian idea of an unmoved mover.[10] This conception of the will as causal power is substantive. It does not merely refer to a general capacity for rational deliberation but attributes to the will rational (as contrasted with natural) powers of causation capable of effecting events in the sensible order of things: such as my decision *now* to rise from the chair on which I am sitting. *Groundwork* II utilizes this speculative metaphysical idea of the will as a power of rational causation

---

[10] I am grateful to Manfred Baum for alerting me to this.

for practical purposes whilst also modifying it. In the above paragraph the will is conceived not as a power of rational causation, but as a power to act in accordance with the representation of laws: independence from nature now lies not in the will's non-natural power to intervene directly in the causality of nature but is conceived as the capacity for law-governed volition. Foreshadowed in this characterization of the will as 'a power to act from the representation of laws' is Kant's subsequent strikingly casual introduction of maxims as 'subjective principles of volition'.[11] The will conceived as a power to act from the representation of laws is a will conceived as a *volitional* as opposed to a *causal* power: the will as a volitional power to act from the *representation* of laws thus contrasts with natural beings' merely passive conformity with natural causal laws.[12]

The will's power to act in accordance with the representation of laws applies in relation to hypothetical imperatives as well as to categorical imperatives. This need not mean that hypothetical and categorical imperatives share the same root, or that we can derive a capacity to act morally from a capacity to act on principles of instrumental rationality.[13] While Kant conceives of both instrumental and moral reasoning as species of practical reasoning – in contrast to theoretical reason, both relate to our 'capacity for desire [*Begehrungsvermögen*]' (*CpV* V 9 fn.; *MdS* VI 211) – this need not mean that every rational being that possesses a capacity for instrumental reason therefore also possesses a capacity for moral reasoning, or vice versa. Kant sometimes entertains the possibility of beings who, though instrumentally rational, lack the capacity for pure practical reason (*G* VI 434); similarly, he frequently invokes a possible perfectly moral being, who lacks all need for instrumental reasoning. Although human beings, in contrast to both these other possible types of rational being, have the capacity for instrumental *and* moral reasoning, this need not imply any necessary connection between the two forms of practical reasoning.

The mistaken assumption that we can arrive at the categorical imperative by means of an analysis of (the conditions of) hypothetical imperatives is encouraged by Kant's order of exposition, which begins with the latter. Instrumental reasoning is law-governed action in relation to a materially

---

[11] *G* IV 421 fn.: 'A maxim is the subjective principle of acting, and must be distinguished from the objective principle, namely the practical law'. A will that acts from the representation of laws is a will that adopts objective law as its subjective principle of volition.

[12] Kant's specification of the rational will as a distinctive causality thus remains metaphysically more demanding than current glosses of it in terms of human beings' capacity for rational deliberation.

[13] But see Christine Korsgaard, 'The Normativity of Instrumental Reason' in Garrett Cullity and Berys Gaut (eds.), *Ethics and Practical Reason* (Oxford University Press, 1997), pp. 215–54.

given object of desire. Determinate laws of instrumental reason are analytically contained in the object as necessary means to its attainment. Thus, 'how [hypothetical imperatives] are possible requires no special discussion', since 'whoever wills the end also wills (insofar as reason has decisive influence on his action) the indispensably necessary means to it that are within his power' (*G* IV 417). By contrast, categorical imperatives have 'not to do with the matter of the action and what is to result from it, but with the form and principle from which the action itself follows' (*G* IV 417). Here, we cannot derive the relevant laws of action from the given object of desire, hence the question as to these laws' 'objectively represented necessity' presents us with 'a difficulty of insight into [their] possibility [that] is very great'. In contrast to the analyticity of hypothetical imperatives, the categorical imperative is an '*a priori* synthetic practical proposition' (*G* IV 420). Kant's comparative discussion of the two forms of practical laws thus leads him to conclude that they are different in kind.[14]

How *should* we conceive the concept of a categorical imperative? Despite the 'great difficulties' surrounding its possible vindication, Kant arrives at this law's first formulation with surprising ease: 'When I think of a hypothetical imperative in general, I do not know beforehand what it will contain; I do not know this until I am given the condition. But when I think of a categorical imperative I know at once what it contains' (*G* IV 420). Since it pertains only to the *form* of an action, a categorical imperative requires no factual information but contains 'only the necessity that the maxim [as subjective principle of volition] be in conformity with this law, while the law [deriving from no sensibly given objects of desire] contains no condition to which it would be limited' (*G* IV 421). When we *think* the concept of a possible categorical imperative, we in fact think FUL: 'act only in accordance with that maxim through which you can at the same time will that it should become a universal law' (*G* IV 421). In FUL, the subjective form of the proposed action (the maxim) is given objective form, i.e. it is given the form of lawlike necessity. This is reminiscent of the specification of duty in *Groundwork* I as 'the necessity to act out of reverence for the law' (*G* IV 400). In so far as FUL represents the form of a practically necessary action in accordance with a universal law, it represents the idea of a rational will as acting in accordance with its representation of the concept of duty. Kant's immediate move from the basic formulation of the categorical imperative (FUL) to its first variant, the law of nature formulation (FULN), introduces no fresh argument but merely continues with the

---

[14] My thanks to Camillia Kong for helpful discussion of this point.

analogy between the causality of nature and the possible causality of morality (conceived as the causality of freedom) (*G* IV 421):

Since the universality of law in accordance with which effects take place constitutes what is properly called nature in the most general sense (as regards its form) – that is, the existence of things insofar as it is determined in accordance with universal laws – the universal imperative of duty can also go as follows: *act as if the maxim of your action were to become by your will a universal law of nature.*

Insofar as we understand by 'nature in its most general sense' any system of law-governed causality, we can think of a will that gives its maxims the form of universal law as a power capable of 'effecting', through such willing, a law-governed system of morality. The reformulation of FUL into FULN thus continues at the level of metaphysical argument and analysis: Kant's claim at this juncture is not, as Rawls maintains, that 'for the categorical imperative to be applied to our situation, it must be adapted to our circumstances in the order of nature', or that 'this adaptation ... takes into account the normal conditions of human life by means of the law of nature formulation'.[15] FULN does not represent a move from metaphysical analysis to applied ethics: the idea of 'nature' employed is Kant's perfectly general one of a law-governed order: FULN continues with the idea of the will as a distinct kind of causality, simply extrapolating the already implicit idea of the will as effecting, through its volitional power, a law-governed order – a 'nature' – that is qualitatively distinct from the sensible order of things. What FULN does add compared to FUL is precisely this idea of law-governed willing as effecting a moral order, or *system*. Where the focus of FUL is on law-governed individual actions, FULN introduces the related idea of multiple such law-governed actions' systemic effects. This idea of the systemic effects of law-governed action recurs, as we shall see, in the kingdom of ends formulation.

With regard to the basic formulation of the categorical imperative (FUL) and its first variant (FULN), Kant claims that 'we have shown at least this much: that if duty is a concept that is to contain significance and real lawgiving for our actions it can be expressed only in categorical imperatives and by no means in hypothetical ones' (*G* IV 425). But this does not show that this law indeed 'contains significance and real lawgiving' for all rational beings, ourselves included. It is at the point of transition from FUL/FULN to FHE that Kant explicitly announces a necessary step into metaphysics (*G* IV 426):

[15] Rawls, *Lectures on the History of Moral Philosophy*, p. 167.

Our question is this: 'Is it a necessary law *for all rational beings* always to judge their actions by reference to those maxims of which they can themselves will that they should serve as universal laws?' If there is such a law, it must already be connected (entirely *a priori*) with the concept of the will of a rational being as such. But in order to discover this connection we must, however much we may bristle, take a step beyond, that is, into metaphysics, although into a region of it different from that of speculative philosophy, namely, the metaphysics of morals.

In order for FUL, as the law of duty, to be binding for us, an *a priori* necessary 'connection' must be shown to exist between this universal law and the concept of the will of a rational being. While in preparation for FUL the rational will was conceived as a 'power to act in accordance with the representation of laws', the argument preparatory to FHE introduces the idea of the will's 'capacity to determine itself to acting in accordance with the *representation of certain laws*' (*G* IV 428). Kant immediately goes on to say that the 'ground' of law-governed self-determination is the 'end' (*Zweck*) of an action, implying that the sought 'necessary connection' obtains between the law and the end which the will of a rational being intends to achieve through acting in accordance with that law.

For Kant, the notion of *purposive* willing is contained in that of *law-governed* willing. Law-governed willing is non-arbitrary: just as in the realm of nature causal laws produce determinate effects, so in the realm of practical reason law-governed willing is directed at the production of corresponding ends. A will that acts in accordance with the representation of laws is a will that acts in accordance with the representation of ends. A will that acts in accordance with hypothetical imperatives has conditionally given ends as the ground of its determination. By contrast, a will that acts in accordance with an unconditional law must have an unconditional end as its ground. The unconditional law of FUL implies an unconditional end in the general form of FHE: to that extent, the second variant of the categorical imperative is simply an extrapolation from that aspect of the basic formulation which, in contrast to the derivation of FULN, implies not the systemic quality of law-governed action, but its purposiveness. But if this is so what does the 'step into metaphysics' consist in, which Kant expects us so to bristle at? The analytic connection between FUL as the unconditional law of pure practical reason and FHE as articulating the idea of its correspondingly unconditional end does not itself yield the substantive content of FHE. While it may be true both that every law implies an end, and that an unconditional law implies an unconditional end, this does not in itself warrant the designation of *rational nature* as the unconditional end in question. In the paragraphs leading up to FHE Kant asks his readers to (*G* IV 428):

Suppose there were something whose existence has in itself an absolute value, something which as an end in itself could be a ground of determinate laws. In it, and in it alone, would there be the ground of a possible categorical imperative.

This corresponds with the foregoing analysis according to which an unconditional law must have an unconditional end as its object. But Kant now abruptly asserts that 'man, and in general every rational being exists as an end in himself' (*G* IV 428). The humanity as an end-in-itself formulation follows immediately as the command to 'act in such a way that you always treat humanity, whether in your own person or in the person of any other, never simply as a means, but always at the same time as an end' (*G* IV 429). The designation of rational nature (or, equivalently, humanity in each our person)[16] as the moral law's substantive unconditional end does not follow from the *analytic* connection between laws and ends; it constitutes a fresh argumentative step. As Jens Timmermann points out, Kant's terminology – 'rational nature' (*die vernünftige Natur*), 'rational being' (*das vernünftige Wesen*) – is ontological, invoking the existence of types of nature and beings distinct from sensible nature.[17] These ontological claims are conditional: the contention that 'rational nature exists as an end in itself' responds to the question as to what a rational will *would have* to will as its unconditional end *if* FUL *were to be* an unconditional law for it. On the one hand, the rational will conceived as a practical power must have a substantive object as its end – it cannot be merely formal but must be thought of as seeking to effect the object of its representation. On the other hand, if the end of an *unconditional* practical law can only be an *unconditional* substantive end, and if nothing that is unconditional can be sensibly given, the unconditional substantive end of an unconditional practical law must be a non-sensible substantive end. Kant's designation of rational nature as existing as an end-in-itself is given conditional warrant by the practical nature of the inquiry itself: *if* there is an unconditional practical law that applies to all rational beings as such, this law *must* correspond with an unconditional substantive end for all rational wills, and the only conceivable such candidate end is rational nature as an end-in-itself. Note that although rational nature is conceived substantively, its precise nature remains indeterminate. The formulation of humanity as an end-in-itself does not tell us what precisely rational nature

---

[16] I follow Friedo Ricken in reading 'humanity' in *Groundwork* II as equivalent in meaning to what *Religion* subsequently terms 'personality'. See Friedo Ricken, 'Homo noumenon und homo phaenomenon' in Höffe, *Grundlegung zur Metaphysik der Sitten*, pp. 234–52.

[17] Jens Timmermann, 'Value Without Regress: Kant's "Formula of Humanity" Revisited', *European Journal of Philosophy* (2006), 69–93, at 75.

looks like or what exactly it consists in; the formulation simply posits rational nature as the only possible unconditional end of an unconditionally valid practical law. I shall return to this point below. More important now is the way in which the limited practical warrant just proffered modifies the ontological status of Kant's claim: while the existence of rational nature as an end-in-itself is a practically necessary presupposition of a rational will's acting in accordance with the categorical imperative, rational nature may have no existential status independently of the rational will's taking FUL as its unconditional practical law, with FHE as that law's unconditional substantive end.[18]

On the above analysis, the derivations of the basic formulation of the categorical imperative (FUL) and its first two variants (FULN and FHE) draw on substantive metaphysical presuppositions concerning the nature of a rational will and the substantive ends of its willing. FUL casts the will as a power to act independently of the causality of nature; FULN introduces the thought of the systemic efficacy of law-governed pure rational willing; and FHE posits the existence of a non-sensible, rational nature as the end to be effected through law-governed willing. In no case is the argument relativized to the human condition; FUL, FULN and FHE are all conceived as applying to practically rational beings *in general*. Yet the ontological status of the conception of the will as non-sensibly efficacious power and that of rational nature as its non-sensible end are relativized to the realm of practical as opposed to that of theoretical reason. Turning finally to FKE, recall the contention that although it results 'in combination with the above principles', this third variant of the categorical imperative is nonetheless non-derivative, requiring a 'special act of [practical] cognition'. What does this special act consist in? As mentioned, FKE sets itself apart both from the basic formulation and from the first two variants in not being articulated in the form of a single second-order principle. Indeed, in contrast to both FULN and FHE, both of which are derived from the basic formulation directly, FKE is derived not from FUL itself but from FULN in conjunction with FHE. Kant speaks of FKE as representing 'a whole of all ends in systematic connection ... in accordance with the above principles' (*G* IV 433), where the reference to 'ends' invokes FHE and that to 'systematic connection' FULN. Interpretation is further complicated by the interpolation of what commentators sometimes designate as the additional 'formula of

---

[18] For a fuller discussion of the nature of such practical as opposed to theoretical warrant see Flikschuh, 'Kant's Indemonstrable Postulate', 8–13.

autonomy' (FA) between the first two variants and the third. FA represents the principle 'of every rational being as one who must regard himself as making universal law by all the maxims of his will, and must seek to judge himself and his actions from this point of view'. It is *this* principle which 'leads to the very fruitful concept of a kingdom of ends' (*G* IV 433). It looks, then, as though FKE is derived from FULN and FHE through the interpolation of FA.

Under FA the will takes FULN as the 'objective rule' and FHE as the 'subjective end' of its legislation (*G* IV 431). Only through giving its maxims the form of a possible universal law of (non-sensible) nature, treating in so doing rational nature as an end-in-itself, is 'the will not merely subject to the law but subject to it in such a way that it must be viewed as giving law to itself' (*G* IV 431). Self-legislation consists in the will's giving its maxims the form of universal law under the idea of a subjectively adopted end which, being 'based on no interest', is therefore 'unconditional' (*G* IV 432). We may say that self-legislation is self-subjection under a universal law whose unconditional end the will adopts as its own through the act of giving its maxims the form of universal law. Here, I want to return to my earlier remark regarding the indeterminate specification of rational nature as an end-in-itself. The idea of the self-legislating will's taking rational nature as the end of its law-making should not be interpreted as the will's regarding its particular rational nature or its particular rational capacities as the end of its moral law-giving. We should not specify 'rational nature in each person' as referring to each person's individually distinct rational self or capacities, construing the self-legislating will as one that legislates universal law on its behalf. To the contrary, FA demands that each rational will give its maxims the form of universal law so as to treat rational nature *in general* as an end-in-itself. It is this idea of the autonomous will as legislating law *to itself* on behalf of *rational nature in general* that gives rise to the 'very fruitful concept of a kingdom of ends'. On the interpretation here suggested, a self-legislating will can arrive at the idea of a kingdom of ends independently of (the willing of) all other rational beings. Yet no rational will, in legislating the moral law to itself, does so on its behalf. This reading of the kingdom of ends formulation conflicts with currently dominant interpretations of it as a normatively co-legislated realm whose purpose is the mutual fostering of one another's capacity for personal autonomy. I shall try to show that the proposed reading better fits Kant's direct argument for FKE as well as the *Maximenethik* of the *Groundwork* more generally.

4 THE KINGDOM OF ENDS AS METAPHYSICAL IDEAL: SELF-LEGISLATION ON BEHALF OF RATIONAL NATURE IN GENERAL

Kant's immediate argument for the kingdom of ends formulation begins with the characterization of the concept of a kingdom in general as representing a 'systematic union of different rational beings through common laws' (*G* IV 433). This fits Kant's general conception of a political union.[19] However, a kingdom *of ends* constitutes the special case of a union of rational wills through *ethical* laws; it represents the ideal of an ethical union that arises when each rational will, in legislating the moral law to itself, abstracts from all personal circumstances and ends (*G* IV 433):

For rational beings all stand under the law that each of them is to treat himself and all others *never merely as a means* but always *at the same time as end in himself*. But from this there arises a systematic union of rational beings through common objective laws, that is, a kingdom, which can be called a kingdom of ends (admittedly only an Ideal) because what these laws have as their purpose is just the relation of these beings to one another as ends and means.

This specification of FKE as a 'systematic union of rational wills through common laws' in which we abstract from personal ends but not from the end-setting capacity of each[20] has given rise to its interpretation as an ideal ethico-political order, established through a deliberate act of co-legislation, the purpose of which is the reciprocal fostering of one another's personal end-setting capacity. According to Korsgaard, 'to join with others as citizens in the Kingdom of Ends is to extend to our inner attitudes and personal choices the kind of reciprocity that characterizes our outer actions in the political state'.[21] Korsgaard goes on to say that 'I must make your ends and reasons mine, and I must choose mine in such a way that they can be yours. But this just is reciprocity. Generalized to the Kingdom of Ends, my own ends must be possible objects of a universal legislation, subject to the vote of all. And this is how I realize my autonomy.'[22]

This is a politicized reading of an ethical ideal. Kant does not speak of individuals as 'joining' the kingdom of ends, nor does he characterize rational beings as 'citizens' of such a kingdom. There is no mention of a 'reciprocal exchange' of inner attitudes, and no requirement that the

---

[19] Cf. *MdS* VI 313: 'A state (*civitas*) is a union of a multitude of human beings under laws of Right.'
[20] If we did abstract from the end-setting capacity of each, we would be abstracting from the capacity of the will to act from maxims. But a will that cannot act from maxims cannot prescribe FUL to itself.
[21] Korsgaard, 'Creating the Kingdom of Ends', p. 192.   [22] *Ibid.* p. 193.

maxims and ends of each be subject to the 'vote' of all. Instead of all this there is an unexpected appeal to God as head of an ethical kingdom of ends (*G* IV 433):

A rational being belongs to the kingdom of ends as a member, when, though legislating universal laws, *he is also himself subject to these laws*. He belongs to it as its head, when, as lawgiving, *he is not subject to the will of any other*. (emphasis added)

The laws of morality are valid for members and head alike: 'a rational being must always regard himself as lawgiving in a kingdom of ends possible through freedom of will, whether as member or sovereign' (*G* IV 434). However, while subjects are additionally subject to the will of the head, the head is not subject to the will of any other. Again, this is broadly consistent with Kant's conception of the relationship between subjects and sovereign in a *political* kingdom, where all are morally subject to the laws of Right but where only the subjects are simultaneously subject to the (coercive) will of the sovereign. The crucial difference is that members of the ethical kingdom are not subject to the head's *coercive* authority. While the political sovereign has the legitimate coercive authority to compel subjects to act in outward conformity with Right, God cannot *coerce* members of an ethical union to legislate the moral law to themselves. What, then, does the relation between God and each rational will as a member of the kingdom of ends consist in?

Formally, God is the only possible unifying principle of a union of wills under ethical laws. A rational being 'cannot hold the position of sovereign merely by the maxims of his will but only in case he is a completely independent being, without needs and with unlimited resources adequate to his will' (*G* IV 434). We saw in connection with the analysis of the basic formulation of the categorical imperative that a maxim is a subjective principle of volition capable of being given universal form through FUL. A rational being who legislates universal law *to himself through his maxims* cannot be sovereign of a kingdom of ends as representing the ideal of a union of *all* rational wills. God does not legislate universal law to himself through his maxims: he simply acts from the moral law. In contrast to the finite wills of dependent beings who give themselves the moral law through their maxims, God's will always already is objectively good. God is that completely independent being without needs and with unlimited resources adequate to his will who, in contrast to the dependent wills of finite rational beings, can act as head of an ideal ethical kingdom of ends.

Yet God cannot legislate the moral law to any member of that union. Dependent rational wills are subject to the independent will of God in relation to their membership in the ethical union, not with respect to their status as self-legislators of the moral law. As we saw from the formulation of FA, it is *through* the act of legislating universal law to himself that the idea of a kingdom of ends arises for each self-legislating rational being. Insofar as one gains access to the kingdom of ends only through legislating the moral law to oneself, God cannot be thought of as legislator of the moral law in the kingdom of ends. But if the ideal arises only for a will that *already* legislates the moral law to itself, what is the contribution of FKE to the metaphysical analysis of duty in *Groundwork* II? What does FKE add to the other formulations of the categorical imperative?

FKE returns us to the opening theme of *Groundwork* – the non-identity of happiness and morality (*G* IV 434):

In the kingdom of ends everything has either a price or dignity. What has a price can be replaced by something else as its equivalent; what on the other hand is raised above all price and therefore admits of no equivalent has dignity.

Human inclinations and needs have a 'market price'; objects of taste and delight have a 'fancy price'. Only that which can be an end-in-itself has 'dignity', i.e. is 'above all price'. But the only condition under which a rational being can be an end-in-itself is morality (*G* IV 435): and only then is a rational being also a member of the kingdom of ends. We saw that a rational being who acts morally legislates the moral law to himself on *behalf of rational nature in general*. In prescribing universal law to himself – and to himself alone! – a rational being treats rational nature in general as an end-in-itself. In so doing a rational being acts morally. But morality is priceless – beyond sensible nature. This is why, in acting morally, we should not expect any sensibly conditioned pay-off, such as happiness. At this point the idea gains importance of our primary relation, as dependent rational beings in the kingdom of ends, to God. When we act morally, each legislating universal law to ourselves, we abstract from our personal needs and quest for happiness, from others' acknowledgement of our efforts, from their co-operation (*G* IV 438–9):

Now a kingdom of ends would actually come into existence through maxims which the categorical imperative prescribes as a rule for all rational beings, *if these maxims were universally followed*. Yet even if a rational being were himself to follow such a maxim strictly, he cannot count on everybody else being faithful to it on this ground, nor can he be confident that the kingdom of nature and its purposive order will work in harmony with him, as a fitting member, towards a kingdom of ends made possible by himself – or, in other words, that it will favour his expectation of happiness. But in spite of this the law 'Act on the maxims of a member who makes universal laws for a merely possible kingdom of ends' remains in full force, since its command is categorical.

Whether others legislate the moral law to themselves, whether I am able to effect any change in sensibly observable relations between persons, whether doing so affords me personal satisfaction, all this is utterly immaterial to my obligation to act so as to effect a *possible* kingdom of ends through the morality of my intentions. Indeed, whenever I legislate the moral law to myself in accordance with FULN and for the sake of FHE I do effect the kingdom of ends: not empirically, but intelligibly so. The kingdom of ends represents the ideal of a spontaneous, non-sensible, ethical order in which each, in systematically legislating the moral law to himself, treats rational nature in general as an end-in-itself irrespective of what anyone else does. The kingdom of ends has practical though non-sensible reality in the will of each rational being in whom this ideal arises from their moral agency. But it *can* have such practical reality for the dependent will of a finite rational being only on the supposition of God as independent head of that union. As a dependent rational being who has no final insight into morality's intelligible nature, my moral agency is, ultimately, an act of moral faith: of faith in the non-futility of my agency even in the face of all available empirical evidence to the contrary. Structurally, the third formulation of the categorical imperative anticipates, not Kant's political philosophy, but the second *Critique*'s doctrine of the postulate of God's existence and the related ideal of the Highest Good.[23]

5   THE KINGDOM OF ENDS AS A
NON-POLITICAL ORDER

I have defended a reading of the kingdom of ends formulation according to which it constitutes an integral part of Kant's metaphysical analysis of duty in *Groundwork* II. This analysis is metaphysical not just in the sense that it abstracts from everything that is merely empirical but also in the sense of introducing a number of substantive metaphysical propositions whose distinctiveness compared to traditional metaphysical approaches lies in their acknowledged theoretical non-vindicability together with their claimed practical indispensability. Thus, in relation to the basic formulation of the categorical imperative – FUL – Kant arrives at the idea of the rational will as an uncaused power to act from the representation of non-sensible

---

[23] Otfried Höffe has suggested to me that the better parallel between a reading of the kingdom of ends and the ideal of an ethical order may lie in Kant's discussion of a possible 'ethical commonwealth' as an 'invisible church' in *Religion*. This strikes me as highly plausible, and an interpretative suggestion worth following up, though I do not, unfortunately, have the space to do so here.

practical laws. In relation to FULN he again utilizes the analogy between the causality of nature and the causality of morality to arrive at the idea of a possible *system* of morality. In relation to FHE he postulates the necessary existence of rational nature as a (substantively indeterminate) end-in-itself. In the context of FKE he has recourse, finally, to the idea of God as the independent unifying principle of a possible ethical union of dependent rational wills. The notion of FKE as a co-legislated moral order plays no role in the text, nor can it plausibly do so given the maxim-based character of Kant's account of self-legislation according to which each legislates the moral law to himself, and to himself alone, irrespective of the co-operation of others. Instead of a co-legislated realm, FKE represents the non-sensible ideal of a spontaneous ethical order of self-legislating rational wills made possible through the unifying principle of God as its head, practical faith in whom assures each dependent self-legislating will of the non-futility of their moral endeavours even in the face of apparent empirical evidence to the contrary: *herein* lies the practical significance of FKE in relation to our moral agency.

On the reading here advocated the ideal of the kingdom of ends cannot function as a blueprint for an empirically realizable moral order. As metaphysical ideal, FKE is analogous to the ideal of the Highest Good in the *Critique of Practical Reason*, which similarly functions to sustain individuals' practical faith in morality in the face of sensibly conditioned adversity, or alternatively, and perhaps more plausibly, anticipates the idea of an *invisible* 'ethical commonwealth' in *Religion*.[24] Certainly, FKE can offer no plausible model for a Kantian *political* order. It cannot do so not because FKE lacks the element of *co-legislation* (although it manifestly lacks that too), but because it lacks the element of *co-ordination*. Co-legislation is as irrelevant to Kant's political philosophy as it is to his ethics, but co-ordination is not.[25] Co-legislation is impossible in Kant's ethics in virtue of its maxim-focused character. Nor is the system of Right co-legislated: a just political order requires a head – an earthly sovereign – who governs in accordance with the idea of a united general will and who is subject to the coercive will of no one. It is the sovereign from whose public will all juridically binding public law emanates. The sovereign is under a moral obligation to pass only those laws which could, in his judgement, be endorsed by each *as a member of the*

---

[24] Cf. *Religion* VI 96 ff.
[25] For an account of co-ordinated action as a distinctive requirement of Kant's political philosophy, see Katrin Flikschuh, 'Nature, Duty, Right: Kant's Answer to Mendelssohn in "Theory and Practice III"', *Journal of Moral Philosophy* 4 (2007), 223–41.

civil union. This moral requirement represents the ideal of a universally valid positive legislation, not of a co-legislated system of public laws. In the *Doctrine of Right* we read that the *a priori* united general will as the ground of any generally legitimate coercive law-giving is possible only through the entrance of all into the civil condition. The moral necessity of establishing relations of Right between persons justifies the compulsion of each into that condition by all others (*MdS* VI 312). Political morality is thus a morality of legitimate public coercion.

The coercive character of political morality is a corollary of its inter-personal nature. For Kant, virtue is a function of the maxim's conformity with universal law: ethics specifies an agent-internal relation between *Willkür* and *Wille*. No one can legislate conformity of maxim with universal law to anyone else. By contrast, the morality of Right abstracts from agents' maxims. It considers only the *outward conformity* of agents' *actions* with universal law. According to the universal law of Right, 'any action is right if it can coexist with everyone's freedom in accordance with a universal law' (*MdS* VI 230). What is morally decisive is the action's outer conformity with universal law, not its maxim. Such outward conformity of action can be externally imposed. The ground of the legitimacy of such external compulsion lies in others' morally valid freedom claims against one. Others' valid claims morally restrict the external freedom of action of each, and the restrictions can permissibly be enforced against the agent even where he fails to acknowledge their validity of his own accord (*MdS* VI 231).

Given the external character of the morality of Right, a political union – a system of rightful relations under the coercive authority of the sovereign – can be thought of as an established, co-ordinated union in a way in which FKE as a maxim-based, spontaneous ethical order cannot. The quotation from the *Doctrine of Right* at the beginning of this chapter indicates as much: Kant there speaks of the (*a priori*) construction of Right as proceeding in analogy with the natural law of the 'equality of action and reaction' (*MdS* VI 232), likening the co-ordinated actions of a plurality of externally free agents to the law-governed interaction of constitutive elements within a system of natural 'bodies'. In the absence of law-governed regulation, such bodies' movements would be arbitrary – unco-ordinated. Only the law-governed structure of relations between them combines all into a coherent natural system. Yet the law does not emanate from these bodies, but is superimposed upon them from 'outside', as it were. Similarly with exter-nally free agents whose co-ordinated interaction in accordance with the universal principle of Right transforms a plurality of otherwise arbitrarily free agents into constitutive members of a system of Right. Here, too, the relevant law, though moral in kind, can be externally imposed upon agents' wills by the sovereign as necessary representative of the idea of the general united will.

Kant's systematic division of virtue and Right into two distinct if co-equal parts of morality is one of the great strengths of his practical philosophy. Virtue pertains to the domain of inner morality – to moral conscience; Right pertains to that of outer morality – to the morally valid claims raised by others which we can be compelled to honour even against our wills. The two domains complement each other but are not dependent on each other. Under Kant's division, it is possible to be virtuous even where the civil condition fails as yet to obtain. It is likewise possible to act justly even if one is not virtuous. Ideally, persons act both justly and virtuously: however, virtue cannot take on the tasks of justice, and justice cannot compel to virtue. The state, in particular, cannot compel persons to be virtuous and should not attempt to do so: any political authority which seeks to impose virtue rather than Right amounts to a paternalistic regime at best and to a moral despotism at worst. The distinctiveness and the limits of political morality, in contrast to ethics, should be taken seriously: never more so than when at a time of liberal overconfidence, self-righteous battle-cries are increasingly heard on behalf of the coercive imposition of an envisaged liberal nirvana upon non-liberal societies. Kant's political philo-sophy appreciates the dangers of such moral despotism; his maxim-based ethics does not in any case lend itself to such a politicization of its ideals. By contrast, current interpretations of the kingdom of ends which represent this ideal of a spontaneous ethical union, under the idea of God as its head, as a plausible model of a co-legislated political order overlook Kant's deep appreciation both of the limits of our capacity to legislate morality to others and of the potentially disastrous political consequences which disregard for these limits may incur.

CHAPTER 8

Kant against the 'spurious principles of morality'

J. B. Schneewind

Philosophers have to think that their predecessors and contemporaries got things wrong. Otherwise what room would they find for their own contributions to the subject? Some philosophers ostensibly ignore earlier work. Spinoza, for instance, wrote his great *Ethics* as if what came before it had not existed. From Socrates on, however, philosophers have more often cleared the way for themselves by trying to demolish other views. Sometimes a philosopher like Hegel will politely claim that without the work of his forerunners he would not have got as far as he has. Others are more purely negative. They do not try to salvage anything from the positions they wreck. In the *Groundwork* Kant takes this kind of stance when he considers alternatives to his own view of the first principle of morals. He lumps them together, not very politely, as 'spurious principles of morality'. And he dismisses them because they are, one and all, 'heteronomous' (*G* IV 441).

He can do this because he thinks he has shown that morality as we all understand it requires autonomy. Its first principle, the moral law or categorical imperative, centres on autonomy of the will. Any other sort of principle just gets morality wrong. So if all alternatives to Kant's principle are heteronomous, they simply miss the point. Now, for anything that Kant has shown up to this point, it might be that morality is itself a chimera or a delusion. He will try in the final section of the *Groundwork* to show otherwise. But even if the principle of morality is chimerical, it is an *autonomous* principle that is so, not a heteronomous one. Heteronomous principles have no right to be called moral. This is the dominant objection Kant makes to them. But he does not leave them alone after this dismissal. Both in the *Groundwork* and in the *Critique of Practical Reason* he gives further arguments against them. Why does he bother?

I am grateful to the Philosophy Department at the University of Oslo for perceptive and helpful discussion. My thanks also to Jens Timmermann and to an anonymous reader for helpful suggestions.

I AN 'ONLY SURVIVOR' ARGUMENT?

Criticisms of mistaken views can be part of an argument to support a philosopher's own position. 'All the other available views have fatal flaws', this kind of argument goes, 'and mine alone survives all the criticisms; so mine is the best'. I will call this an 'only survivor' argument. It has several potential weaknesses. There is always the possibility that there are positions the philosopher has not considered and which are not flawed. There may be other flaws, which the alleged survivor itself contains. Or the question itself to which all these views are answers may be hopelessly confused. Then perhaps none of the alternatives is worth considering. And, obviously, any criticism of views to be eliminated must not presuppose the truth of the view to be defended.

An 'only survivor' argument can avoid these weaknesses. The philosopher using it may argue that the positions she is criticizing completely exhaust all the possibilities outside her own view. If she also argues that there must be an answer to the question under consideration, then a dismissive shrug won't do. There must be an answer, and this is the only survivor, so this is it. The success of the argument thus turns on the specific objections the philosopher makes to the positions to be eliminated.

Kant makes several remarks indicating that he is thinking in terms of this kind of argument.[1] He plainly thinks that there must be an answer to the question he wants to answer in the *Groundwork*: what is the single basic principle of morality? In *CpV* he sets his *formal* principle of morals apart from 'all previous *material* principles'. He gives a schematic listing of the

---

[1] The criticisms of proposed alternatives are given in several places. (All references to Kant's writings are to the Academy Edition, citing volume and page number. Hereafter references will be given in the text.) The main published statements are in the *Groundwork* IV 441–5, and the *Critique of Practical Reason* V 33–41. Kant frequently discussed the history of moral philosophy in his lectures on ethics. Some of the surviving lectures notes have been published. Paul Menzer edited one set, which was translated by Louis Infield and published as *Immanuel Kant: Lectures on Ethics* (1930). Other lecture notes were published by Gerhard Lehmann in vol. 27 of the Academy edition of Kant. A substantial selection from the lectures has been translated by Peter Heath: *Immanuel Kant, Lectures on Ethics* (Cambridge University Press, 1997). The main passages containing Kant's criticisms of other moral philosophers are XXVII 100–6, 247–54, 482–4, 646–50, 1400–6; and XXIX 603–4, 621 and 626 (many of these are translated in Heath). Volume XIX of the Academy edition contains occasional remarks about the history of moral philosophy and numerous sketches of exhaustive classifications of possible positions, found in marginal notes written in the textbook from which Kant taught and in manuscript remains. I will draw on the two published sources and on the lecture notes.

In the essay *On the Common Saying: 'That May Be Correct in Theory, But It is of No Use in Practice'*, Kant replies to criticisms of his ethics by Christian Garve, published in 1792 (VIII 275–89). He also discusses Hobbes' political theory, but not the part of Hobbes' work that bears more directly on morality (VIII 289–97). The essay is translated in Mary Gregor, *Immanuel Kant: Practical Philosophy* (Cambridge University Press, 1996).

alternatives to his principle, saying that here 'all possible cases are actually exhausted' (*CpV* V 39). If each of these material principles is shown to be unsuited to serve as the single basic principle, then, he says, 'the *formal practical principle* of pure reason ... is the *sole* principle that can *possibly* be fit' for the job (*CpV*V 41). Kant thus comes close to describing his criticisms of other views in terms of a 'sole survivor' argument.

If Kant meant his wholesale dismissal of heteronomous principles to be an argument in support of an autonomous principle, he would be begging the question in his own favour.[2] There are some passages in which Kant does seem to be begging the question in this way. But in many of the separate arguments against the various proposed heteronomous principles he does not seem to be doing so. Kant's targets in these arguments are drawn from the moral philosophy of (roughly) his own time. To see the focus of the criticisms it will help to compare them with his handling of ancient views.

2 ANCIENTS AND MODERNS

Kant is famous, or infamous, for claiming that 'before the coming of the critical philosophy there was as yet no philosophy at all' (*MdS* VI 207; see

---

[2] Although Kant cannot appeal directly to the moral law to support independent arguments against alternative possible principles, he may be able to use points he has made in the *Groundwork* prior to his criticism of them. In one of the most detailed English-language examinations of the critique of spurious principles, Samuel Kerstein lists a number of what he takes to be Kant's criteria for a supreme principle of morality (Samuel J. Kerstein, *Kant's Search for the Supreme Principle of Morality* (Cambridge University Press, 2002), ch. 7, especially pp. 139–40). Kerstein thinks Kant might appeal to these to test proposed alternatives to his favoured principle. The first four criteria are that the principle must be '(i) practical, (ii) absolutely necessary, (iii) binding on all rational agents and (iv) the supreme principle'. Kerstein finds four further criteria. Three relate to moral motivation: (v) whatever act is willed because of the principle has moral worth; (vi) the moral worth of acting from the principle 'stems from its motive, not from its effects'; and (vii) the thought that the principle is a law gives the agent a sufficient motive to conform to it. Finally, (viii) a 'plausible set of duties ... can be derived from the principle'. It seems to me that this list is overly generous to Kant. Criteria (i) and (iv) state what may be common ground between Kant and those he is criticizing. Some philosophers, however, like Butler and Reid, would object that morality cannot be so tidily accommodated in a single supreme principle. Criterion (viii) could be common ground if 'derived' does not point only to duties obtained from the principle by reasoning alone. Criteria (ii) and (iii) seem to rule out any empirically based principle and therefore seem question-begging. Criteria (v), (vi) and (vii) encapsulate distinctively Kantian ways of putting views about the centrality of motivation. Proponents of other views on moral motivation might object to the terminology, even if in some sense they agree. Hume, for instance, thinks that moral worth requires special sorts of motivation, but he would not say that the motive must always be devotion to a principle. Kerstein considers many possible counter-examples to Kant's criticisms. But he often considers proposed ethical principles that are more indicative of current discussions than of work that Kant could have known.

Another valuable commentary is that by Friedrich Kaulbach, *Immanuel Kants 'Grundlegung zur Metaphysik der Sitten'* (Wissenschaftliche Buchgesellschaft, 1988), ch. II.9. Kaulbach's comments follow the text more fully and closely than Kerstein's.

also *CrV* B xv). He alone, he holds, has put the theoretical part of the subject on a firm footing. In matters involving practical reason he is not so sweepingly dismissive of the past. Quite the contrary. 'In moral philosophy', he says in the lectures that became his textbook on logic, 'we have come no further than the ancients' (IX 32; cf. XXVIII 540). From the surviving lecture notes we can see that his courses on ethics frequently start with a survey of ancient moral philosophy. The ancients, he holds, were agreed about the issue to be addressed. They asked about the highest good. 'All ethical systems of the ancient world were founded on the question of the *Summum Bonum*' (*Lectures* XXVII 247). The Cynics, the Stoics, and the Epicureans each portrayed an ideal of a person living a good life; and so also, he adds, perhaps surprisingly, did Christ, whom he sometimes describes as one of the ancient moral philosophers. 'With these four ideals', Kant says, 'the whole topic is exhausted' (XXIX 604–5).

When Kant discusses modern moral philosophers he does not examine their views of the highest good. He treats them as having pursued a different quest. They have sought a principle.[3] By this he means the kind of directive he describes in a footnote in the *Critique of Practical Reason*. In it Kant is replying to a critic (Tittel) who objected that the *Groundwork* offers no new principle of morals. It gives only a new formula. Kant asks: who could want to introduce a new principle? One would have to think that the world had been ignorant of morality up until now. 'But whoever knows what a *formula* means to a mathematician, which determines quite precisely what is to be done to solve a problem... will not take a formula that does this with respect to all duty in general as something that is insignificant' (*CpV* V 8 fn.). If a principle of this kind is to have any practical effect, there must be a motive or motives that reliably lead us to follow its guidance. Kant's examination of the moderns focuses on principles of duty in general and on motives to do one's duty.

Henry Sidgwick is often credited with having shaped a widely held view of the main difference between ancient and modern ethics. The ancients, he said, argue 'from first to last' about the answer to the question, 'Which of the objects that men think good is truly Good or the Highest Good?'. The moderns instead take a 'quasi-jural' notion of duty as the main object of investigation. The ancients saw ethics as basically concerned with what

---

[3] Klaus Düsing, 'Das Problem des höchsten Gutes in Kants praktischer Philosophie', *Kant-Studien* 62 (1971), 5–42, discusses Kant's views on ancient moral philosophy and on Christian moral philosophy, making the same points I make. Düsing draws his evidence more from notes from Kant's manuscript remains than from the ethics lectures. I am indebted to Eckart Förster for drawing my attention to this article.

most fundamentally attracts us. The moderns fix on what provides the most
basic authoritative directive for action.[4] Kant seems to have anticipated
Sidgwick's understanding of the main difference between ancient and
modern moral philosophy.

When Kant discusses ancient moral philosophy in his early lectures, he
does not examine either views of virtue and the virtues, or any principles of
duty. Even so, he is clear about what sort of principle for decision-making
he thinks desirable. After he has explained the ancient views, he says that
'since we must all have a principle of moral judgement, whereby we can
unambiguously decide what is morally good or bad, we perceive that there
must be a single principle emanating from the ground of our will' (XXVII
252). This remark points toward the kind of principle Kant gives us later.
The first full exposition of such a principle comes in the *Groundwork*, in
Kant's account of the categorical imperative.

3 ALTERNATIVES TO KANT'S PRINCIPLE

In the *Groundwork* Kant argues that a formal moral law is the basic law of
morality. For finite beings like us the moral law takes the form of the
categorical imperative. Both the law and the imperative are tied to autonomy
of the will. In Sections I and II, Kant says, he has done no more than to
show that the moral law, the categorical imperative, and autonomy are
central to what we all think of as morality. If morality is a chimera, then
so are these three. That question is to be settled only in Section III.

In Section II Kant takes on alternatives to his view proposed by other
modern moral philosophers. The passage in which he chiefly does this, from
G IV 441 to the end of *G* IV 444, begins with the assertion that all proposed
principles of morals other than the categorical imperative are
heteronomous.

The first section on *G* IV 441 simply restates the distinctive mark of
heteronomous principles. They all direct us to will something because we
already will something else. A categorical imperative tells us, by contrast, to
will something whether or not we have willed anything else. To decide to do
or not do something because of something we already want or have chosen
is to decide heteronomously. The will in this kind of case does not give itself

---

[4] Henry Sidgwick, *The Methods of Ethics* (7th edn, London: Macmillan, 1907), Bk I, ch. ix, §1, pp. 105–6.
For critical assessment of this historical position see Nicholas White, *Individual and Conflict in Greek
Ethics* (Oxford University Press, 2002).

the law or principle by which it decides. It is determined by its object. It is governed either by an inclination toward the object, or by a 'representation of reason' that determines choice because of some property of what is represented.

The example Kant gives is interesting, if only because it should have prevented a long series of criticisms based on the supposition that Kant objects to pursuing the happiness of others. I ought, he says, to 'try to further the happiness of others'. I might want to do so out of a feeling of benevolence, or because I find the idea of general happiness (a representation of reason) appealing. In both cases I would pursue general happiness because my will is determined by the object. But the proper reason for pursuing it is that I cannot rationally will a maxim that excludes pursuing it. In this case my will determines itself.

Before Kant gives his classification of all possible heteronomous principles he makes a suggestion about the history of thought. Reason, he says, hits on the right path only after it tries every other possible path – all the wrong paths. The suggestion here is in line with the dismissal of all previous efforts at philosophy as failures.[5] And it is a strong claim: reason has not missed a single wrongheaded option. If the criticisms are effective, it will indeed be 'futile to look around for any other principle than the one now presented' (*CpV* V 39), that is, the categorical imperative.

In the *Groundwork* (*G* IV 442–3) Kant divides heteronomous principles in two ways. One division is between empirically based principles and rationally based principles. The other division is between principles based on something internal to us and principles based on something external to us. In the *Critique of Practical Reason* there is a counterpart division. He there considers 'material principles', which he classifies as either subjective or objective, and as either external or internal (*CpV* V 40).

In the *Groundwork* Kant finds two sorts of internal empirical principle. There are those instructing us to pursue happiness or pleasure, and those telling us to follow the direction of our moral feelings or moral sense. There are also two kinds of external empirical principle. Some tell us to live according to the customs of our time and place; others tell us to obey the ruler of our country.

---

[5] In the Preface to the second edition of the *Critique of Pure Reason*, Kant says that before reason enters on the sure path of a science it shows only 'unfounded groping and frivolous wandering about' (*CrV* B xxxi; cf. B vii). He does not there say that reason exhausts all possible errors before getting things right. On this point I am indebted to Kaulbach, *Immanuel Kants 'Grundlegung zur Metaphysic der Sitten'*, p. 109, who helpfully discusses the relation of the claim about moral error to Kant's claims about metaphysical error.

One kind of internal principle directs us to pursue pleasure – our own, or that of others. Kant mentions Epicurus as holding the view (*CpV*V 40). He would have had no difficulty in finding other exponents among his German and French predecessors and contemporaries. To mention only one, Johann August Eberhard, in his *Sittenlehre der Vernunft* (*Rational Theory of Morals*) of 1781, declares in chapter I.1 that 'if there is an art of human happiness there must also be an essence of the rules of this art. The science of these rules is ethical theory or morality in an extended sense. (Moral science, moral discipline, practical philosophy).'

The other kind of internal empirical principle tells us to do as our moral feeling or moral sense directs. In the *Critique of Practical Reason* Kant gives Hutcheson as an instance. He was also familiar with the work of Shaftesbury and Hume, whom he thought of as moral sense philosophers. He treats the moral sense as a source of pleasure, different from the source in satisfaction of desires. When we comply with the moral sense we are pleased with ourselves. Thus, when we follow the moral sense, we are trying to obtain the pleasant feeling of self-approval. Kant treats sympathetic concern for the happiness of others in the same way. We are pleased when they are happy, and this pleasure is our end in acting sympathetically (*G* IV 442 fn.). These two views tell us to treat morality as means to an end. Our nature makes us desire happiness. We do not choose that end. Hence the principles are heteronomous.

So also are the two external empirical theories. The principle that we are to live according to the customs in which we have been raised points us to an external source of guidance about which only experience can teach us. Kant thinks Montaigne held this view (*CpV*V 40). Another external empirically based principle tells us to obey the ruler or the civil constitution. Kant points to Mandeville (and elsewhere to Hobbes) as proposing this view. In both cases morality has the aim of complying with some external authority.

Kant finds alternatives to these empirically based principles in doctrines whose principle is that we are to increase perfection. Christian Wolff's perfectionism dominated German philosophy teaching in the early part of the eighteenth century, and his followers published innumerable textbooks in the latter part. Kant himself used those by Baumgarten. Perfection, on this view, relates to the harmonious working of a complex entity. The ultimate purpose of everything in the perfect world God created is to express God's glory. Each kind of thing does so in a special way. Its parts are more or less harmoniously organized to carry out this function. The more parts an entity has and the more harmoniously they function, the more perfect the entity is. The Wolffians all held that we are so constituted that we necessarily strive to increase our own perfection. And every increase in perfection is an increase in pleasure. So what the principle 'Maximize perfection' directs is co-extensive with what is required by the principle 'Maximize pleasure'. But we can only find out about what increases perfection through the study of *a priori* metaphysics. Hence, perfectionist views are rational, not empirical. What metaphysics shows us is that we increase our perfection by increasing the clarity and distinctness of our thoughts. Kant can thus consider Wolffian perfectionism as resting on a rational internal principle. And Kant would think that it is a heteronomous principle because it requires us to comply with an order of perfection that is determined by the nature of things, not by our own will.

The chief critic of Wolff and his followers was Christian August Crusius, who restated the Lutheran doctrine that morality results from the will of God. Luther taught that what is right is so because God wills it. We must not suppose that God wills it because it is right. That would subject God to something other than himself. Crusius gives a philosophical defence of this kind of view. He then argues that *a priori* metaphysics can tell us enough about God's will to give us guidance. Thus, he advocates what Kant calls a rational external principle, and one which plainly subordinates our will to the will of another.

4 AGAINST EMPIRICIST ALTERNATIVES

Has Kant shown all of these principles to be, in his terms, heteronomous? The point is arguable, because there are different conceptions of what counts as being autonomous, or imposed by oneself.[6] We can allow at least that if he is right about them, all the 'spurious principles' are teleological. They derive principles about what to do from a view about an end to be achieved. And this is probably enough for his purposes. Now he suggests that these views all fail *just because* they 'set up heteronomy of the will as the first ground of morality' (*G* IV 443). As I said above, in a 'sole survivor' argument he would be begging the question if this were his only reason for

---

[6] Wolff, for example, would argue that clear and distinct ideas are fully our own, while confused and indistinct ones are much less so: hence the clearer and more distinct the ideas that move us to action, the more we are self-directed. In contemporary discussion there are many, hotly contested, conceptions of autonomy. For the recent literature, see James Stacy Taylor (ed.), *Personal Autonomy: New Essays on Personal Autonomy and its Role in Contemporary Moral Philosophy* (Cambridge University Press, 2005), and John Christman and Joel Anderson (eds.), *Autonomy and the Challenges to Liberalism* (Cambridge University Press, 2005).

rejecting them. We must ask to what extent his other arguments escape this charge.

He has one argument against all empirical principles. Moral principles, Kant believes, must hold universally, for all rational beings. But empirically based principles cannot have this universality. Kant holds this to be true of empirical principles in all domains of thought. It is an important part of his attack on empiricist conceptions of causality in the first *Critique*. In the *Groundwork* he is arguing that we cannot assume that all rational beings share the human nature on which empirical moral principles are based. We can, for instance, think of a deity who is rational but otherwise not constituted as we are. Empirical principles, therefore, cannot be moral principles.

This is a quite general argument against empirical principles of morality. Empiricists, of course, would reject it. They hold that universal principles, both in science and in morality, can be established on empirical grounds. They would claim that the general argument begs the question. The issue here cannot be settled without deciding the whole controversy between Kant and the empiricists. But Kant goes on to offer more specific arguments as well.

Among the spurious principles, that which directs us to pursue our own happiness is, Kant says, the worst. He then offers a series of reasons for rejecting the principle:

(H1) It is false, Kant says, because experience shows us that people who are prosperous and happy are not always good. Pursuing happiness is not pursuing goodness.

(H2) There is a plain distinction between making someone happy and making him good. But the egoist's happiness principle cannot account for the distinction.

(H3) There is a clear distinction between being shrewd and far-sighted about one's own advantage and being virtuous. Who could deny that these are distinct? Yet the happiness principle cannot allow them to be so. In the *Critique of Practical Reason*, Kant gives two illustrations of this point. No one would believe a man who claimed that in successfully committing perjury he was carrying out a 'true human duty'. One would be disgusted by him. And it would be no recommendation of someone to be the manager of all your affairs to praise his ruthlessness and shrewdness in pursuing his own ends. The boundaries of morality and self-love, Kant says, are so sharp and clear that 'even the most common eye' can see them with no trouble (*CpV* V 32–3).

(H4) The happiness principle tells us that the motive to pursue virtue is the same as the motive to pursue vice. In each case we are pursuing what we think to be our own good. In some cases we calculate that virtue will pay better than vice, in other cases the reverse. On this view there is no other difference. But these two motives, Kant says, are different in kind. So the happiness principle has got things wrong.[7]

It will seem to contemporary readers that Kant pays very little attention to the principle that we ought to do what most increases happiness generally. He is more concerned about egoism than about what we call utilitarianism. But he has more to say about the general happiness principle. He allows that it is a possible principle. But he plainly did not know Bentham's work, and he did not consider Bentham's forerunners. A comment in the *Critique of Practical Reason* shows us, however, what he would say about their kind of view. Even if universal happiness were to be the object of moral directives, it could at best give us general rules, not binding principles necessarily holding for everyone (*CpV* V 36). This is because happiness comes from satisfaction of desire. Desires are inconstant and fluctuating, and consequently happiness can never provide a firm and fixed target.[8] We cannot derive firm action-guiding rules by taking it as the goal.

Kant himself thinks everyone has an obligation to help other people satisfy their morally permissible desires. He also holds that we are not to use our own conception of happiness as a guide when we help others. We should help them get what *they* want. He is not, as I pointed out above, opposed to the pursuit of happiness. He might rest his rejection of the general happiness principle on the general argument against empiricist views. But the objection here is more specific. It concerns just happiness. Happiness is too unstable an aim to generate universal moral laws. We cannot get moral guidance by taking happiness as our end.

In the *Critique of Practical Reason*, Kant gives some additional objections to views like utilitarianism and to hedonism generally. On his own view, it is easy to tell what one morally ought to do. Even those of 'the most common understanding' can think it out for themselves. But it is very hard to figure out what will make one happy. So these cannot be the same thing. And this is not an unimportant difference. Since morality binds everyone, morality must be such that everyone can know what it requires. We all do in fact

---

[7] Note that this is not applying any of Kerstein's criteria concerning motivation.

[8] It is perhaps for this reason that Kant does not criticize ancient conceptions of happiness or wellbeing. They simply reflect one or another set of desires. That not everyone shares them is, for Kant, hardly worth mentioning.

pursue happiness, so it would be absurd to say we are obligated to pursue it. Moreover, Kant holds, we can always do what morality tells us to do. But we can't always bring happiness to ourselves (or, he might have added, to others). The pursuit of happiness, again, fails to capture essential points about morality (*CpV* V 36–7).

This gives us three additional arguments against principles of pleasure-seeking:

(H5) Happiness cannot be a stable and useable goal.

(H6) We cannot easily know what brings happiness, but we can easily know what morality requires. The two cannot be the same.

(H7) We can always do what morality requires but we cannot always bring about happiness. The two cannot be the same.

In the *Groundwork*, after dismissing egoistic hedonism or pleasure-seeking, Kant turns to the other internal empirical principle, that of the moral sense. The principle says that we are to do what our moral sense feels approval of. Here, we might expect Kant to bring in the general argument against empirical principles. It is only a contingent fact about our nature that we have the capacity for feeling approval. So the moral sense principle fails because it relies on features of human nature that we cannot suppose to be universal. But Kant does not give this argument:

(MS1) His objection is rather that feeling cannot do the job that morality needs. Morality needs a universal law. But feelings differ indefinitely in degree. So they cannot furnish a universal standard.

(MS2) Kant adds that 'one cannot judge validity for others by means of one's feeling'. I think he has in mind something like this. I don't like liver. On this basis I conclude that I should reject it when it is offered. I can't on this basis conclude that you should reject it. If you like it, then what is valid for me – rejecting liver – is not valid for you. But morality, for Kant, requires a universal principle. What is to be rejected in my case must be rejected in a like case by you.

(MS3) In a footnote at *G* IV 442 Kant adds another reason to reject moral sense theories. Doing as the moral sense directs, he says, is just another case of gratifying an empirical interest, an interest that our nature causes us to have. Gratifying *any* interest contributes to our wellbeing. In some cases the gratification is a contribution to our wellbeing. When I have an interest in increasing my wealth, its gratification (unless I am a hoarder of money for its own sake) contributes to my wellbeing by enabling me to purchase things I want. When I gratify my moral feelings, it is the gratification itself that contributes to my wellbeing. It pleases me when I act as the moral feeling urges. So the moral sense theory is in the end just a variant on the egoistic happiness principle.

(MS4) Kant adds that 'the principle of sympathy with the happiness of others' falls under the moral sense principle and so can be rejected for the same reason. Sympathy makes me share the happiness or unhappiness of others. Kant thinks this means that I feel happy when the relevant others are happy, and unhappy when they are not. These feelings move me to act, either to support the happiness of others or to diminish their unhappiness. Gratifying these interests is, again, just gratifying an empirically given urge, and doing so always increases our own happiness. We like helping others, so in helping them we are increasing our own enjoyment.

5 AGAINST RATIONALIST ALTERNATIVES

Kant deals with rational principles other than the categorical imperative in a paragraph consisting of one very long sentence filled with important and somewhat obscure parenthetical remarks (*G* IV 443). He concentrates on principles about perfection, and begins by objecting to the 'ontological' conception of it. By this he means a conception of perfection that applies to all things in the universe without distinction:

(P1) This conception, he says, is empty and indeterminate. The principle 'Maximize perfection' is therefore useless in practice. It cannot guide us because it does not tell us how to calculate the greatest amount of perfection that we (as distinct, say, from God) should pursue. In the *Critique of Practical Reason* Kant elaborates on this a little. Perfection in a theoretical sense is just the completeness of a thing considered as a kind. A perfect baking apple has all the attributes a baking apple should have to be exemplary. A perfect adultery would similarly be an exemplary case of infidelity. But knowing what it takes for something to be perfect of its kind will not, by itself, guide us. It would guide us only if we desired a thing of that kind; but then we would be back to heteronomy.

Practical perfection, Kant continues, in the case of humans, is the possession of talents and skills. But this gives no guidance unless we first have a goal to reach where these would be helpful. And once again we have left autonomy behind (*CpV* V 41):

(P2) For morality we presumably need to pursue a perfect life. What perfections are specifically required to make a life perfect? Kant thinks perfectionists are bound to get caught in a vicious circle. They will have to bring in some moral attributes in order to explain human perfection. But to justify picking those attributes they will have to show them to be more perfect than others. Kant thinks that they cannot show moral attributes to be more perfect than alternatives without presupposing the superior perfection of the very moral attributes they seek to justify. So perfectionists either can say nothing about moral perfection or can only go in circles.

(P3) The theological conception of perfection is worse. It tries to show that morality is compliance with God's will. But we cannot know intuitively what God's will is. So we have to reason out what it is. To do this we must use other concepts. If theological moralists use moral concepts they will be reasoning in a circle. They will be using moral concepts to show that God wills us to act in accordance with moral concepts.

(P4) If theological moralists leave out moral concepts, thus avoiding circularity, they are in still worse shape. All they can say of God is that he is all-powerful, punishes disobedience, and seeks glory and mastery. No decent morality can be expected from the commands of an amoral being of that kind.

6 ASSESSMENT OF KANT'S CRITICISMS

How successful are Kant's criticisms of the 'spurious' principles? Has he given sufficient reason to reject them, without begging the question by presupposing the truth of his own view? Has he truly exhausted all the alternatives to his view?

Kant's basic argument against empirical views rests on the argument that moral principles must hold universally, for all rational beings. This is not the same as the general argument, found in the first *Critique*, that only *a priori* necessary principles can be truly universal. It concerns practical principles; and Kant does not offer any argument in favour of it. The closest he comes to supporting it is a remark in the Preface to the *Groundwork* (*G* IV 389):

Everyone must grant that a law, if it is to hold morally, that is, as a ground of an obligation, must carry with it absolute necessity; that, for example, the command 'thou shalt not lie' does not hold only for human beings, as if other rational beings did not have to heed it...; that, therefore, the ground of obligation here must not be sought in the nature of the human being or in the circumstances of the world in which he is placed, but *a priori* simply in concepts of pure reason.

From this it follows that any moral principle based on experience is inadequate. So also is any principle based on 'the circumstances of the world', even if this is the best possible world and created by God – which is what the Wolffian perfectionists held.

Must everyone grant this? To some readers it may seem obvious that morality makes this kind of *a priori* claim. But for some of Kant's readers the point would not have been obvious, or even acceptable. We get a clue about their resistance if we ask who the 'other rational beings' are on whom moral claims are binding. In an early work on cosmology Kant imagined rational beings living on other planets. If gravity exerts a stronger force on these planets, their inhabitants might find it harder to comply with the categorical imperative than we do. But they would still be obligated by it. They are not, however, the main 'other rational beings' Kant has in mind. The chief one, of course, is God. And this causes a problem for Kant. Crusius, following his highly influential predecessor Samuel Pufendorf, holds that God is rational but not bound by obligations. God imposes morality on us by willing us to obey certain commands, but he is not himself bound by any constraints except those of abstract rationality: his legislation cannot be self-contradictory. Kant was raised as a Lutheran and he had studied Crusius (and probably Pufendorf). So he must have known that theological moralists would not have found it 'clear of itself' that there must be an *a priori* moral law valid for all rational agents. It is therefore puzzling that he could have thought his position to be so obvious as to need no defence.

Kant may be appealing here, as he does elsewhere, to the convictions of the ordinary person. Once the terms '*a priori*' and 'necessity' are explained, he may think, plain people will take it as an obvious *a priori* truth that moral demands necessarily bind every rational agent. We may leave aside the doubts that arise from an attempt to conjecture what ordinary people would think about a proposition with whose terms they are unfamiliar. We cannot, however, leave aside the fact that large numbers of ordinary people in Kant's Prussia were raised on orthodox Lutheran doctrine. If these ordinary people understood that Kant's claim entails that God has moral obligations just as they do, would they find the position obvious? I cannot answer the question; but we cannot just disregard the possibility that Lutheran teaching was effective among many of those raised under it. This reading opens up the large question of the extent to which there is, or was in Kant's time, a single, unified common sense morality. But even leaving this aside, Kant's assurance on the point remains puzzling.

Another challenge to Kant's view arises from a quite different direction. Hume sees morality as arising from emotional responses to our own motives and those of others. He also thinks that we do not know anything about God's feelings. So we cannot say that God and we share a common morality.[9] Kant knew about Hume's views and thought highly of them. Again, it is hard to see how he could have taken his own view to be obvious.

Hume also worked out a highly original idea about what are often considered the strictest of obligations, those involved in justice. For him, justice arises as a solution to a recurrent practical problem. Human beings need to live together and to co-operate. We are all also aware that if we do, there will be enough material goods to go around, more or less. But food, clothing, shelter, and so on, will never be so plentiful that we never have to worry about them. We don't live in a natural paradise. Moreover, although people are sometimes generous they still always look out for themselves. We want to be secure in our possession of tools, housing, food, clothing and partners. But we can't rely on our own physical strength to give us security. The principles of justice, Hume suggests, arise as a human convention. We set up rules about the acquisition and transfer of property. We create ways of enforcing the rules, and we all come to expect everyone to abide by them. The rules of justice may be costly for each of us in some circumstances or in some transactions. But we are all better off with such rules than we would be without them. So we tacitly agree that they are to be binding on us regardless of our desires in particular cases. Of course, as a whole the conventions of justice are based on needs arising from our own nature and our situation in the world. But this need is common to all humans. And the result is rules that are as close to being unconditionally binding as human beings need or can get.

Hume thus offers an alternative to Kant's account of the rigorous strictness of moral obligation. And it is an alternative that Kant does not take into account.

This brings us to Kant's particular criticisms of the 'spurious principles'. The first three objections to egoism hedonism, H1, H2 and H3, point out in different ways that we all make a distinction between what we think of as morality and what we think of as prudence in the conduct of our own affairs. The argument here is that the egoist has simply failed to find what we set out to find – a principle of morality. H4 pursues this further. We would agree that the desire to be good or virtuous is not the same as the desire to increase one's own happiness. But the egoist thinks they must be the same desire. So, again, the theory fails to connect with what is distinctive about morality. We might treat the egoist as offering a form of denial that there really is such a thing as

---

[9] See my 'Hume and the Religious Significance of Moral Rationalism', *Hume Studies* 26 (2000), 211–23.

morality. If the egoist thinks that morality as Kant has identified it is just a 'phantom' (*G* IV 445) then she must wait until Section III of the *Groundwork* for an answer. But taken just as showing that egoism is a bad theory about the distinctive practice we call 'morality', the objections are effective.

The next objection, H5, is that happiness cannot be a stable and useable goal. We cannot derive specific directives by reasoning from it. But Kant himself points to part of a reply to this objection. The utilitarian can say that what we ought to do is help people satisfy their legitimate desires. Even if these change, there are general principles to guide us in offering help. Kant even offers one: never foist off your own conception of a good desire on the person you want to help. Liberalism enshrines this principle, and Kant's objection to fluctuations in conceptions of happiness does not harm it. Utilitarians have, of course, said much more to show how their principle can give guidance, not least on large-scale social and political problems. Kant's criticism is not effective.

The next objection, H6, is that because we cannot easily know what brings happiness, but can easily know what morality requires, the two cannot be the same. Kant here makes a point that is far more important than it seems. It involves rejecting technical expertise as having the last word in morality. Christian Wolff explicitly declared that ordinary people need the kind of guidance that only learned folk, like himself, could give. Against such pundits, Kant is defending the ability of ordinary people to figure out for themselves what morality asks of them. John Stuart Mill went to great lengths to show how utilitarian theory could accommodate this point. He agreed with Kant that no moral theory requiring an elite of learned or technically trained leaders to settle moral issues could be acceptable. Most ancient moral philosophers would plainly not have taken this position. The Stoics, to be sure, would have agreed with Kant in principle. They held that even a slave or a woman could acquire the knowledge needed to live wisely. But they also held that almost no one had in fact achieved the ideal, and Kant thinks it is a common ability.

The emergence of belief in the equal ability of normal adults to guide their own moral lives is a major feature of modern moral philosophy. It marks a decisive difference between ancient and modern morality. Kant is one of the first and most articulate of its proponents. It is still controversial. A decision about the effectiveness of H6 requires a decision on this matter.[10]

---

[10] For a recent important discussion of this matter, tying it to debates about 'internal' and 'external' reasons, see John Skorupski, 'Internal Reasons and the Scope of Blame' in Alan Thomas (ed.), *Bernard Williams* (Cambridge University Press, 2007), pp. 73–103 especially pp. 97–102.

Finally, H7 says that we can always do what morality requires but we cannot always bring about happiness. Hence the two cannot be the same. A ready answer here is that we can always *try* to bring about happiness, our own or that of others; and that morally speaking trying is what counts. The objection seems quite weak.

Among the objections to moral sense theory, MS1 and MS2 are like H1, H2 and H3. They point out that there are aspects of the morality we are trying to explain that the moral sense theory cannot handle. Moral judgements are not like judgements of taste or feeling. Some people like pink wallpaper and polkadot shirts, others don't. We just say: everyone to his taste. But we don't say that about those who like child abuse. And mere feeling isn't enough to explain the difference. There is a large literature on this topic. I think Kant points in the direction of valid objections to this kind of theory, but a detailed discussion would be needed to take into account all the ways in which moral sense theorists and their modern descendants could defend their views.[11]

MS3 and MS4 both tell us that moral sense theories are after all variants of egoism as a psychological theory. If we act because we take pleasure in the thought that we are acting rightly or helping others, we are really acting to increase our own enjoyment. These objections point to a serious weakness, or at least a grave wavering, in Kant's own psychology. He sometimes – as here – talks as if aside from acting from duty, anything one does willingly one does for the sake of the pleasure one takes in doing it. Bishop Butler worked out powerful objections to this view, which Kant seems not to have known. Butler pointed out that sometimes we simply desire something with no thought of our own pleasure or good. When we are hungry, what we want is food, not the pleasure of eating. Indeed, if we didn't want food we would take no pleasure in eating. So there must be simple, direct desires for something other than enjoyable states of yourself. And if so, a direct desire for the good of another is also possible.[12] Kant himself sometimes seems to admit the possibility of this desire; if he allows it, then even on his own view these objections fail.

Against the form of perfectionism Kant knew, objection P1 amounts to the charge that it always involves heteronomy. If so, Kant begs the question by supposing that autonomy is basic. Perfectionism, Kant says, does not tell us how to choose between different sorts of perfect things unless we want one but not the others. A Wolffian might reply to the charge that the

[11] For one of the best of these, see Allan Gibbard, *Wise Choices, Apt Feelings* (Harvard University Press, 1990).
[12] Joseph Butler, *Sermons* (J. H. Bernard (ed.), London, 1900), especially I, fn. 7.

directive 'Increase perfection!' is empty by saying: 'Not so. We tell you to increase the clarity and distinctness of your thoughts. That is pretty specific!' But the question that then arises is: which thoughts? Those that tell me I am on the trail of a new mathematical proof, or those that tell me I might help ward off starvation in Africa by giving to Oxfam? It is not clear what answer the Wolffian will have that does not require some sort of heteronomy.

P2, the vicious circle argument against perfectionism, seems effective against Wolff's form of the doctrine. But it would not hold against recent versions which Kant cannot have considered.[13]

P3 and P4, Kant's criticisms of theological perfectionism, pick up on a heated debate in early modern moral philosophy. Luther and Calvin revitalized views making morality depend on the absolute will of God. Philosophical defences of their kind of position were offered and these in turn stimulated philosophical critiques. Leibniz's attack on Pufendorf called forth a reply from Pufendorf's translator Barbeyrac. This exchange is the most thorough of the available controversies of the period on this point.[14] The theological view lost adherents steadily, though John Stuart Mill felt called upon to repudiate the view even in the later nineteenth century.[15] But voluntarism is still alive. New variants of the view have appeared in the recent literature. Robert Adams and Philip Quinn, for instance, have offered differing voluntarist theories of considerable sophistication.[16] There is no point in considering them here. Kant has nothing new to add to this debate.

In his criticism of the 'spurious principles' of morality, did Kant in fact consider all the possible positions other than his own? Even leaving aside views developed after his, which are not relevant, the answer has to be that he did not. Among the British moralists there were those who held that morality rests on *a priori* rational principles that we come to know by intuition. Samuel Clarke and Richard Price developed quite sophisticated versions of this view. They put forth, moreover, principles that did not depend on our prior acceptance of an end. Kant seems not to have known of

---

[13] See Thomas Hurka, *Perfectionism* (Oxford University Press, 1993), and David O. Brink, *Perfectionism and the Common Good: Themes in the Philosophy of T. H. Green* (Oxford University Press, 2003), for differing contemporary accounts.

[14] See Samuel Pufendorf, *The Whole Duty of Man* (Ian Hunter and David Saunders (eds.), Liberty Fund, 2003), pp. 267–307, which contains Leibniz's criticisms of Pufendorf and Barbeyrac's replies. The two are discussed in my *The Invention of Autonomy* (Cambridge University Press, 1998), pp. 250–9.

[15] John Stuart Mill, *Examination of Sir William Hamilton's Philosophy* (Longman, 1866), ch. 7.

[16] See Robert Merrihew Adams, *Finite and Infinite Goods* (Oxford University Press, 1999), and Philip L. Quinn and Christian B. Miller (eds.), *Essays in the Philosophy of Religion* (Oxford University Press, 2006).

their views.[17] In any case, Kant would have objected to the very idea of a substantive *a priori* principle that could be known by intuition. He would also have been strongly opposed to the intuitionist view that morality requires an irreducible plurality of equally fundamental principles. He would have thought that this destroys the possibility of keeping morality rational; and the defenders of this kind of intuitionism disagree.[18]

7 CONCLUSION

Kant's criticisms of the 'spurious principles of morality' are best understood as parts of a 'sole survivor' argument. The objections to hedonistic egoism are telling, as are those to Wolffian perfectionism and Crusius' divine command view of morality. Many of them do not depend on Kant's specific views about morality and so do not beg the question against their targets. They do often depend on his account of features of the practice of morality that distinguish it from other practices, such as looking out for oneself. Kant thinks this is neutral ground as between himself and those he criticizes. Not everyone would agree. Bernard Williams, for example, argues that what Kant calls 'morality' is a 'peculiar institution' belonging to modernity and not present in antiquity. And like Nietzsche, Williams deplores the change.[19] Kant did not find any challenge like this in the philosophy he knew nor did he invent it for himself and try to reply.

Some of Kant's criticisms of the 'spurious principles' could have been answered in terms of philosophical resources available in his lifetime. Some of his contemporaries published views that he did not consider. We therefore have to conclude that Kant's 'sole survivor' argument fails. Nonetheless, only Hume matches him in trying to give fair-minded and often trenchant responses to the main contemporary alternatives to his own view.

---

[17] Would these count as non-heteronomous principles? A Kantian might say that they are heteronomous because they subject the will to moral realities that bind regardless of our willing.

[18] For recent work on intuitionism and pluralism, see the collection edited by Philip Stratton-Lake, *Ethical Intuitionism: Re-evaluations* (Oxford University Press, 2002).

[19] Bernard Williams, *Ethics and the Limits of Philosophy* (Harvard University Press, 1985).

CHAPTER 9

Autonomy and impartiality: Groundwork *III*

John Skorupski

I KANT'S GRAND PROJECT

Kant's project in the third section of the *Groundwork* is exhilaratingly bold. He seeks to obtain, from the idea of acting *freely* – which (we shall see) is the same as the idea of acting *from reasons* – a principle governing how rational beings should act. It consists in a requirement of impartiality of a particular kind. We human beings, Kant thinks, in virtue of our sensuous nature, experience this principle as a 'categorical imperative', a constraint to be obeyed whatever our inclinations and actual aims may be. However, the principle as such applies to all reason-responsive beings – as it must, given that it is derived from the mere idea of acting for a reason.

Kant gives a number of formulations of the principle, holding them to be equivalent. From these, he has already argued in the two previous sections, we can obtain the imperatives of morality. In fact, he believes his principle gives us *all and only* the universal principles of morality which govern the behaviour of *all* reason-responsive beings; it is, he claims, morality's 'supreme principle' (*G* IV 392), hence, *the* categorical imperative.[1]

Thus, the argument has two steps: from acting for a reason to the categorical imperative, and from that to morality. Taken together in their full strength, the two steps would produce a truly extraordinary result: any being capable of acting for reasons is bound by principles whose content can be deduced from that very idea. No wonder the *Groundwork* has proved inspiring. However, both steps have been widely and devastatingly criticized. Each of them is stoutly defended by some Kantians; it is rare to find them simultaneously defended.

One common view is that the categorical imperative can only have implications for morality if it itself already has moral content, and that no

---

I have been helped by comments from Amanda Perroneau-Saussine and Jens Timmermann.
[1] He does not mean that it can tell you how to act in concrete circumstances. That, he points out, also requires *a posteriori* knowledge and 'a judgement sharpened by experience' (*G* IV 389).

principle that has moral content could be derived from the idea of acting for a reason alone. Now even if we accept this view and abandon the first step, serious difficulties remain in showing the categorical imperative to be *the* supreme principle of morality in the way that Kant intended. That would require a formulation that yielded all and only the principles of morality: not an easy task, as those who have seriously tried it have found. Some defenders of the categorical imperative would, however, only make a more modest claim, though still an interesting one: that it should be seen as being a highly general principle *within* morality, with far-reaching implications to be sure, but not one that on its own generates the whole of morality. This is often argued with particular reference to the formulation of humanity (see *G* IV 429 and p. 166 below). If we give up the ambition of deriving this version of the categorical imperative from its alleged source in the idea of acting for a reason, we are free to acknowledge its full richness; this is especially so if we also stop trying to see it as the basis for *every* moral principle. Undoubtedly, the idea that it is wrong to treat people merely as means – to *use* people, as we say – even put as baldly as that can be the source of some moral guidance; the hope is to deepen and sharpen it by careful consideration of examples.

However, I am not going to discuss any of these matters here. My interest is entirely in the first step.

One reason for taking an interest in this first step is that it is so important to the argument of the *Groundwork*. To relinquish it is to move far indeed from Kant's position. It is to cut off his ethics from his critical philosophy as a whole, in a way that Kant could not have contemplated. If we simply accept the categorical imperative as a substantive, albeit broad, principle *within* morality, and focus our efforts on bringing it into reflective equilibrium with the rest of our considered moral convictions, we are adopting the method of what is called 'moral intuitionism'. We are taking the normative authority of morality as a whole for granted, and investigating its more general features from inside it. This may turn out to be the wisest way; it is definitely not Kant's way. I do not mean that Kant favours scepticism about our moral convictions: he takes them to be largely sound. But neither does he think they should simply be granted. He thinks it is both possible and necessary to consider them as a whole and ask how any convictions of this kind can be sound. The aim of his critical stance in ethics, as in epistemology, is to answer this question: to show *how* it is possible that our moral convictions should be sound, not just to accept dogmatically that they are.

To this end Kant tries to show in the third section of the *Groundwork* that morality follows from freedom, and that it is at least possible that we are free. To some extent, it is true, he may seem to follow a more intuitionistic method in the first two sections, where he seeks to show how we can pass from our shared moral convictions to knowledge of the categorical imperative. In these sections he considers some famous examples which, he suggests, confirm the applicability and implicit presence of the categorical imperative in our everyday moral reasoning. All this, however, is consistent with his overall critical method: it is one part of the overall critical inquiry into the foundations of our moral thinking of which the third section is the other. Furthermore, his main thrust in those sections is to derive the categorical imperative from our concept of duty, rather than to base it simply on its congruity with our moral thinking. So even in these two sections, where he is proceeding 'analytically from common cognition [of morality] to the determination of its supreme principle' (Preface, *G* IV 392), he turns out to have ambitions which an intuitionist would disclaim.

Section III is even more philosophically daring. Even if Kant succeeded in deriving moral content from the very idea of duty it would remain open to a moral sceptic to deny that there is any such thing as duty. The sceptic might find that very tempting. In contrast, it is plainly vastly less tempting to deny that there is any such thing as acting for a reason. Moreover, at this point Kant has a clever move to make. He points out that whenever we deliberate about what to do we must be taking ourselves to be capable of acting for reasons; it will follow, if the rest of his argument is sound, that whenever we deliberate we must take ourselves to be bound by morality.

There is a second reason to examine the first step, which is at least as important. We should not ignore the possibility that both steps might have force in some weakened form, so that from the idea of acting for a reason we can get to some principle weaker that Kant's categorical imperative, but still strong enough to give significant shape to practical deliberation. Specifically, the question I want to ask is whether Kant found a way to derive a requirement of impartiality from the idea of acting for a reason. I shall argue that by his own standards the answer is 'no'. But that is not the end of the story. We can still ask whether a requirement of impartiality is necessarily accepted by any being that is thinking and acting autonomously. Here, the answer is less clear-cut, as we shall see. Does thinking and acting that is autonomous freely acknowledge constraints of impartiality, just in virtue of being autonomous? If Kant has shown that impartiality is somehow grounded in autonomy, even in this broader way, that is itself important and inspiring.

We shall concentrate, then, on the first step in Kant's argument as it is found in *Groundwork* III. It can itself be broken down into two. The first sub-step takes us from acting from a reason to autonomy. The second takes us from autonomy to the categorical imperative. I begin by considering the first.

2 FROM ACTING FROM A REASON TO AUTONOMY

We talk about animals as acting for reasons, but we do not think they deliberate about them. They do not think about the reasons for doing something, assess their strength, consolidate them into an overall conclusion as to what to do. For example, we say that the cat's reason for waiting at the mouse hole is that it expects a mouse to come out. But in saying so we do not think that it deliberates about how good a reason that is – about whether there is any reason to expect a mouse, or whether there is in anycase more reason to do something else, instead of waiting around for a mouse, nor do we think that *it* thinks of itself as acting for a reason.

This is not the kind of acting for a reason that interests Kant. He would no doubt have said that it is not really acting *for*, or *from*, a reason at all. The capacity for assessing reasons *as* reasons is essential to what he is interested in: I shall call it *reason-responsiveness*. Reason-responsiveness is recognizing reasons and acting from them because one recognizes them as reasons to act. It is not that whenever we act reason-responsively we have explicitly deliberated about reasons; the point is only that we always have that capacity to assess whether something really is a reason, and how strong a reason it is.

Since deliberation is thinking about what reasons there are to do something, and how strong they are, when we deliberate we must be thinking of ourselves as reason-responsive, at least with respect to the decision we are deliberating about. We are considering what, all things considered, we should do – with a view to doing it. So we are practically committed to thinking that in this case at least there may be an answer to that question, and that we can succeed in recognizing it and acting on it. Suppose we do succeed: in that case our action is caused by our recognition that it is what we should do, and by no other cause.

Consider an example. You are thinking about whether to go on a diet. You take stock of some relevant facts: that you are in imminent danger of a heart attack if you don't, that for you life is definitely worthwhile, etc. You come to believe that these facts entail that you should go on a diet, and the reason you come to believe it is that that is what they *do* entail. Accordingly, you go on a diet. In this sequence no cause other than reason-recognition has played a role. You arrive at a correct assessment of what you should do – not accidentally but because you see that it is correct – and that correct assessment fully explains what you do.

It might not work out like that. In a second scenario, having decided you should go on a diet, you fail because you like eating so much. Here, there is reason-recognition but failure to execute. In a third, you come to believe that you should go on a diet only because you want to look like the people in celebrity magazines. Suppose for the sake of argument that this is not a good enough reason to go on a diet; you are just succumbing to peer pressure. So in this third scenario there is failure of reason-recognition, though no failure to execute: either you incorrectly took that to be a good reason to go on a diet, or you didn't even think about whether or not it was a good reason. In these two scenarios your action springs from causes *alien to reason*, in the sense that they are causes outside pure reason-responsiveness. There are many possible alien causes: you may be diverted by inattention, inertia, self-delusion, overpowerful inclination, and so on. These are alien causes in the sense that their existence is irrelevant to assessing what you should do, except insofar as you may have to recognize and cope with them as obstacles. They do not in themselves give you reasons to act, but they can divert you from what you should do.

Kant thinks that this ability to act rationally – from pure reason-responsiveness without being diverted by alien causes – is what freedom is. If freedom exists, this is its causality: *the causality of freedom*, as he calls it. That is what the first sentence of Section III says (*G* IV 446):

Will is a kind of causality of living beings insofar as they are rational, and *freedom* would be that property of such causality that it can be efficient independently of alien causes *determining* it.

He immediately takes another important step; he argues that reasons must be universal laws because (*G* IV 446):

the concept of causality brings with it that of *laws* according to which, by something that we call a cause, something else, namely an effect must be posited.

Natural causes, Kant thinks, operate in accordance with universal laws of nature. When we act freely, a different causal story applies. To act freely is not just to act in accordance with a universal law but *from your recognition* of a universal law. What you are recognizing is a universal law, but not a law of nature. What you recognize in recognizing what you should do, explicitly or implicitly, are universal *normative* principles. For example, you see someone swimming in a pool where they are in danger of getting sucked under and drowning, but clearly unaware of it, and so you shout out a warning. You probably don't formulate to yourself the principle 'When someone is in danger of drowning and unaware of it, one should warn them', but that is the principle on which you act.[2] So you act from your awareness of a universal principle, not just in accordance with one.

This is autonomy. You 'give' the law to yourself in the sense that you act because *you* recognize that there is a law of reason, a normative requirement, that requires you to do this action, and you do it from that recognition, even though, perhaps, you don't feel like doing it.[3] In contrast, a fire acts in accordance with some laws of physics when it burns things, but it is not autonomous. It does not burn things because it is recognizes that a law of reason says that it should do so. Note, by the way, that it doesn't really matter whether Kant is right to think that natural causes are universal. The important point on which he relies is that reasons are.

Note also that the notion of autonomous action is stronger than that of acting for a reason. When you get an ice cream out of the fridge and eat it, even though you know you are on a diet, you are not necessarily over-powered by an addiction you cannot resist. You may still be acting for a reason, though not the best reason; the fact that the ice cream is going to taste really good *is* a reason to eat it. You may also think to yourself that this will be the last one, that one more won't make a difference, etc. In that case you are kidding yourself: your assessment of reasons is distorted or rendered ineffective by alien causes, but some reason-recognition is still in play.

We can say that you are free when you act autonomously, or we can say that you are free so long as you have the capacity to act autonomously. The latter formulation seems better, in that it allows that a person can freely do the wrong thing – what they should not have done. When you eat the ice cream you do so freely, but not autonomously. Kant sometimes puts it in the latter way; however, he also sometimes identifies freedom with autonomy; for example, when he says that morality can be derived from freedom he means it can be derived from autonomy. On this way of

---

[2] It is not really as simple as that. Those facts just give you reason to warn them. It might be false that you should warn them, because there may be even stronger reasons not to, for example, that an even bigger disaster would occur if you did. Complicated questions about how to formulate the universal principles involved would arise. But for our purposes we can ignore all that. I agree with Kant's essential claim, which is that what you should do is always determinable by universal principles of which you can be aware (even if you find it hard or impossible to formulate them in advance).

[3] Kant distinguishes between the author of a law and its law-giver. See e.g., *MdS* VI 227. No one is literally the *author* of a law of reason, but we *give* it to ourselves in the sense of 'commanding' ourselves to follow it, whatever our inclination.

speaking, when you eat the ice cream you do not act freely. It remains true that you could have acted freely, and so you are still responsible.[4]

So far, so good. The problem, Kant thinks, is that he has only shown that *if* we think of ourselves as reason-responsive we must think we are capable of autonomy. He hasn't shown that we *are* ever reason-responsive. Strictly speaking, at least in the *Groundwork*, he thinks we cannot ever know that we are. Nonetheless, insofar as we deliberate about what we should do we must in practice be seeing ourselves as reason-responsive: capable of coming up with the right answer, and acting on it.

We need not go too far into why Kant thinks we can never know that we are acting from reasons. As we have seen, he thinks that acting from reasons requires the 'causality of freedom', and this causality, he thinks, is irreducible to natural causality. At the same time, when we take the standpoint of natural science and consider ourselves as a phenomenon, we can truly say that everything about this phenomenon is the product of natural causes. These two standpoints, Kant thinks, can only be reconciled by his doctrine of 'transcendental idealism', to which he alludes at *G* IV 450–3 and 457–9. On the one hand, this doctrine entails that we cannot know ourselves to be free, or to be reason-responsive at all, since an essential feature of the doctrine is that phenomena are all we can know. On the other hand, in Kant's opinion, it establishes the possibility that we are free – a possibility we can make no sense of so long as we conceive human beings solely in an empirical, scientific, phenomenal perspective. For, according to transcendental idealism, even though we can only *know* the phenomenal aspects of ourselves, we *are* that (the 'noumena') of which these phenomenal aspects are appearances. Furthermore, and very importantly for Kant, this doctrine makes room for the possibility that as noumena we are all equally free, i.e. equally capable of autonomy. Thus, on the one hand, freedom is strictly unknowable, on the other, it is possible that everyone is equally, absolutely, free.[5] And although these are only possibilities, they are possibilities we must take as truths when we deliberate.

Suppose we hold (*contra* Kant, but in my view sensibly) that acting from reasons is compatible with natural causality, without the need for his

---

[4] This is different from saying that you are only free if you could have acted otherwise. If you were *incapable* of acting otherwise than autonomously, you would on Kant's view still be free. If you simply cannot tell a lie, for example, that does not, on Kant's view, restrict your freedom (since according to him it is always wrong to tell a lie).

[5] It seems that Kant later held that we can know, or in some way be aware, that reason is active within us. That would only strengthen the argument of the *Groundwork*, inasmuch as Kant could now argue from this awareness to our capacity for autonomy.

transcendental idealism, and that we can often know perfectly well that we are acting from reasons and what reasons we are acting from. This view will also make it an empirical question whether different people have different capacities for autonomy, with potentially important consequences for Kant's substantive moral views. However, as far as the argument we are concerned with goes – from reason-responsiveness to the categorical imperative – it simply gives it a stronger base, since on this view we sometimes know ourselves to be responding to reasons. In any case on either view, when I think about what I have reason to do I must be taking it that I am capable of working out what I have most reason to do, should do, and doing it. I am committed to the idea that I can act autonomously.

So if the next stage of the argument works, we would have a great result, irrespective of 'transcendental idealism'.

3 FROM AUTONOMY TO IMPARTIALITY?

That the categorical imperative incorporates a requirement of impartiality is clearest in the formulation of humanity, which is for many people its most resonant and inspiring version (G IV 429):

> So act that you use humanity, whether in your own person or in the person of any other, always at the same time as an end, never merely as a means.

This requires us to treat *all* rational beings impartially as ends and not merely as means.[6]

There is indeed more to the categorical imperative than just a requirement of impartiality. Impartiality as such can be upheld in otherwise very different moral schemes. For example, the utilitarian principle is impartial: 'Maximize happiness, counting everyone for one and no one for more than one'. Kant requires, as one may put it, impartial *respect* rather than impartial *concern*, and these two approaches are usually thought to have different implications for ethics. Contemporary Kantian perspectives are mostly interested in developing these different implications. Nonetheless, Kantians and utilitarians agree in taking impartiality to be a requirement of practical reason.

Our question, however, is whether we can get even impartiality, let alone the distinctive doctrine of impartial *respect*, from autonomy.

---

[6] Although in this formulation Kant refers to 'humanity' he means 'rational nature': 'the human being and in general every rational being *exists* as an end in itself' (G IV 428); 'Rational nature exists as an end in itself' (G IV 429, emphasis omitted).

At this point we must recognize an old and indisputable point. You cannot get to a requirement of impartiality from the mere universality of reasons. The point was made by Henry Sidgwick,[7] and by many other commentators since. We can make it vivid by considering the standpoint Sidgwick calls 'rational egoism'. Rational egoists follow the maxim 'Always do the action that is best for you'. They readily acknowledge the universality of that principle: everyone should always do the action that is best for them.

The rational egoist's reasons are *agent-relative*. A fact is an agent-relative reason for an agent to act if its reason-giving force is essentially due to its involving some relation between the agent and the act. For the rational egoist, the relation in question is that the act will advance his, the agent's, good. Let us say that a reason is 'agent-neutral' if it is not agent-relative. Suppose we claimed, for example, that there is reason to promote anyone's good, or that there is reason to respect any rational being as an end, irrespective of any relation they may or may not have to the agent, then we would be claiming that there are agent-neutral reasons. Alternatively put, we would be claiming that there is something that is agent-neutrally good, or that is an agent-neutral end.[8] Thus, the utilitarian holds that the good or wellbeing of people is agent-neutrally good. The Kantian holds that rational nature is an agent-neutral end. It would still follow from these standpoints that there is reason for the agent to advance his own good, or respect himself as an end – but these would be agent-neutral reasons. In contrast, the rational egoist denies that there are any agent-neutral reasons, goods or ends. That is a consistent position. Thus, we cannot get from universality to impartiality by analysis alone. Impartiality requires not just the universality of reasons but also the existence of agent-neutral reasons.

Is there perhaps something else about the very idea of a reason, other than universality, some further formal feature of the concept of a reason as such, or of the good as such, that enables us to conclude that reasons cannot be merely or fundamentally agent-relative? We can already see that any grounds for thinking that reasons must be agent-neutral cannot be *merely* formal, since the rational egoist's reasons are in perfectly good formal shape to be reasons. Rational egoism may be and in my view is mistaken, but it is

---

[7] Henry Sidgwick, *The Methods of Ethics* (London: Macmillan, 1907), pp. 208–10, 420–1, 497–8. Sidgwick's point is directed at Mill's 'proof' of the principle of utility as much as at Kant: it is interesting that neither philosopher provides any clear ground for the impartial element in his fundamental principle.

[8] We could also say that it was 'absolutely' good, good 'in itself', or an end 'in itself'. In that case we would need to distinguish these notions from both the notion of a *final* and the notion of an *unconditional* good or end. Rational egoism says that every person's good is a final and unconditional end – not absolutely, or in itself, but for that person.

not a misunderstanding of the very notion of a reason. If our substantive insight into practical reasons reveals to us that all or some reasons are agent-neutral, what it reveals is a substantive normative truth. This insight is not analytically derivable from the very notion of a reason. So if we interpret Kant as arguing to impartiality from the sound formal point that reasons are universal, we have to conclude that his argument is fallacious.

Let us turn instead to a promising observation made by Henry Allison.[9] Recognizing the force of the Sidgwickian objection, Allison acknowledges that no impartial principle can be deduced from the universality of reasons *alone*. However, he denies that that is Kant's intention. Instead, he points out that Kant means to derive impartiality from *autonomy*: that is, from the idea of acting solely from recognition of what one should do.

Acting thus means that one accepts no aim for one's action, and no constraint on it, unless one sees reason to pursue that aim or observe that constraint. For anyone who accepts an aim or a constraint which they see no reason to accept is not acting from reason-responsiveness alone; they are being driven heteronomously by non-rational factors, 'alien causes'. This is an important feature of Kant's account. It generates (in my view) a sound objection to an instrumental, means-end conception of rationality, according to which rationality consists in adopting efficient means to one's ends. Against this conception we can ask: why *should* we pursue our ends if there *is* no reason to pursue them? This may be your or my end, but it remains an open question whether it should be. Strictly speaking, in fact, one should deny that an instrumental conception of rationality is a conception of *rationality*, the capacity to come to a purely reason-responsive conclusion about what one should do, at all. Rationality thus understood – free and unconstrained rational deliberation – requires that we should be able to pursue reasons all the way down, never accepting an end or constraint simply as given: there must be no end, no constraint, that practical reason cannot put in question, by asking and answering whether there is reason to accept it.

This is a plausible interpretation of Kant's notion of autonomy, and of why he thought it so important. Autonomy itself entails the existence of categorical, not merely hypothetical, imperatives. It is the crucial thing an instrumental conception of rationality omits. The instrumentalist maxim is 'Do whatever will most efficiently advance your actual ends'. The objection

---

[9] Henry E. Allison, *Kant's Theory of Freedom*, (Cambridge University Press, 1990) pp. 204–10. See also Thomas Hill, 'Kant's Argument for the Rationality of Moral Conduct', *Pacific Philosophical Quarterly* 66 (1985), 3–23.

to it is not that it cannot be universalized, for it can be: everyone should act in a way that most efficiently advances whatever ends they seek to advance. The objection is that this principle simply takes ends for granted, without asking whether they should be adopted in the first place, and so cannot be the principle of an autonomous, fully free rational agent.

The instrumentalist conception of practical reason is agent-relative, and is ruled out by the 'open-question' requirements of autonomy. It does not follow that *all* agent-relative principles are ruled out by autonomy. In particular, appeal to autonomy provides no effective argument against the rational egoist. Rational egoists do not hold that you cannot deliberate about ends. They hold that there is reason for everyone to pursue their own good and they deliberate about what constitutes that good; thus about what ends there is reason to pursue. They accept that autonomy requires recognition of categorical imperatives; they think pursuit of one's own good is a categorical imperative. Each person's own good is a rational end for that person. For all that mere analysis of the notion of autonomy can tell us it may be the only rational end; it may be that for each person their own good is the only final and unconditional end – in which case a rational egoist acts autonomously. We must conclude, therefore, that an argument purely from the very idea of autonomy does not get us to impartiality, any more than an argument from the universality of reasons does.

Does the universal law formulation help us? This says (*G* IV 421):

Act only according to that maxim through which you can at the same time will that it become a universal law.

This formulation contains a very suggestive idea: the idea of what you *can will*. We shall investigate it below. But for the moment we encounter another familiar objection. The notion of acting from reasons alone can, we have seen, yield the conclusion that if you act as you should then you act from universalizable maxims. Now, is the universal law formulation meant to rule out only those maxims that we cannot will to be universal laws because they cannot, as a matter of logic, be *formulated* as universal laws? In other words, is it to be read weakly, as simply saying that if you act on a non-universalizable maxim you are not acting as you should? Or is it saying something stronger than that: is it meant to cut out some universalizable maxims because although they can indeed be universalized without self-contradiction we cannot *will* them in their universalized form? In which case, where does this stronger proposal come from?

Kant holds that the inference from autonomy to morality is analytic: 'if freedom of the will is presupposed, morality, together with its principle, follows by mere analysis of the concept of freedom'.[10] A possible explanation of why he holds this would be that he thinks it is morally permissible to act on any maxim that is not self-contradictory when universalized – in the strict sense of 'self-contradictory' in which a self-contradictory proposition must be false. The thought would be that any maxim is an application to oneself of some universal normative proposition about what should be done; if the underlying universal proposition is literally self-contradictory then it is false. Hence, you cannot autonomously will it to be a universal law: where (let's assume for the moment) willing it to be a universal law is simply accepting it as true. That is the weaker reading of the formula of universal law. If morality were simply the rejection of such maxims, it would follow analytically from autonomy.

This is quite obviously far too weak to yield morality, however, and Kant does not try to make anything of it. The most one can say is that his interest in the notion of a maxim being 'self-contradictory' when universalized probably arises from the idea that morality follows analytically from freedom. In practice, he works with a looser notion of contradiction, in which a maxim is 'self-contradictory' when it is impossible for everyone to act on it. But to introduce this new sense is to abandon the project of showing that morality follows *analytically* from autonomy; it presents a stronger reading of the universal law formulation, which brings in a new idea.

And again it is open to some familiar difficulties. Take the maxim 'Always give way to others before you go through a door'. That is 'self-contradictory' when universalized – 'Everyone should give way to everyone else before going through a door' – in the new and stronger sense that it is impossible for everyone to follow it (not in the strict sense in which it would follow that it must be false). Does this entail that it is morally wrong to follow this maxim? In any case, as many have pointed out, the maxims Kant wants to reject on the grounds that they are self-contradictory when universalized are not self-contradictory even in this way. This applies even to the examples most favoured by defenders of Kant. It is, for example, not *impossible* that everyone acts on the maxim 'Break your promise when it is to your advantage to do so'. True, in our actual world, and given human nature, it is very unlikely that disadvantageous promises could always be broken without people knowing, and hence if everyone tried to act on that maxim the institution of promises might well cease to be taken seriously. But this is clearly a matter of our social circumstances, not of logic, whereas the universal law of reason is meant to hold for all rational beings in all possible

[10] G IV 447. Compare CpV V 31.

worlds. There certainly are logically possible worlds in which everyone follows the promise-breaking maxim; for example, they may not believe that everyone else is doing so too, or immediately forget, or the circumstances in which breaking a promise is advantageous may be so few and far between as not to be noticed. And finally, it is quite obvious that the egoist's universalized maxim is not impossible for everyone to act on.

These points refute any attempt to derive morality analytically from the very idea of autonomy. In contrast, of course, they fall away as irrelevant if one thinks that the categorical imperative is simply a way of testing for fairness, and that we have a pre-existing obligation to act fairly. *Given* that obligation, we could bring in the idea of what I can will in the way that it is often brought in, and which Kant often seems to intend: as a way of testing whether our maxim is fair. I can ask myself whether, given my necessary needs and limitations as a human being, I can will a society in which everyone cheats whenever they can get away with it, in which there is no mutual aid, and so on. If I would not want everyone to do that kind of thing, because of the bad consequences such behaviour would have for me, or for people in general, then I am taking unfair advantage of others if I do it myself. I am using them. This is good moral thinking; but it makes no attempt to derive the obligation of fairness from autonomy; nor does it show any other way in which pure practical reason itself can be said to bring fairness, impartiality, onto the scene.

Is there a way in which one might show a connection between autonomy and impartiality by considering the idea of what can be willed by an autonomous will? This idea remains intriguing. It is the idea of what can be willed by a will that is free of alien causes, free of non-rational influences on its willing. We must consider it more closely.

4 THE DISINTERESTED WILL

Before doing so let us take stock of three possible ways to develop Kant's ideas. They are as follows:

(1) Derive the categorical imperative from the very idea of autonomy; that is, show it to be an analytic truth that if a being has the capacity of autonomy the categorical imperative applies to it, so that when that being acts autonomously it is acting in a way that acknowledges that imperative (the *analytic* interpretation).

(2) Derive it as a principle which any being capable of autonomy wills ('gives itself as a law') so far as it is thinking and acting autonomously (the *disinterested* interpretation).

(3) Present it as a very general moral principle: perhaps not the only one, perhaps not one that all rational beings would accept, whatever their interests and needs, but one that we human beings (or we modern people with our morality, etc.) do on reflection accept (the *moral intuitionist* interpretation).

(1) is what Kant says is his view. However, even though (1) is the view that Kant says he holds, it may be that we can find materials for a better view that is still closer to Kant's ambitions than is (3). Our guideline is to find a line of thought between (1) and (3), as it were, neither analytic nor simply a form of moral intuitionism. Hence (2).

The question on this approach is whether there is anything, and if so what, that a being can will inasmuch as it wills autonomously but without knowledge of the *content* of rational ends, its own or those of others, to work on.

What I am asking can be illustrated by a thought-experiment. You are contemplating a world of people that does not include you. All you know about them is that they are pursuing some rational ends or other. In other words, you know that whatever these ends may be they are ends they should pursue, and hence ends they would autonomously pursue. You have some green buttons you can press, one per person, to assist them to achieve their ends. You have some red buttons you can press, one per person, to frustrate their pursuit. Pressing any of these buttons has no other effect. You know nothing else; in particular you know nothing about who these people are or any relation they might have to you, or about your own current inclinations. Is there anything you can autonomously will? Is there anything there is still *reason* to will?

I myself think you should press as many green buttons as you can, chosen at random if you can't press them all, and that you should not press any red buttons. (A weaker view would say: 'Don't press the red buttons' – either would do for our illustrative purposes.) If I am right, then that is something an autonomous will can will *purely* as autonomous, that is, before any further material is brought in that might give it further or different reasons for action. This answer effectively says that achievement by anyone of their rational goals has value not just for them, agent-relative value, but agent-neutral value, value 'in itself'. It is good in itself that people should achieve their rational goals. There is agent-neutral reason to press the green buttons, chosen impartially.

To accept this answer is to accept that everyone's rational ends, considered comprehensively and impartially, have standing as ends for the autonomous will, ends there is reason to further. The rational egoist denies that. In this thought-experiment, he will say, there is no reason for you to press any buttons at all, green or red. He agrees, to be sure, that your interests have no special importance just because they are yours. But that is because he denies that anything has importance in this sense – an importance that is not agent-relative. Your interests have rational importance for you; my interests have rational importance for me. There are no agent-neutral ends.

If, contrary to the rational egoist, we *accept* the answer, we have certainly not shown that reasons must be agent-neutral just by deriving that conclusion from the notion of a reason. We have not even shown that all reasons must be agent-neutral. Once you bring knowledge about your inclinations and relations to other people back into the picture, you may well bring back agent-relative reasons. The claim is not that the autonomous will can *only* will agent-neutral ends. The claim is that when we focus on whether there is anything that an autonomous will can will purely in virtue of its property of autonomy, disinterestedly, we find that there is indeed still something, and that something is the achievement of any being's rational ends as such. The moment of impartiality that is (on this view) contained in the will exercises a constraint of some form on our pursuit of our own, agent-relative ends.

I am not suggesting that this is the only line of thought available to a Kantian. The autonomous will, in its disinterested moment, wills to further rational ends impartially. It is therefore committed to accepting that everyone should further rational ends impartially. However, this is not literally a case of willing others to act. Compare the rational egoist, who is committed to accepting that everyone should pursue their own rational ends alone – he does not literally will that others should do that. To will is to be disposed to act; to will someone else to do something is to be disposed to make them do it if you can. (Consider 'willing someone on.') Let us say: to *demand* that they do it. The egoist certainly does not demand that others act egoistically, even though he thinks they should.

But may it be the case that the autonomous will, in its disinterested moment, does make demands on others? Does it perhaps make the second-order demand that everyone refrains from demands on others, except in circumstances characterized by a theory of rights? This line of thought is more difficult to develop than the one we have considered, but it fits rather well with Kant's universal law formula, since it gives his idea of the autonomous will as universal legislator real work to do.

But don't these lines of thought just get us back to a form of moral intuitionism? By the standard of Kant's strictly formal ambition the answer may seem to be 'yes'. However, I am inclined to argue that neither the term 'moral' nor the term 'intuitionism' fits.

'Moral' does not fit because *moral* intuitionism works from within morality – but moral concepts did not enter our thought-experiment. For all that has been said, it may be that morality has sources not only in impartiality but also in the feelings, so that only when you bring these back in, and join them to purely rational constraints of impartiality, do you get morality proper. This is not Kant's picture, for he denies the feelings any place in determining moral obligation and purports to derive moral obligations from the categorical imperative alone. Nonetheless, he does hold that it is in virtue of our emotional nature that we experience the universal law of reason *as* a categorical imperative: because we are beings with emotional lives, this requirement of impartiality, which is a requirement of pure practical reason, is felt by us as a constraint: an *imperative* of fairness. A further step in this direction would be to say that human morality is a joint product of the purely rational demands of impartiality and of our needs as social and emotional beings. Although Kant does not actually take this step at the level of his abstract moral theory, he does in practice have a lot to say in other writings about these human needs, and their impact on ethics and politics.

Isn't this view of the connection between autonomy and impartiality nevertheless describable as a form of intuitionism? An intuitionist would say that it amounts to asserting as self-evident an axiom of impartiality. To discuss this properly we would have to go into meta-normative questions about the relation between practical reasons and the will. Intuitionists hold that there is a world of normative facts that we know by normative intuition, in the way that we know the world of space and time by spatio-temporal perception. On the basis of that knowledge of normative facts, we then choose what to do. In other words, they treat normative knowledge and dispositions of the will as quite distinct. For Kant there is no such separation. Pure practical reason is will, will is pure practical reason. From this standpoint, talk of self-evident practical axioms is somewhat misleading. Normative cognition in the practical sphere is epistemically grounded in spontaneous dispositions of the *will* (in Kant's sense of spontaneity)[11] and for just that reason it can itself be practical: i.e. give rise to action via the

---

[11]   The contrast is with 'receptivity'. In the theoretical sphere, purely normative cognition also originates in spontaneous dispositions – in this case spontaneous dispositions to *believe*. (Cognition in general involves an interplay between spontaneous normative judgement and material supplied by receptive sensibility.)

causality of freedom. Furthermore, freedom is nothing but spontaneity of the will; so freedom and normative cognition are but aspects of one thing. Among the spontaneous dispositions of an autonomous will there is a pure or disinterested disposition which structures or frames all other dispositions. That, I suggest, is the sense in which we should ask whether we *can will* our maxim to be a universal law: we are asking whether we can will it in the presence of that pure or disinterested disposition, which is the spontaneous disposition of pure autonomy itself.

CHAPTER 10

Problems with freedom: Kant's argument in Groundwork *III* and its subsequent emendations

Paul Guyer

I PROBLEMS WITH FREEDOM

In the first two sections of the *Groundwork for the Metaphysics of Morals*, Kant has offered an analytical argument for his claim that the categorical imperative is the fundamental principle of morality. In Section I, he has argued that the imperative 'I ought never to act except in such a way that I could also will that my maxims should become a universal law' (*G* IV 402)[1] is derivable by the analysis of 'common rational moral cognition', specifically from common-sense conceptions of the good will (*G* IV 393–6) and of duty, which is the concept of good will with the addition of 'certain subjective limitations and hindrances' (*G* IV 397) that are inescapable for human beings, namely the fact that our inclinations do not always and only coincide with the demands of morality. In Section II, he has argued that the categorical imperative, which has now been represented as a system of formulas of which the specific formulation derived in Section I is only the first,[2] is derivable by analysis of the 'universal concept of a rational being as such' (*G* IV 412), or, more accurately, from the general concept of a rational being with a will, or a rational agent (*G* IV 412 and IV 427). But in both cases, Kant claims, the mere analysis that suffices to determine the content of the fundamental principle of morality does not by itself prove that this principle is binding for us actual human beings. He makes this clear after his derivation of the first formulation of the categorical imperative in Section II, the formulation that is the same as that reached in Section I, when he says that 'We have not yet advanced so far

[1] Translations from Kant will be drawn, with occasional modifications, from Kant, *Practical Philosophy* (Mary J. Gregor (ed. and trans.), Cambridge University Press, 1996), and Kant, *Religion and Rational Theology* (Allen W. Wood and George di Giovanni (eds. and trans.), Cambridge University Press, 1996).
[2] See Allen W. Wood, 'The Moral Law as a System of Formulas' in Hans Friedrich Fulda and Jürgen Stolzenberg (eds.), *Architektonik und System in der Philosophie Kants* (Hamburg: Meiner, 2001), pp. 287–306, and 'The Supreme Principle of Morality' in Paul Guyer (ed.), *The Cambridge Companion to Kant and Modern Philosophy* (Cambridge University Press, 2006), pp. 342–80.

as to prove *a priori* that there really is such an imperative ... which commands absolutely of itself and without any incentives' (*G* IV 425); he does so again in Section II, after he has completed the presentation of the system of imperatives and summed them up in the conception of 'autonomy as the supreme principle of morality', when he says that 'That this practical rule is an imperative, that is, that the will of every rational being is necessarily bound to it as a condition, cannot be proved by mere analysis of the concepts to be found in it, because it is a synthetic proposition' (*G* IV 440); and at the beginning of the third Section, when he says, reverting to the initial formulation of the categorical imperative, that 'the principle of morality – that an absolutely good will is that whose maxim can always contain itself regarded as a universal law – is nevertheless always a synthetic proposition, for, by analysis of the concept of an absolutely good will that property of its maxim cannot be discovered' (*G* IV 447). Section III of the *Groundwork* is then supposed to provide a 'critique of the subject, that is, of pure practical reason' (*G* IV 440), that is, of *our* pure practical reason, which will prove the synthetic proposition that the fundamental principle of morality, as analysed in the first two Sections, really is a categorical imperative *for us*, that is, a practical principle that is universally and necessarily binding or categorical for us but that also presents itself to us as a constraint or imperative because we are not always and only inclined to do what it demands. The question, of course, is how Section III of the *Groundwork* is supposed to accomplish this proof of a synthetic rather than analytic proposition.

My thesis here is that the 'critique of the subject' that is supposed to provide this proof is a metaphysical argument depending upon a claim about our real, 'noumenal' selves, not a further analysis of the concept of agency, as it is often represented in recent literature, that would yield merely another analytical statement of the content of the categorical imperative.[3] This metaphysical argument is intended to prove that the moral law is the *causal* law of the real self, because the freedom of the will that is attributed to the

---

[3] To be sure, my thesis that, contrary to a currently popular approach, Kant's argument in Section III is not an analysis of the concept of agency but a metaphysical argument is not unique; others who have presented such an interpretation, although with differences of detail, include Henry E. Allison, in *Kant's Theory of Freedom* (Cambridge University Press, 1990), ch. 12, pp. 214–29; Karl Ameriks, 'Kant's *Groundwork* III Argument Reconsidered' in his *Interpreting Kant's Critiques* (Oxford: Clarendon Press, 2003), pp. 226–48, previously published as 'Zu Argumentation am Anfang des Dritten Abschnitts der *Grundlegung*' in Hans-Ulrich Baumgarten and Carsten Held (eds.), *Systematische Ethik mit Kant* (Freiburg: Alber, 2001), pp. 24–54; and Dieter Schönecker and Allen W. Wood, *Kants 'Grundlegung zur Metaphysik der Sitten': Ein einführender Kommentar* (Paderborn: Schöningh, 2002), ch. 4, pp. 170–206; this chapter is based on Schönecker's previous book, *Kant: Grundlegung III: Die Deduktion des kategorischen Imperativs* (Freiburg: Alber, 1999).

noumenal self, 'although it is not a property of the will in accordance with natural laws, is not for that reason lawless but must instead be a causality in accordance with immutable laws but of a special kind' (*G* IV 446). That Kant's argument in Section III is a metaphysical argument that the moral law is the causal law of the noumenal self immediately raises several objections, however. First, how could a critique of our pure practical reason possibly yield a positive, synthetic *a priori* claim about our real, noumenal selves, when the entire argument of the *Critique of Pure Reason* has apparently proven that we can have no metaphysical cognition of the noumenal realm at all, only empirical, synthetic *a posteriori* knowledge of its appearance in experience, synthetic *a priori* cognition of the logical and mathematical structure of appearance, and synthetic *a priori* knowledge of the transcendental conditions of the possibility of experience, that is, the necessary conditions for the representation of objects in experience? Secondly, if, as Section III appears to argue, our noumenal self is the *ground* or *basis* – '*noch etwas anderes zum Grunde liegendes*' – of the 'constitution' of the subject 'that is made up of nothing but appearances' (*G* IV 451), how can there be any *tension* or *conflict* between the inclinations of the phenomenal, empirical self and the will of the real, noumenal self? How can my noumenal, moral self be, as it were, only a *part* of my whole self, so that 'if I were only this, all my actions *would* always be in conformity with the autonomy of the will, but since at the same time I intuit myself as a member of the world of sense' I can only say that 'they *ought* to be in conformity with it' (*G* IV 454)? Thirdly, if the moral law is really the causal law of our noumenal selves, and if a causal law is genuinely universal and necessary, a 'rule', as Kant says in the *Critique of Pure Reason*, 'in accordance with which [an] occurrence always and necessarily follows' (A 193/B 238), then how can anyone ever act *contrary* to the moral law, that is, how is *immoral* action possible at all?

My further thesis will be that Kant attempted to address these three questions in his works on the foundations of morality subsequent to the *Groundwork*, that is, the *Critique of Practical Reason* and *Religion Within the Boundaries of Mere Reason*. In the *Critique of Practical Reason*, I will argue, Kant addresses the first two questions, the first by introducing a conception of 'practical' knowledge that is an alternative to the purely 'theoretical' knowledge of the noumenal that was banned by the first *Critique*,[4] and the second by introducing the thesis that one must regard one's entire empirical

---

[4] The second *Critique*'s conception of practical cognition was anticipated by Kant's famous statement in the Preface to the second edition of the first *Critique* that 'I had to deny *knowledge* in order to make room for *faith*' and thereby make possible a '*practical extension* of pure reason' (B xxx); but since the

character, inclinations and all – 'in general every determination of his existence changing conformably with inner sense, even the whole sequence of his existence as a sensible being' – 'as nothing but the consequence and never as the determining ground of his existence as a *noumenon*' (*CpV* V 97–8). According to this thesis, there is indeed nothing in anyone's phenomenal self that is not grounded in his noumenal self. However, I will argue, in spite of a famous change in direction in the argument of the *Critique of Practical Reason*, its switch from the *Groundwork*'s inference from our noumenal self to the moral law as its causal law to an inference from the fact of our consciousness of the moral law to our noumenal freedom (see *CpV* V 47), Kant does not in fact change his conception of the moral law in the second *Critique*: it remains the causal law of the noumenal self or will. Thus, the problem of how such a self could ever violate the moral law remains, or, given that the noumenal self is now clearly recognized to be the ground of everything in the phenomenal self, the problem of how the latter could even *appear* to violate the moral law becomes pressing. I will argue that Kant addresses this problem only in the *Religion*, although he does so there not by explicitly retracting anything that he has previously argued about the noumenal self and will but rather simply by heavily relying on the principle that 'ought implies can' and the implicit corollary that 'ought does not imply *does*' – this pair of principles will yield the result that if it is our duty to make the moral law our fundamental maxim, then we are free to do so, but we are equally free to choose not to, that is, to make self-love our fundamental maxim instead, which in turn implies the points Kant is concerned to make in the *Religion*, namely that even if we have already chosen evil, as we all seem to have done, we are still free to choose good, but that even if we seem to have chosen good, not only can we never be sure of that, but we are also still free to relapse into evil, and thus must not rely on any external guarantee of the completeness of our conversion but must remain constantly vigilant to preserve it. This position requires a fundamental departure from the conception of the freedom of the noumenal will that is common to both the *Groundwork* and the *Critique of Practical Reason*.

2 THE ARGUMENT OF *GROUNDWORK* III

Not what but how Kant intended to argue in Section III of the *Groundwork* is as controversial as any issue in Kant interpretation. I will take the position,

second *Critique* apparently grew out of Kant's work on the revision of the first, and was indeed intended as part of the second edition of the first *Critique* rather than as a separate work, this does not undermine my thesis but if anything supports it.

first, that Section III begins with a recapitulation of the analytical approach of Sections I and II that is expressed in the statement that 'If freedom of the will is presupposed, morality together with its principle follows from it by mere analysis of its concept' (*G* IV 447), but which then leads to the worry about a circle, which entails a *petitio principii*,[5] namely that we may 'take ourselves as free in the order of efficient causes in order to think ourselves under moral laws in the order of ends' but 'afterwards think ourselves as subject to these laws' only 'because we have already ascribed to ourselves freedom of the will' (*G* IV 450); and, secondly, that Kant then attempts to prove[6] the synthetic proposition that we really are free *qua* rational beings and thus that the moral law really does apply to us, thereby breaking the circle or averting the *petitio principii*, by an appeal to his doctrine of transcendental idealism, specifically to its distinction between the phenomenal and noumenal self, but an appeal which is affirmative in character, making a positive assertion about the noumenal self, rather than, as we might have expected from the *Critique of Pure Reason*, merely negative in character, restricting the scope of our assertions about the phenomenal self but not positively asserting anything about the noumenal self.

The first phase of *Groundwork* III (*G* IV 446–50) is the most confusing, because Kant says very early (*G* IV 447) that 'the principle of morality' is 'always a synthetic proposition' but that it can be grounded in the third term (the 'third thing' necessary to bind subject and predicate in any synthetic proposition; see *CrV* A 155/B 194) provided by 'the *positive* concept of freedom' (*G* IV 446), which might suggest that the section is meant to be a synthetic rather than analytic argument from the outset. However, Kant immediately says that 'What this third thing is, to which freedom points us and of which we can have an idea *a priori*, cannot yet be shown here and now; nor can the deduction of the concept of freedom from pure practical reason, and with it the possibility of a categorical imperative, as yet be made comprehensible; instead some further preparation is required' (*G* IV 447);

---

[5] See Marcel Quarfood, 'The Circle and the Two Standpoints' in Christoph Horn and Dieter Schönecker (eds.), *Groundwork for the Metaphysics of Morals* (Berlin and New York: de Gruyter, 2006), pp. 285–300, especially pp. 287–92.

[6] Both Jens Timmermann and Samuel Fleischacker have objected to my claim that the central argument of Section III attempts to *prove* that we are noumenally free, suggesting instead that Kant is only trying to make philosophical space for our pre-philosophical conviction that we are free to do as morality requires, which would conflict with our pre-philosophical as well as critical commitment to determinism in the natural world. I think that this more modest interpretation of Kant's aim in *Groundwork* III, though it may have much to recommend it, does not make sense of his subsequent attempt to create a category of practical or 'practico-dogmatic' knowledge, so I will stick to my more radical account of Kant's aim.

he heads the immediately following paragraph with the still provisional statement that 'Freedom must be *presupposed* as a property of the will of all rational beings' (emphasis added), thus remaining at the level of conceptual analysis; and by raising the threat of a 'circle' three pages later (*G* IV 450) he again reminds us that the argument is still merely analytical. So I take it that everything through that statement is meant to be merely analytical, thus a recapitulation of the analytical arguments of the first two Sections although perhaps with a new twist, and that the positive, synthetic 'deduction' of the concept of freedom and with it of the moral law to which Kant refers at *G* IV 447 is meant to be found only in the argument from transcendental idealism that begins, following the worry about the circle, at *G* IV 451.[7]

If this is right, the first two subsections of Section III (the first of which concerns negative and positive concepts or definitions (or 'explications', *Erklärungen*) of freedom and the second of which expands upon the statement that freedom must be presupposed as a property of the will of all rational beings) are both merely analytical, as is signalled not only by the heading for the second subsection but also by the heading of the first, i.e. 'The *concept* of freedom is the key to the [definition or explication] of the autonomy of the will' (*G* IV 446, emphasis added). Kant begins the first subsection with what is clearly intended to be the non-controversial statement that '*Will* is a kind of causality of living beings insofar as they are rational, and *freedom* [of the will] would be that property of such causality that it can be efficient of alien causes *determining* it'. He then says that this definition or explication of freedom is '*negative* and therefore unfruitful for insight into its essence' (given how he uses this terminology, he could also have said that it is merely a nominal definition of freedom). 'But there flows from it a *positive* concept of freedom, which is so much the richer and more fruitful', namely that even though freedom of the will as negatively defined (i.e. as freedom from external determination of the will) must not be 'a property of the will in accordance with natural laws, it is not for that reason lawless but must instead be a causality in accordance with immutable laws of a special kind'. Since another way of describing the determination by external factors that is excluded is as 'heteronomy', Kant next says that the

---

[7] In the works previously mentioned, Allison, Ameriks, and Schönecker and Wood all agree that Kant's actual attempt at a deduction of the moral law in Section III does not come until after he has stated the danger of a circle, although Ameriks does not actually discuss the metaphysical argument that follows and Schönecker and Wood claim that the actual deduction comes only after the appeal to transcendental idealism, when Kant explains how the difference between our noumenal and phenomenal selves explains the imperatival character of the principle of morality (Schönecker and Wood, *Kants 'Grundlegung zur Metaphysik der Sitten'*, pp. 197–9). I regard this as a statement of a consequence of the deduction rather than the attempted deduction itself.

positive conception of the will must be the concept of 'autonomy', which is in turn nothing but the 'will's property of being a law to itself'. This in turn means that the principle of the will under the positive conception of its freedom is the moral law, because, according to Kant, the 'proposition, the will is in all its actions a law to itself, indicates only the principle, to act on no other maxim than that which can also have as object itself as a universal law' (*G* IV 446–7). Presumably this follows by the same sort of argument by elimination that Kant used in Sections I (*G* IV 402) and II (*G* IV 421): once heteronomous grounds or objects for laws are eliminated, nothing is left to serve the will as a law except the requirement of the lawlikeness, that is, the universalizability of its maxims itself. Thus, Kant infers from the negative conception of freedom to the positive conception of freedom and from the positive conception of freedom, or autonomy, to the moral law. The reason why he now says that the principle of morality is a synthetic proposition that cannot be discovered 'by analysis of the concept of an absolutely good will' must be that he is here equating the concept of an absolutely good will with the initial, negative conception of freedom; which would be consistent with his initial, negative characterization of action from duty (which is, again, just the good will subject to certain hindrances) as action that is not motivated by inclination (*G* IV 398), which also could not have proved and was not intended to prove that we are in fact subject to the moral law. Thus, the positive conception of freedom becomes a third term linking the negative conception of freedom and the moral law in a synthetic proposition. But then Kant's claim that 'what this third cognition is, to which freedom points us … cannot yet be shown here and now' can only mean that it has not yet been proven that we have freedom positively conceived, so it has not yet been proven that we actually have freedom negatively conceived, on the one hand, nor that we are actually subject to the moral law, on the other.[8] Everything thus far is still at the level of conceptual analysis.

The title of the next subsection (again, 'Freedom must be presupposed as a property of the will of all rational beings') cannot be the deduction of our positive freedom that is still needed, because Kant introduces it precisely by saying that 'some further preparation is required' (*G* IV 447). Rather, the function of this subsection is to show that the positive conception of

---

[8] Here, I differ from Allison's interpretation that the 'third cognition' to which Kant refers us here is 'the idea of an intelligible world' (*Kant's Theory of Freedom*, p. 215). In my view, Kant is referring to the reality of freedom as understood through the positive concept of it, although his proof of that reality will depend upon his proof of the reality of the intelligible world.

freedom and therefore the moral law can be connected to the concept of every rational being, which Kant has claimed is a condition on any derivation of the moral law in the Preface (e.g. *G* IV 389) and in Section II (*G* IV 412). Here, Kant says that 'since morality serves as a law for us only as rational beings, it must also hold for all rational beings', thus that since morality 'must be derived solely from the property of freedom' (under its positive conception), 'freedom must also be proved as a property of all rational beings'. This excludes any proof of *our* freedom from 'certain supposed experiences of human nature', which would in any case be 'absolutely impossible' (*G* IV 447–8). It is at this point that Kant makes his famous, or notorious, claim that 'every being that cannot act otherwise than *under the idea of freedom* is just because of that really free in a practical respect, that is, all laws that are inseparably bound up with freedom hold for him just as if his will had been validly pronounced free also in itself and in theoretical philosophy' (*G* IV 448). Kant's reason for this claim is that a rational being that conceives of itself as acting freely cannot 'consciously' (*mit ihrem eigenen Bewußtsein*) think of itself as 'receiving direction from anywhere other' than its own reason, 'since the subject would then attribute the determination of its judgement not to its reason but to an impulse'. Any rational being that thinks of itself as free must therefore 'regard [*ansehen*] itself as the author of its principles independently of alien influences', that is, must regard the moral law rather than any heteronomous source as the principle of its action.[9] This argument, which turns on attributing to any rational being the positive conception of freedom and therefore the moral law, serves the purpose of showing that any rational being is bound by the moral law. But it is still just 'preparation' for the deduction of the moral law *because it has not yet been shown that we are actually rational beings*. Kant is not here claiming that for us to act 'under the idea of freedom' is sufficient to prove that we are rational beings; rather, he is still, as he explicitly says, preparing the way for a subsequent proof that we are rational beings which will demonstrate that we are not acting *merely* under the *idea* of freedom but are actually free and therefore, in accordance with the positive conception of freedom, bound by the moral law. This is why he can still be worried about the threat of a circle entailing a *petitio principii*, at *G* IV 450: he has not yet attempted to prove that *we are* rational beings, but has only proven what will follow, namely the validity of the moral law for us as for all rational

---

[9] Schönecker and Wood point out that this argument, which Kant had made the previous year in his 'Review of Schulz's *Essay toward an Introduction to the Doctrine of Morals*', can be traced back to Epicurus (*Kants 'Grundlegung zur Metaphysik der Sitten'*, pp. 184–5).

beings, *if* we are. It is because Kant so clearly says that this argument about what must be presupposed by and about any rational being is still part of the preparation for the deduction, not the deduction itself, that I cannot, as a matter of historical interpretation, join in the contemporary tendency to regard it as intended by Kant to be the real basis for the proof that the moral law applies to us.[10]

Kant expresses the threat of the circle by stating that 'freedom and the will's own lawgiving are both autonomy and hence reciprocal concepts', thus neither can be used as a 'ground' for proving the other (*G* IV 450). His strategy in the second main stage of *Groundwork* III (*G* IV 451–4) for escaping this threat is now to prove that we really *are* rational beings, and *therefore* positively free beings bound by the moral law, by means of an appeal to transcendental idealism. Kant begins this stage by asking whether we might not escape the threat of the circle by taking up 'a different standpoint when by means of freedom we think ourselves as causes efficient *a priori* than when we represent ourselves in terms of our actions that we see before our eyes', i.e. when we represent ourselves empirically or *a priori*. The kind of interpretation I reject reads this question as if it were itself the answer, that is, as if Kant is claiming that we *can* take a practical standpoint or think of ourselves as agents independently of any metaphysical argument. But it is clear that in Kant's own view, only the metaphysical argument that follows will *allow* us to adopt the practical standpoint of agency.

Kant introduces the metaphysical argument with the remarkable claim that 'no subtle reflection is required' to accept its first premise, which is that in all involuntary representation, such as sensory representation, we must distinguish 'objects only as they affect us' from 'what they may be in themselves', or 'appearances' from 'things in themselves' (*G* IV 451). Kant does not allude explicitly to the *Critique of Pure Reason* nor to any of the

---

[10] The two most influential proponents of this tendency have been Thomas E. Hill, Jr, beginning with 'Kant's Argument for the Rationality of Moral Conduct', *Pacific Philosophical Quarterly* 66 (1985), pp. 3–23, reprinted in his *Dignity and Practical Reason in Kant's Moral Theory* (Ithaca and London: Cornell University Press, 1992), pp. 97–122, and continuing in the 'Editors' Introduction to Kant' in *Groundwork for the Metaphysics of Morals* (Thomas E. Hill, Jr and Arnulf Zweig (eds.), Oxford University Press, 2002), pp. 97–8; and Christine M. Korsgaard, in e.g. 'Morality as Freedom' in Yirmiahu Yovel (ed.), *Kant's Practical Philosophy Reconsidered* (Dordrecht: Kluwer, 1989), pp. 23–48, reprinted in her *Creating the Kingdom of Ends* (Cambridge University Press, 1996), pp. 159–87, especially pp. 173–4. Other prominent proponents of this interpretation include Barbara Herman and Andrews Reath. Referring to an earlier paper by Robert Pippin, 'Kant on the Spontaneity of Mind', *Canadian Journal of Philosophy* 17 (1987), pp. 449–75, Karl Ameriks also raises doubts about attempts to find Kant's deduction of the moral law in this analysis of what must be presupposed in the concept of rational agency; see 'Kant's *Groundwork* III Argument Reconsidered', in his *Interpreting Kant's Critiques*, pp. 236–7.

specific arguments for transcendental idealism that he made there, nor does he elaborate much of an independent argument for it here; he says only that this distinction will be made 'perhaps merely by means of the difference noticed between representations given us from somewhere else and in which we are passive, and those that we produce simply from ourselves and in which we show our activity'. If he is not assuming any *a priori* and metaphysical activity here that would entirely obviate the need for any further argument, he must be assuming a merely empirical distinction between some states or events in which we seem active and others in which we seem passive (like the difference between a state in which I seem to raise my arm merely because I want to, and a state in which, because my eyes are open, I see the sun whether I want to or not) and then assuming that in the latter sort of state my representation is the effect of a cause from which it must differ; indeed, differ not merely numerically but in such a profound qualitative way that I cannot ascribe to the cause even the same sorts of properties that I find in the effect. Kant may have meant to state such an argument in the inaugural dissertation of 1770,[11] but he did not make such an argument in the first *Critique* nor does he go beyond this hint here. Nevertheless, we are supposed to accept that there must be a difference between the way objects of perception appear and the way they are in themselves as the premise for everything that follows.

Kant's next step is to apply this distinction to our empirical cognition of ourselves through inner sense: 'Even as to himself, the human being cannot claim to cognize what he is in himself through the cognizance that he has by inner sensation'. Thus, everything the human being knows about himself by means of inner sense, presumably including (although Kant does not explicitly say so) everything we know about the causal determination of our choices and actions by antecedent incentives, is merely 'the appearance of his nature and the way in which his consciousness is affected', yet 'beyond this constitution of his own subject, made up of nothing but appearances, he must necessarily assume something else lying at their basis, namely his self [*Ich*] as it may be constituted in itself' (*G* IV 451). Thus (*also*), one must count oneself as belonging not merely to the 'sensible world' but also to the 'intellectual world'. Kant's use of *also* or 'therefore' here makes it plain that one does not simply adopt a conception of oneself as an agent without

---

[11] See *On the Form and Principles of the Sensible and Intelligible World*, §4, 2:392; in Kant, *Theoretical Philosophy, 1755–1770* (David Walford (ed.) with the collaboration of Ralf Meerbote, Cambridge University Press, 1992), p. 384.

metaphysical presupposition, but can do so only on the basis of the present distinction between oneself as appearance and oneself as thing in itself.

Now Kant also says that one 'has no further cognizance' of the intellectual world to which one assigns one's self as it is in itself, which would seem to bring the whole argument to a halt. However, this claim must be provisional, for the third step of Kant's argument is to claim that because we find '*reason*' (his emphasis) to be 'a capacity by which one distinguishes oneself from all other things, even from oneself insofar as one is affected by objects' (*G* IV 452), we can take reason to be a property of ourselves as we really are rather than as we merely appear. This is because reason goes entirely beyond sensibility: unlike understanding, which is a form of 'self-activity' but merely brings sensible representations 'that arise when we are *affected* by things' under rules, reason is a 'pure self-activity' or 'spontaneity so pure that it thereby goes far beyond anything that sensibility can ever afford it, and proves its highest occupation in distinguishing the world of sense and the world of understanding' (*G* IV 452). The key inference of Kant's argument is thus that while sensibility and understanding can be thought of as faculties of our merely empirical selves, we must think of reason as a faculty of our selves as they are in themselves: thus, we really are rational beings, and everything that is contained in the concept of a rational being really does apply to us.

One might well think that the claim that reason distinguishes us from all other things and even from ourselves insofar as we are merely affected by things, that is, insofar as we are engaged in mere sense-perception, could only be an empirical claim: we do not find reason in any other creatures, nor do we find reason to be involved in mere sense perception, but we do find ourselves able to reason in ways that cannot be reduced to sense perception. But discovering empirically that we have a unique capacity for reasoning would not seem to entitle us to make any metaphysical claims about our selves as they are in themselves. However, Kant does not pause to consider such an objection to the *nervus probandi* of his argument, but instead proceeds directly to its conclusion: namely, that if we really are rational, then we really can attribute to ourselves negative freedom, its ground in positive freedom, and the moral law that is the principle of positive freedom. Thus he writes, as the fourth step of his argument, in which the 'third thing' that will prove the synthetic proposition that the moral law does apply to us is finally revealed (*G* IV 452–3):

As a rational being, and thus as a being belonging to the intelligible world, the human being can never think of the causality of his own will otherwise than under the idea of freedom; for, independence from the determining causes of the world of sense (which reason must always ascribe to itself) is freedom. With the idea of freedom the concept of *autonomy* is now inseparably combined, and with the concept of autonomy the universal principle of morality, which in idea is the ground of all actions of *rational* beings, just as the law of nature is the ground of all appearances.

The suspicion that we raised above is now removed, the suspicion that a hidden circle was contained in our inference from freedom to autonomy and from the latter to the moral law.

The suspicion is now removed because by proving ourselves to be *rational* beings we have proved, not just assumed, that we are (negatively) free to act independently of the 'determining causes of the sensible world' and (positively) free to act in accordance with the 'universal principle of morality'. We have proved that what applies to all rational beings 'in the idea' actually applies to us as we really are. '*Hence*', as Kant says (but I emphasize) we have 'two standpoints from which' we can regard ourselves (*G* IV 452).

This completes Kant's argument that the moral law as analysed in Sections I and II of the *Groundwork* really does apply to us, and the remainder of Section III only clarifies some implications of this argument. First, Kant claims that it answers the problem that was left dangling in Section II – how is a categorical imperative possible (*G* IV 419–20) – because it explains why my actions conform to the laws of the sensible as well as the intellectual world, and thus why my inclinations can provide resistance to the requirements of the moral law, thereby making it seem like an imperative to us.[12] Kant says that (*G* IV 453–4):

All my actions as only a member of the world of understanding would … conform perfectly with the principle of the autonomy of the pure will; as only a part of the world of sense they would have to be taken to conform wholly to the natural law of desires and inclinations, hence to the heteronomy of nature … And so categorical imperatives are possible by this: that the idea of freedom makes me a member of an intelligible world and consequently, if I were only this, all my actions *would* always be in conformity with the autonomy of the will; but since at the same time I intuit myself as a member of the world of sense, they *ought* to be in conformity with it

---

[12] This is the argument that Schönecker and Wood characterize, in my view misleadingly, as the deduction of the categorical imperative itself (*Kants 'Grundlegung zur Metaphysik der Sitten'*, p. 197). In my view, this argument explains the phenomenologically imperatival character of the fundamental principle of morality for us, that is, that it presents itself to us as a constraint, but not the underlying fact that it obligates us. But since Schönecker and Wood also admit that this argument presupposes the 'validity' of the moral law for us (p. 199), the difference between my view and theirs is more verbal than substantive.

but apparently are not necessarily always in conformity with it. Secondly, Kant spends the remaining pages of Section III explaining that his argument for our rationality as things in themselves does not violate the strictures against knowledge of things in themselves established in the *Critique of Pure Reason* because it is not based on any claim to an *experience* of our rationality and freedom: 'By *thinking* itself into a world of understanding, practical reason does not overstep its boundaries, but it would certainly do if it wanted to *intuit* or *feel itself* into it' (*G* IV 458).

There are grave problems with Kant's metaphysical argument in *Groundwork* III, however. First, there is what we might call the epistemological problem. This can in turn be divided into two parts. The first part has already been suggested, namely that the premise for the crucial third step of Kant's argument, that we find reason to be that which distinguishes us from everything else in nature and even from ourselves as mere perceivers, might seem to be exactly the sort of empirical premise on which he has just denied that his argument rests; the second part is that assuring us that the argument he has offered does *not* rest on any empirical premise hardly seems sufficient to explain how we can have knowledge of the self as it is in itself, even through a faculty of reason that is not reducible to sense perception or some operation on it. We need a more positive account of the possibility of knowledge of the in-itself than Kant offers in the *Groundwork*. Secondly, there is what we might think of as a metaphysical problem, namely, Kant's explanation that if we were solely denizens of the intelligible world we would not find the moral law to be a constraint in accordance with which we ought to act, but that we do find it a constraint that we wish to resist because we are *also* creatures of the sensible world makes it seem as if our nature is genuinely bipartite, part rational and part irrational, with these two parts contending for control of our will; but if our noumenal self is supposed to be the *ground* of our empirical self, then it ought to be the source for *everything* in that phenomenal self, and while we might be able to make sense of the idea that for some reason the phenomenal self *appears* different from the noumenal self, it seems very hard to make any sense of the idea that the phenomenal self could in any way actually be *opposed* to the noumenal self, or more precisely to the will of the noumenal self. Thus, it seems hard to understand how anything in the phenomenal self could offer *resistance* to the will of the noumenal self, even a resistance that can be overcome by the noumenal will. And thirdly, if the noumenal self is entirely rational, not just negatively free but positively governed by the moral law – if, as Kant said at the outset of Section III and now takes himself to have proven, 'freedom ... must be causality in accordance with immutable laws but of a special kind' – then the question inevitably arises, how could the noumenal will ever choose in opposition to the moral law? Kant forces this question upon us when he writes (*G* IV 457–8, emphasis added):

the human being claims for himself a will that lets nothing be put to his account that belongs merely to his desires and inclinations, and on the contrary thinks as possible by means of it – *indeed as necessary* – actions that can be done only by disregarding all desires and sensible incitements. The causality of such actions lies in him as intelligence *and in the laws of effects and actions in accordance with the principles of an intelligible world* ... in it reason alone, and indeed pure reason independent of sensibility, *gives the law*, and, in addition, that since it is there as intelligence only, that he is his proper self [*der eigentliche Selbst*] (as a human being he is only the appearance of himself), those laws apply to him immediately and categorically, so that what inclinations and impulses (hence the whole nature of the world of sense) incite him to *cannot* infringe upon the laws of his volition as intelligence.

This makes it unmistakable that Kant holds the moral law to be the causal law of the noumenal self. But if the moral law is the causal law of the noumenal self, how could the noumenal self ever will an immoral action (that is, immoral maxim)? And then, combining this question with the previous one, how could the phenomenal self even appear to be acting immorally?

My argument now will be that Kant attempted to address the first two of these questions in the *Critique of Practical Reason*, but that he did not address the third question there nor modify his position in any way that would resolve the third question. He addresses the third question only in the *Religion*, although not so much by retracting the argument that gives rise to it, as by skirting it.

3 ANSWERING THE FIRST TWO QUESTIONS

In the *Critique of Practical Reason*, Kant restates the 'reciprocity thesis'[13] that he had already stated in the *Groundwork* when he said that a circle could arise precisely because 'freedom and the will's own lawgiving are ... reciprocal concepts' (*G* IV 450), now asserting that 'freedom and unconditional

[13] Henry Allison has made this name for Kant's analytical connection canonical; see 'Morality and Freedom: Kant's Reciprocity Thesis', *Philosophical Review* 95 (1986), pp. 393–425, and his *Kant's Theory of Freedom* (Cambridge University Press, 1990), ch. 11, pp. 201–13. Dieter Schönecker refers to it as Kant's 'analyticity thesis'; see his *Kant: Grundlegung III: Die Deduktion des kategorischen Imperativs* (Freiburg and Munich: Alber, 1999), ch. 3, pp. 147–95, and 'How is a Categorical Imperative Possible? Kant's Deduction of the Categorical Imperative' in Horn and Schönecker, *Groundwork for the Metaphysics of Morals*, pp. 301–24.

practical law reciprocally imply each other' (*CpV* V 29), but then appears to reverse the direction of his previous argument, stating that (*CpV* V 29–30):

> our *cognition* of the unconditionally practical ... cannot start from freedom, for we can neither be immediately conscious of this ... nor can we immediately conclude to it from experience. It is therefore the *moral law* of which we become immediately conscious (as soon as we draw up maxims of the will for ourselves), that *first* offers itself to us and, inasmuch as reason presents it as a determining ground not to be outweighed by any sensible conditions and indeed quite independent of them, leads directly to the concept of freedom.

Kant himself implies that there is a reversal of the direction of the argument from the *Groundwork* here several pages later, when he says that the 'moral law is given, as it were, as a fact of pure reason of which we are *a priori* conscious and thus which cannot be deduced from anything else', but that 'something different and quite paradoxical takes the place of this vainly sought deduction, namely that the moral principle conversely itself serves as the principle of the deduction of an inscrutable faculty which no experience could prove... namely the faculty of freedom' (*CpV* V 47). Here, Kant suggests that any attempt to derive the validity of the causal law from the fact of our freedom, which one might have thought was the strategy of the *Groundwork*, is doomed, because no theoretical proof of our freedom can be given, but that the attempt to derive the fact of our freedom from our consciousness of our obligation under the moral law will succeed, because the latter is a 'fact of reason' which needs no deduction.[14] Presumably, what now allows Kant to derive our freedom from our consciousness of the moral law is the premise that 'you can because you ought to', that one 'judges that one can do something because he is aware that he ought to do it' (*CpV* V 30):[15]

---

[14] The literature on the 'fact of reason' is of course extensive. For a survey of the relevant texts, see Lewis White Beck, *A Commentary to Kant's Critique of Practical Reason* (University of Chicago Press, 1960), pp. 166–70; for a classic statement of the reversal interpretation, see Karl Ameriks, 'Kant's Deduction of Freedom and Morality', *Journal of the History of Philosophy* 19 (1981), pp. 53–79, and his *Kant's Theory of Mind: an Analysis of the Paralogisms of Pure Reason* (Oxford: Clarendon Press, 2000), ch. VI, pp. 189–233; and for another statement of the reversal interpretation, see John Rawls, *Lectures on the History of Moral Philosophy* (Barbara Herman (ed.), Harvard University Press, 2000), Kant lecture VIII, pp. 253–72. Those who have argued against the reversal interpretation by arguing that the 'fact of reason' argument of the second *Critique* is actually already implicit in the *Groundwork* include H. J. Paton in *The Categorical Imperative: a Study in Kant's Moral Philosophy* (London: Hutchinson, 1947), and Dieter Henrich, in 'Die Deduktion des Sittengesetzes' in Alexander Schwan (ed.), *Denken im Schatten des Nihilismus* (Darmstadt: Wissenschaftliche Buchgesellschaft, 1975), pp. 55–112, partially translated in Paul Guyer (ed.), *Kant's Groundwork of the Metaphysics of Morals: Critical Essays* (Lanham: Rowman and Littlefield, 1998). See Allison, *Kant's Theory of Freedom*, p. 228.

[15] See Jens Timmermann, 'Sollen und Können: "Du kannst, denn du sollst" und "Sollen impliziert Können" im Vergleich' in *Philosophiegeschichte und logische Analyse* (*Logical Analysis and History of Philosophy*) 6 (2003), pp. 113–22.

if we genuinely have an obligation, then we must be able to fulfil it, no matter what everything else about our character and conduct might suggest, that is, we must be able to free ourselves from any other determinants of our behaviour and be free to fulfil our obligation.

But the relation between the *Groundwork* and the second *Critique* may not be as simple as it initially seems and as indeed Kant makes it seem. For as we have now seen, in the *Groundwork* Kant does not in fact simply attempt to deduce our obligation under the moral law from the alleged fact of our freedom, but rather infers both our freedom and our necessary conformity to the moral law from the alleged fact of our membership in the intelligible world, and thus our rationality. Meanwhile, in the *Critique of Practical Reason* Kant does not appeal to the principle 'you can because you ought to' for his primary inference of freedom from the moral law, but only in the course of showing that 'experience also confirms this order of concepts in us' (*CpV* V 30). In fact, Kant's primary proof of our freedom in the second *Critique* depends upon a claim about the *purity* of our knowledge of the moral law, its status as a principle of *pure* practical reason, and this suggests that the primary datum of his argument is our consciousness of the *rationality* of the moral law rather than its *obligatoriness*: he does, after all, state that his argument begins from a fact of reason (*CpV* V 31). But the fundamental premise of his argument in the *Groundwork* was also the fact of our rationality. The real difference between the two arguments is that, in the *Groundwork*, Kant appeals to transcendental idealism to establish our rationality, while in the second *Critique* he appeals directly to the character of the moral law to establish the fact of our rationality and therefore our freedom.

This is clear in how Kant continues the passage in which he says that it is the moral law of which we become immediately conscious and that then leads to the concept of freedom (*CpV* V 30):

But how is consciousness of that moral law possible? We can become aware of pure practical laws just as we are aware of pure theoretical principles, by attending to the necessity with which reason prescribes them to us and to the setting aside of all empirical conditions to which reason directs us. The concept of a pure will arises from the first, as consciousness of a pure understanding arises from the latter. That this is the true subordination of our concepts and that morality first discloses to us the concept of freedom ... is clear from the following: that since nothing in appearances can be explained by the concept of freedom and there the mechanism of nature must instead constitute the only guide ... one would never have ventured to introduce freedom into science had not the moral law, and with it practical reason, come in and forced this concept upon us.

It is following this that Kant says that we can appeal to experience to confirm this, for anyone will admit that he can do something he knows he ought to do, such as refuse to bear false witness against an honest person even when that will cost him his life, even though he does not know whether he will do it. The preceding argument does not directly appeal to an ought, and thus to the principle that you can because you ought to, at all. Instead, it infers from the *necessity* of the moral law that it must have a *pure* source within us, just as we can infer from the necessity of the laws of logic that we must have a pure understanding (and for that matter, although Kant does not mention it, as we can infer from the necessity of the laws of mathematics that we must have a faculty of pure intuition). In making this inference, it should be noted, Kant observes the constraint of the *Groundwork* (*G* IV 447–8) that the argument for the validity of the moral law cannot turn on any specifically human feature of experience. His argument is not that we infer to the purity of the will from our experience of *necessitation* (*Nötigung*) *by* the moral law, that is, the experience of the moral law as a constraint on our non-moral or only contingently moral inclinations ('the relation of objective laws to a will that is not thoroughly good' (*G* IV 413)), but is rather that the *necessity* (*Notwendigkeit*) of the moral law is self-evident (something that would be self-evident for any rational being, not just a human being) and that from the purity of the faculty that apprehends the necessarily true moral law we can also infer the purity of the will, the executive faculty that determines the maxims of our actions.

Now if he does not in the first instance appeal to the principle that you can because you ought to, how does Kant get from the necessity of the moral law and therefore the purity of its source to our freedom? The answer is that he does this by equating pure practical reason with a pure will, when he says that the consciousness of a pure will arises from the necessity of pure practical laws just as that of a pure understanding arises from the necessity of pure theoretical principles. That is, since he does not think that any additional step is needed to get from pure practical reason as the source of pure practical laws to the existence of a pure will, independent of empirical determinants, he must be equating pure practical reason with a pure will. But if he does this, of course, then the law of pure practical reason, that is, the moral law, must also be the law of the pure will, and the problem that there is then no way that a being with a pure will could choose to violate the moral law is still with us in full force.

So in the *Critique of Practical Reason* Kant does not exploit the possibility of avoiding this problem that is opened up by the strategy of basing an argument for freedom on the principle that you can because you ought to, namely the fact that you ought to do something does not imply that you will. That move will have to await the *Religion*. Nevertheless, Kant does address the first two questions left outstanding by the *Groundwork*. First, each half of the epistemological problem is addressed. The first half of the problem, namely that the *Groundwork*'s metaphysical argument seems to depend upon an empirical claim about the uniqueness of our faculty of reason, is not addressed explicitly, but is tacitly avoided by the inference to our pure faculty of reason from the *necessity* of the moral law. This move does not depend upon any empirical claim, but quite to the contrary on the principle that genuine necessities are *never* known empirically, but only by means of a pure, non-empirical faculty (see *CrV* B 3–4). Thus, the present argument does not paradoxically try to infer something about the noumenal self from something about the phenomenal self, but instead depends upon the thoroughly Kantian principle that knowledge of necessity is never empirical. Of course, insofar as the argument depends upon the assumption of the necessity of the moral law (that is, presumably, in analogy to pure theoretical principles, its necessary truth), the argument might seem to commit precisely the circularity that Kant was trying to avoid in the *Groundwork*, taking for granted what is supposed to be proved – but in the doctrine of the fact of reason Kant seems to have set aside his fear of this circle and instead embraced the indubitable necessity of the moral law.

Kant addresses the second half of the epistemological problem, that of giving a positive account of how we can have knowledge of anything about the noumenal self, explicitly and at length in the second *Critique*. He does this in his account of the 'Deduction of the Principles of Pure Practical Reason' and the ensuing section 'On the Warrant of Pure Reason in its Practical Use to an Extension which is not Possible for it in its Speculative Use' (*CpV* V 42–57) and in the famous section on the 'Primacy of Pure Practical Reason' in the 'Dialectic' (*CpV* V 119–21). In the latter section, he argues that in the case in which 'practical reason has of itself original *a priori* principles with which certain theoretical positions are inseparably connected', then as long as those theoretical principles do not contradict any other theoretical principles that can be proven to be true, practical reason's need for those theoretical principles is sufficient for it to 'accept' (*annehmen*) them, not to be sure as theoretical 'insights' but as 'extensions of [their] use from another, namely a practical perspective', which is not in the least opposed to the 'interest' of critical philosophy, 'which consists in the restriction of speculative mischief' (*CpV* V 121). The proposition that we have free noumenal wills, just like the proposition that an author of nature exists who makes its laws consistent with the moral law (what Kant is about to argue in the 'Dialectic'), is a theoretical proposition, that is, it asserts a predicate of an object, but a theoretical proposition that cannot be proven by experience. But neither does it contradict any other theoretical proposition that can be proven, because all that can be proven theoretically is that phenomena are completely subject to deterministic causal laws (and the phenomena of human behaviour to deterministic causal laws of inclination), not that noumena are. But then practical reason is free to assume that our noumenal selves are free, and thus to gain an 'extension' even if not an 'insight'.

Kant makes a subtler point in his discussion of the deduction of the principles of pure practical reason. Here, he says that not only need I not bring my noumenal actions under the causal laws of nature that apply to phenomena but that I cannot bring them under such laws, 'For the moral law is not concerned with cognition of the constitution of objects that may be given to reason from elsewhere but rather with a cognition insofar as it can itself become the ground of the existence of objects and insofar as reason, by this cognition, has causality in a rational being' (*CpV*V 46). That is, the ordinary categories of experience, including the ordinary category of causality in accordance with laws of nature, are applied to objects that are given to us; but since in the case of practical reason we are not concerned with objects that are given to us but with objects that we ought to produce (and, according to the *Groundwork*, not physical states of affairs that we ought to produce but strictly speaking the intentions we ought to produce (*G* IV 399–400)), in thinking about practical reason we do not have to concern ourselves with the categories that apply to the appearances of sensible, that is, given objects at all. In the following discussion of the 'extension' of which reason is capable in its practical but not theoretical use, Kant goes on to argue that while the problem about knowledge of things in themselves is ordinarily that our claims about them must be vacuous or indeterminate, the moral law actually makes our concept of the noumenal self determinate: while the 'category of causality' which is by itself indeterminate is in its ordinary theoretical use made determinate only by experience, and therefore only for phenomena, not for things in themselves, the moral law actually makes the category determinate for things in themselves. That is, while this category 'is not capable of being determined so as to represent a *determinate object* for the sake of theoretical cognition, yet for the sake of something else (the practical, perhaps) it could be capable of being determined for its application' (*CpV*V 54). By thus construing the general problem of knowledge of things in themselves as a problem of determinacy or informativeness, Kant allows himself the possibility of claiming that the moral law resolves this general problem about knowledge of the noumenal by making the concept of the noumenal will determinate in a way that our other concepts of the noumenal are not.

I will not comment on the plausibility of this solution other than to observe that it once again confronts us with the third problem for the *Groundwork*, the problem about the possibility of violating the moral law if the moral law is the causal law of the noumenal self, in full force. I will now turn to the *Critique of Practical Reason*'s response to the second problem for the *Groundwork*, the problem that it is not clear how there can be any conflict between the law of the noumenal self and the laws of the phenomenal self if the former is the sole ground of the latter. Kant addresses this problem in the second *Critique* by maintaining that there cannot be any such conflict, but rather that the whole of any agent's phenomenal character must always be regarded as determined by his noumenal character. Kant makes this point in the 'Critical Elucidation [literally, 'illumination', *Beleuchtung*] of the Analytic of Pure Practical Reason' (*CpV* V 89–106). The heart of this section is Kant's explanation of how his theory of freedom is to be reconciled with his thoroughly deterministic theory of experience. On this theory of experience, every event is caused by antecedent conditions which themselves have antecedent causes *ad infinitum*, and human actions are no exception. Thus, the standard compatibilist model of the freedom of the will, according to which free actions are those due to internal causes in the agent, such as preferences, rather than external causes, is a sham, a 'wretched subterfuge' granting the agent no more freedom than a projectile once it is in flight (*CpV* V 96) or the freedom of an 'automaton' or a 'turnspit' (*CpV* V 97), because no matter what sort of internal cause is posited in the agent, that will be part of a chain of causes and effects extending far into the past, and the agent's actions will still be determined by antecedent conditions beyond his current control.[16] The only solution to this, Kant claims, is the transcendental idealist thesis that 'The concept of causality as *natural necessity* as distinguished from the concept of causality as *freedom*, concerns only the existence of things insofar as it is *determinable in time* and hence as appearances, as opposed to their causality as things in themselves' (*CpV* V 94). Transcendental idealism makes it possible to

---

[16] Jochen Bojanowski puts this point by saying that Kant is worried about 'predeterminism' rather than 'determinism'; see *Kants Theorie der Freiheit: Rekonstruktion und Rehabilitierung* (Berlin and New York: de Gruyter, 2006), p. 5. That could be misleading if predeterminism is equated with fatalism, that is, the doctrine that what an agent will do at some time in his life is determined by events prior to his own choices no matter what choices he makes in the meantime; but that is clearly not what Bojanowski thinks Kant is worried about.

'ascribe the existence of a thing so far as it is determinable in time, and so too its causality in accordance with the law of *natural necessity, only to appearance, and to ascribe freedom to the same being as a thing in itself* ' (*CpV*V 95). In particular, transcendental idealism makes it possible for the 'acting subject as appearance', for whom 'the determining grounds of every action ... lie so far in what belongs to past time and *is* [*sic*] *no longer in his control*', to view 'his existence *insofar as it does not stand under conditions of time* ... as determinable only through laws that he gives himself by reason', and further to view his *entire existence in time* as the product of the noumenal determination of his will (*CpV*V 97–9):

in this existence of his nothing is, for him, antecedent to the determination of his will, but every action – and in general every determination of his existence changing conformably with inner sense, even the whole sequence of his existence as a sensible being – is to be regarded in the consciousness of his intelligible existence as nothing but the consequence and never as the determining ground of his causality as a *noumenon* ... the *sensible life* has, with respect to the *intelligible* consciousness of its existence (consciousness of freedom), the absolute unity of a phenomenon ... this whole chain of appearances, with respect to all that the moral law is concerned with, depends upon the spontaneity of the subject as a thing in itself, for the determination of which no physical explanation can be given.

On this model, there can be no genuine conflict between any feature of the appearance of an agent, at least any with which the moral law is concerned, thus any possible motivation to action, and his noumenal will, because his entire phenomenal character is a consequence of his noumenal will. If the agent acts on non-moral motivations or, apparently, even feels the pull of non-moral motivations, that must somehow reflect the determination of his noumenal will, its failure to make any or a complete commitment to morality. Indeed, to carry Kant's thought to completion, everything in the phenomenal world that would appear to be a determinant of an agent's actions must in fact be a reflection of his noumenal choice, so either events that are phenomenally antecedent to his birth but appear to determine his choices or, more plausibly, the laws of his character which link his prior condition to his present choices must in fact reflect his noumenal will.

This position may not be plausible in its own right, but it is clearly a more consistent application of transcendental idealism than was the model suggested in *Groundwork* III, which characterized the human being as only partly in the intelligible world and as also acted upon by causes in the sensible world, as if these two worlds were fighting for control of his will. But of course, it also makes all the more pressing the third problem with the *Groundwork* account of freedom, namely that if the phenomenal character of the agent is entirely the consequence of his noumenal will but if the moral law is the causal law of the noumenal will, then how can there be any violation of the moral law at either the noumenal or phenomenal level? In the passage from the 'Elucidation' that we have been discussing, Kant clearly assumes that there is a possibility of immoral as well as moral choice at the noumenal level: he claims that considered as a *noumenon*, 'a rational being can now rightly say of every unlawful action he performed that he could have omitted it even though as appearance it is sufficiently determined in the past' (*CpVV* 98), which implies that (what appears as) his past choice of an unlawful action was free and could have been otherwise. But how could the noumenal will be free to choose either to comply with the moral law or to violate it if the moral law is its causal law?

4 ANSWERING THE THIRD QUESTION

This is the question that drives Kant's *Religion Within the Boundaries of Mere Reason*, particularly its first part. This question is thought to have been made pressing for Kant in 1792 by Karl Leonhard Reinhold's objection to the 'friends of Kant', in the second set of his *Letters on the Kantian Philosophy*, that since 'the freedom of the *pure will* consists merely in the self-activity of practical reason, one must also concede that the *impure will*, which is not effected through practical reason, is by no means free';[17] but since Part One of the *Religion* appeared in the *Berlinische Monatsschrift* in April of that year, Kant may have written it before he had seen Reinhold's work. However, the question had already been bruited by Carl Christian Erhard Schmid in 1790,[18] so Kant may have already been prompted by him to worry about the question, or indeed might simply have begun to worry about it himself. One might be tempted to say that this is the question that Kant *addresses* in the *Religion*, except for the fact that Kant does not so much directly address this problem with his previous account of noumenal freedom as simply side-step it by appealing only to the principle that *ought implies can* in support of his position that the very nature of freedom is the possibility of choosing either good or evil, so that one who has chosen evil has done so freely but is still always able to choose good, while there is also nothing to prevent one who has chosen good, or more precisely converted from his prior choice of evil, from relapsing and once again choosing evil – Kant

[17] Cited from Rüdiger Bittner and Konrad Cramer (eds.), *Materialen zu Kants 'Kritik der praktischen Vernunft'* (Frankfurt am Main: Suhrkamp, 1975), p. 255.
[18] See *ibid.* p. 249.

explicitly rejects any conception of divine grace on which God is supposed to ensure the unchangeableness of an agent's fundamental moral disposition once he has converted from evil to good (*Religion* VI 67–8).

This is hardly the place for a detailed interpretation of the *Religion*. But some of the key points of Kant's argument are these. First, Kant maintains that an agent's moral evil or goodness is never a product of mere nature, that is, what inclinations the agent happens to have: the mere occurrence of inclinations as such is morally indifferent, although in fact natural inclinations on their own would be a force for at least externally good outcomes (*Religion* VI 28, VI 58). For both good and evil are 'imputable', that is, something for which the agent is justly held responsible, and in order to be imputable they must be a product of free choice: the subjective ground of either evil or good 'must itself always be a deed [*Actus*] of freedom (for otherwise the use or abuse of the human being's power of choice [*Willkür*] with respect to the moral law could not be imputed to him, nor could the good or evil in him be called moral)' (*Religion* VI 21). The agent's free choice always takes the form of a maxim, and it is only by being 'incorporated' into his maxim (that is, made into a reason for action by means of a freely chosen 'universal rule for himself, according to which he wills to conduct himself') that an agent can make a naturally occurring incentive morally significant. An agent accepts or rejects an incentive as a sufficient reason for action by means of the maxim that he adopts regarding the action it suggests: 'Only in this way can an incentive, whatever it may be, coexist with the absolute spontaneity of the power of choice (of freedom)' (*Religion* VI 24). But Kant also maintains that an agent cannot simply adopt some particular maxims that have one moral quality and others that have the other, that is, adopt some evil maxims and some good ones. Rather, the agent must adopt a fundamental maxim on the basis of which he adopts his particular maxims, and this fundamental maxim, 'the first subjective ground of the adoption of [his particular] maxims, can only be a single one, and it applies to [his] entire use of freedom universally. This disposition too, however, must be adopted through the free power of choice, for otherwise it could not be imputed' (*Religion* VI 25). Now, because Kant holds both that every human being is aware of the moral law (his entire manner of argument in both the *Groundwork* and the *Critique of Practical Reason* would collapse if he did not maintain this), but also that no human being is free of self-love, he does not characterize moral goodness as the choice of the moral law as one's fundamental maxim in the sheer absence of self-love, nor moral evil as the choice to make self-love one's fundamental maxim in sheer ignorance of the moral law. Instead, he holds that 'whether the human being is good or evil, must not lie in the difference between the incentives that he incorporates into his maxim (not in the material of the maxim) but in their *subordination* (in the form of the maxim): *which of the two he makes the condition of the other* (*Religion* VI 36): that is, a good person is one who makes it his fundamental maxim to act out of self-love only when that is consistent with the demands of the moral law, while an evil person is one who makes it his fundamental maxim to act in compliance with the moral law only when that is consistent with his self-love. Finally, for what appear to be, broadly speaking, empirical reasons (*Religion* VI 32–3),[19] Kant holds that everyone initially chooses evil, and that his choice of evil is radical in the sense of being the choice of a fundamental maxim that corrupts all of his particular maxims, but that since it is also radical in the sense of being the product of a completely free choice, everyone is also free to reverse their choice of fundamental maxim, and convert from evil to good (*Religion* VI 37):

Now if a propensity to this [inversion] does lie in human nature, then there is in the human being a natural propensity to evil; and this propensity is itself morally evil, since it must ultimately be sought in a free power of choice, and hence is imputable. This evil is *radical*, since it corrupts the ground of all maxims; as natural propensity, it is also not to be *extirpated* ... Yet it must equally be possible to *overcome* this evil, for it is found in the human being as acting freely.

Since the human being is free to choose either self-love or morality as his fundamental maxim, the human being is free to choose either evil or good. This means that one who has chosen evil is still always free to choose good, although conversely one who has already chosen to be good rather than evil is still free to relapse into evil.

Now Kant's insistence that all of a human being's particular maxims are grounded in the choice of a fundamental maxim is sometimes read as meaning that each human being has only a *single* opportunity to choose that maxim, and thus that if every human being's initial choice of fundamental maxim is evil, then no human being can ever escape that choice, and can at most progress toward a genuine conversion, a genuine reversal of

---

[19] Seiriol Morgan, 'The Missing Formal Proof of Humanity's Radical Evil in Kant's *Religion*', *The Philosophical Review* 114 (2005), pp. 63–114, has argued that Kant calls for a 'formal proof' of our universal initial choice of evil and then supplies it by means of the argument that we necessarily initially misrepresent freedom as merely negative freedom from constraint (see especially 64–5 and 79–85). I do not think the text supports the demand for a 'formal' proof, nor that Morgan supplies any *a priori* reason why every human being should initially misunderstand the true nature of freedom. For further discussion, see my chapter 'The Crooked Timber of Humankind' in Amelie Rorty and James Schmidt (eds.), *Philosophy as History: Essays on Kant's Idea for a Universal History* (Cambridge University Press, 2009).

fundamental maxim, but can never actually complete it.[20] But obviously the inapplicability of the temporal form of our experience to our noumenal self precludes such an inference, because to claim that a human being has only a single opportunity to change his fundamental maxim and can at most progress toward conversion but never actually convert would be to individuate noumenal acts in a temporal way. If we take transcendental idealism and Kant's theory of the *practical* determination of our concept of the noumenal self seriously, we simply cannot say whether the noumenal self is capable of one or multiple acts of choice *on any theoretical ground*, but we can and must say about the noumenal self everything but only what is required *on practical grounds*. And what is required on practical grounds, according to Kant's conception of imputability, is simply that the human being is always free to choose either evil or good, no matter what has previously happened at the level of his phenomenal self and what we might therefore infer has 'previously' (but not literally previously) been chosen by his noumenal self.

But now we must return to the question, how can Kant suddenly maintain that we are free to choose either good or evil, and always free to choose the other no matter what we have, as it appears phenomenally, previously chosen, when he has previously argued that the moral law is the causal law of the noumenal self? The answer to this is that in the *Religion*, although Kant obviously presupposes transcendental idealism and the possibility of a noumenal choice not determined by temporal causal laws of nature, he simply does not reproduce either the *Groundwork*'s argument for our noumenal rationality or the *Critique of Practical Reason*'s inference from the necessity of the moral law to the purity of the noumenal will. He just assumes the binding force of the moral law and appeals exclusively to the principle that *ought implies can* for assurance of the possibility of choosing good even if we have previously chosen evil, as well as for the danger of once again choosing evil even if we have already chosen to convert from evil to good – which this principle allows because, of course, 'ought implies can' does not imply that 'ought implies does'. Thus, while in the second *Critique* Kant appealed to the principle that *ought implies can* only

---

[20] According to David Sussman, Kant holds that 'since there can be only one disposition that characterizes each life in its entirety, no one can, in time, undergo any real conversion from depravity to goodness or fall from goodness into depravity. Kant seems to think that all ordinary moral progress or deterioration is purely epiphenomenal, being nothing more than the empirical manifestation of a unique and timeless act of noumenal self-determination'; see 'Perversity of the Heart', *Philosophical Review* 114 (2005), 153–78. As I argue, Kant's transcendental idealism actually disallows any such assertion.

for the empirical confirmation of our knowledge of the purity of our will that was itself derived directly from our *a priori* cognition of the necessity of the moral law, in the *Religion* Kant appeals directly to the principle that *ought implies can* every time he needs to assure us of our freedom to convert or to relapse – and he appeals to it no fewer than seven times. The first invocation of the principle comes in Part One, where Kant says that 'However evil a human being has been right up to the moment of an impending free action ... his duty to better himself was not just in the past: it is still his duty *now*; he must therefore be capable of it' (*Religion* VI 41). He then amplifies in the General Remark to Part One of the *Religion*, where he is rejecting the need for grace (*Religion* VI 44–5):

How it is possible that a naturally evil human being should make himself into a good being surpasses every concept of ours. For how can an evil tree bear good fruit? But, since by our previous admission a tree which was (in its predisposition) originally good but did bring forth bad fruits, and since the fall from good into evil (if we seriously consider that evil originates from freedom) is no more comprehensible than the ascent from evil back to good, then the possibility of this last cannot be disputed. For in spite of that fall, the command that we *ought* to become better human beings still resounds unabated in our souls; consequently, we must also be capable of it.

Kant reiterates the principle three more times in this General Remark (*Religion* VI 47, VI 49 fn., VI 50), and then invokes it twice more in Part Two, where he is arguing that we have no need or use for the idea of someone else who can remit or redeem our sins, although the figure of Jesus Christ is a necessary symbol of our own capacity to convert from evil to good and of the suffering that we must pass through in order to do that (*Religion* VI 62, VI 66). But the character of his argument is evident in the long quotation from Part One: here he simply asserts that the command of the moral law 'resounds unabated in our souls' without attempting to derive it from anything at all, and then derives the actuality of our freedom to fulfil this demand from the principle that we must be able to fulfil our duty, which is also asserted without any argument at all. Since he does not derive the command of morality from anything at all, it is not derived from any conception of the pure rationality of the noumenal self or will that would make the moral law the causal law of the noumenal will, so that the will is free to choose evil as well as good. And since 'ought implies can' does not imply 'ought implies does', as far as that principle too is concerned the noumenal self is free to choose evil as well as good. The problem of the possibility of immorality simply disappears.

Thus, while there is certainly some change in the style of Kant's argument between the *Groundwork* and the second *Critique*, the real caesura in Kant's thought comes between the latter work and the *Religion*. It is only here that Kant adopts the strategy of simply assuming the moral law and then arguing to our freedom through the principle that *ought implies can*, which raises no problem about the possibility of immoral choice and action. Remarkably, or perhaps predictably, in the *Religion* Kant is actually reverting back to the position about the moral law and freedom originally stated in the *Critique of Pure Reason*. In the 'Canon of Pure Reason' in the first *Critique*'s Doctrine of Method, he had written (*CrV* A 807/B 835):

I assume that there are really pure moral laws, ... and that these laws command *absolutely* (not merely hypothetically under the presupposition of other empirical ends), and are thus necessary in every respect. I can legitimately presuppose this proposition by appealing not only to the proofs of the most enlightened moralists but also to the moral judgement of every human being, if he will distinctly think such a law.

Pure reason thus contains – not in its speculative use, to be sure, but yet in a certain practical use, namely the moral use – principles of the *possibility of experience*, namely of those actions in conformity with moral precepts which *could* be encountered in the *history* of humankind. For since they command that these actions ought to happen, they must also be able to happen.

Perhaps Kant's last word on the proof of both the moral law and freedom was his first word – that the moral law is self-evident to anyone who will simply think clearly about it, and that it directly implies freedom by the principle that *ought implies can* – and the intervening attempts of the *Groundwork* and the second *Critique* to prove either the moral law or our freedom by metaphysical arguments for or from our pure rationality were noble but failed experiments.

Freedom and reason in Groundwork III

Frederick Rauscher

Section III of Kant's *Groundwork* has achieved near legendary status as the murkiest of his writings on ethics, comparable perhaps to the 'Transcendental Deduction of the Categories' in the *Critique of Pure Reason*. This chapter will offer a way to cut through the murky material that differs from most in two ways. First, I will work my way from the end of *Groundwork* III with Kant's final explanation of his solution and its limitations, back to his specification of the key to the solution, and finally back to the identification of the problem itself. Secondly, I will present an interpretation, which I call the 'validation of reason' interpretation, that centres on the role of reason as legislator of the moral law rather than on any choice in the will.

I THE STANDARD INTERPRETATION

A standard approach to *Groundwork* III is to view Kant as attempting to provide an argument for the validity of the moral law for human beings by invoking a theoretical argument borrowed from the *Critique of Pure Reason* about the nature of reality. This theoretical argument is taken to invoke transcendental idealism to show that human beings are not merely sensible beings but are also members of another ontological order, the 'intelligible', that grounds the sensible world. As members of the intelligible world, human beings are active and rational, able to initiate action independent of causal determination in the sensible world, that is, as things in themselves they possess a free will understood as an ability to choose. As free in themselves, humans then recognize that they are both obligated and able to conform to rational constraints on their actions. The argument is said to fail, and Kant is said to have realized this failure before writing the *Critique of Practical Reason*, in which he abandoned any hope of a deduction of morality in favour of a very different approach, an assertion of the validity of the moral law as a 'fact of reason' which requires, and is susceptible to, no deduction.

In describing a monolithic 'standard approach' I am simplifying a very complex set of interpretations, not all of which fit each of the parts listed above. Their variety is shown through the following four examples. The locus classicus of the approach is Dieter Henrich, who in a series of articles specifies that Kant seeks to provide a justification for morality he deems 'moral insight' which must be 'essentially ontological'.[1] Regarding *Groundwork* III in particular, Henrich claims that Kant must have two different conceptions of freedom, and that his problem is trying to argue from one kind of freedom to the other, from a freedom of judgement to a freedom of the will. Freedom of the will is then used as justification for the validity of the moral law. Kant's attempt to provide an argument for the validity of the moral law in *Groundwork* III fails because morality, and 'moral insight' itself, cannot be based upon theoretical premises, and the argument for freedom of the will would stem from theoretical premises. Kant is then forced to invoke the 'fact of reason' in the second *Critique* as a *sui generis*, purely practical basis for the moral law.

Karl Ameriks takes Kant to offer a strongly rationalist deduction of freedom in *Groundwork* III, one compatible with similar strong rationalist tendencies in the first edition of the *Critique of Pure Reason* with regard to self-knowledge.[2] His interpretation of *Groundwork* III holds that Kant relies on a pre-critical claim that the self can be aware of its own free activity, that is, become aware of itself as a thing-in-itself, as a member of the intelligible world. This apperception echoes language from the Third Antinomy of the first *Critique* in which, in contrast to the more critical Paralogisms, Kant holds that a transcendentally free causation must exist, and that human beings can attribute this transcendental freedom to themselves because of the mental activities they experience. He later comes to realize that this form of self-knowledge violated the limits of critical philosophy, so in the *Critique of Practical Reason* he abandoned an argument for freedom and accepted instead a 'fact of reason'.

---

[1] Dieter Henrich, 'The Concept of Moral Insight and Kants Doctrine of the Fact of Reason' in his *The Unity of Reason: Essays on Kants Philosophy* (Harvard University Press, 1994), pp. 256–7. The German original is 'Der Begriff der sittlichen Einsicht und Kants Lehre vom *Faktum* der Vernunft' in Gerold Prauss (ed.), *Kant: Zur Deutung seiner Theorie von Erkennen u. Handeln*, Neue Wissenschaftenliche Bibliothek, 63: Philosophie (Köln: Kiepenheuer und Witsch, 1973), pp. 223–54. His direct work on *Groundwork* III is in 'the Deduction of the Moral Law: the Reasons for the Obscurity of the Final Section of Kant's *Groundwork of the Metaphysics of Morals*' in Paul Guyer (ed.), *Kants Groundwork of the Metaphysics of Morals: Critical Essays*, Critical Essays on the Classics (Lanham, MD: Rowman & Littlefield, 1998), pp. 303–41. The German original is Dieter Henrich, 'Die Deduktion des Sittengesetzes: Über die Gründe der Dunkelheit des Letzten Abschnittes von Kants "Grundlegung zur Metaphysik der Sitten"' in Alexander Schwan (ed.), *Denken im Schatten Des Nihilismus: Festschrift für Wilhelm Weischedel* (Darmstadt: Wissenschaftliche Buchgesellschaft, 1975).

[2] Karl Ameriks, *Kants Theory of Mind: an Analysis of the Paralogisms of Pure Reason* (Oxford: Clarendon Press, 1982), esp. p. 189 ff.

Henry Allison's discussion of the argument in *Groundwork* III depends upon a claim that human beings can view themselves as free in each particular act of choice, a 'practical spontaneity' that differs from the 'epistemic spontaneity' attributed to the understanding and reason in their theoretical roles.[3] To move from one to the other by means of the concept of an intelligible world, Kant must use a hidden premise, namely that membership in the intelligible world is what can make a claim to consciousness of possessing a will feasible by providing a way of comprehending that active will without recourse to the mechanism of nature. Regarding freedom of the will, Allison quite explicitly places 'the location of this activity in the intelligible world' in the same way that epistemic spontaneity is supposed to be located there.

Dieter Schönecker's understanding of *Groundwork* III has Kant asking for moral justification and answering in the strongest possible moral realist terms, claiming that morality must be seen as part of the complete reality of the universe.[4] When Kant holds that human beings must consider themselves as members of the 'intelligible world', he means that the genuine human being is a thing-in-itself that also appears as a phenomenon in the sensible world. This ontological 'superiority' of the intelligible world gives the moral law a higher value than laws of the sensible world; and hence human beings are subject to moral obligation.

These four interpretations, although disparate on many counts, raise some common points. First, each holds in different ways that Kant is invoking some theoretical consideration in *Groundwork* III: epistemic freedom or spontaneity, knowledge of myself as I am in myself. Each also links Kant's argument to a conception of freedom of the will or ability to choose that can act and make decisions on its own, independent of any causal determinism in the sensible world. Each interprets Kant's term 'intelligible world' to stand for an order of existence radically distinct from the sensible order (although they differ regarding whether to interpret this as an

---

[3] Henry E. Allison, *Kants Theory of Freedom* (Cambridge University Press, 1990), p. 222 ff. See also the discussion of *Groundwork* III and the corresponding claims in the *Critique of Practical Reason* in Guido Antonio de Almeida, 'Critique, Deduction, and Fact of Reason' in Daniel Omar Perez and Frederick Rauscher (eds.), *Brazilian Work on Kant* (Rochester University Press, in preparation). De Almeida holds that Kant's attempt to link a spontaneity of judgement with the freedom of the will in *Groundwork* III cannot succeed because the concept offered as a link between them, the 'intelligible world', is an indeterminate concept that 'allows no positive determination of whatever object to which it may be applied'.

[4] Dieter Schönecker, *Kant: Grundlegung III: Die Deduktion des kategorischen Imperativs* (Freiburg: Alber, 1999). See a shorter version of his argument in English: Dieter Schönecker, 'How is a Categorical Imperative Possible? Kants Deduction of the Categorical Imperative' in Christoph Horn and Dieter Schönecker (eds.), *Groundwork for the Metaphysics of Morals* (Berlin: de Gruyter, 2006).

ontological claim about a distinct 'world' of things-in-themselves or a viewpoint on an equal standing with a viewpoint of things as sensible).

2 THE 'VALIDATION OF REASON' INTERPRETATION

In contrast to this approach, I will offer a less ontological interpretation that I call 'validation of reason'.[5] This interpretation holds that Kant does not provide a deduction of the objective reality of morality, only of the inescapability of the ascription of this morality to human beings who take themselves to be rational agents. Kant invokes theoretical conclusions from the *Critique of Pure Reason*, but methodological rather than ontological ones concerning the nature of pure reason itself rather than the nature of the faculty of choice. These considerations justify human beings in viewing themselves and their experience as rational, but not in claiming that the world independent of human beings is itself rational. The corresponding conception of the 'intelligible world' is simply a conception of the sensible world as if, contra what can be known, it were governed by reason.

The central claim of this interpretation is that in *Groundwork* III Kant invokes the transcendental freedom not of the whole person but only of the faculty of reason as a way of explaining the freedom of the will.[6] As Kant argues in the first paragraphs of *Groundwork* III, freedom of the will is

---

[5] The interpretation builds on the work of several other interpreters while not claiming the full endorsement or agreement of any of them. I am indebted in particular to the work of Marcus Willaschek on the nature of practical reason and the *Factum* of Reason (Marcus Willaschek, *Praktische Vernunft: Handlungstheorie und Moralbegründung bei Kant* (Stuttgart: Metzler, 1992)); Julio Esteves' argument that Kant does not invoke theoretical arguments in *Groundwork* III and that his claims are fully compatible with the *Critique of Practical Reason* (Julio Esteves, 'The Non-Circular Deduction of the Categorical Imperative in Groundwork III' in Perez and Rauscher, *Brazilian Work on Kant*); Mieth and Rosenthal's interpretation of the nature of the freedom of reason itself in relation to justification (Corinna Mieth and Jacob Rosenthal, 'Freedom Must be Presupposed as a Property of All Rational Beings' in Horn and Schönecker, *Groundwork for the Metaphysics of Morals*); and Jens Timmermann's assessment of freedom of the will that shows it as merely a capacity to be determined by principles of reason rather than a free choice among open possibilities (Jens Timmermann, *Sittengesetz und Freiheit: Untersuchungen zu Immanuel Kants Theorie des Freien Willens*, Quellen und Studien zur Philosophie Bd. 60 (Berlin: de Gruyter, 2003)).

[6] As is generally understood in Kant interpretation, the English term 'freedom of the will' is one not well applied to Kant. His term 'Wille' is often used interchangeably with 'Willkür', and he did not clarify the distinction between the two until the 1797 *Metaphysics of Morals*. Nonetheless, it is generally clear that Kant employs two distinct conceptions of freedom that correspond to those two terms, first 'the power of legislation' of pure practical reason in generating the moral law, and 'the power of decision' of the faculty of desire in choosing particular maxims for actions. Most philosophical discussion of freedom of the will concerns the latter sense. In Kant, however, most discussion of freedom concerns the former sense. The extent to which the faculty of decision is called 'free' is dependent upon the extent to which particular maxims for actions can be said to be 'caused by reason', that is, somehow a product of reason's power of legislating the moral law. (See Timmermann, *Sittengesetz und Freiheit*.)

nothing other than autonomy. The autonomy of the will that culminates the second section of the *Groundwork* is 'The property of the will by which it is a law to itself (independently of any property of the objects of volition)' (*G* IV 440). And since reason is required for any derivation of actions from laws, and reason is itself the source of the moral law (which we finite sensible rational beings experience as a categorical imperative) (*G* IV 412–13), autonomy of the will is the property of the will of being determined by reason alone. Freedom of the will as autonomy is not a matter of the causal power of the will itself but of the causal power of reason to determine that will. The final paragraph of *Groundwork* II, setting up the problem for the following final section, notes that the 'autonomy of the will unavoidably depends upon' the categorical imperative, but 'How such a synthetic practical proposition is possible a priori and why it is necessary' has not yet been shown. The crucial topic for *Groundwork* III, then, is the justification of reason's law itself. The argument Kant provides in *Groundwork* III is primarily a justification of reason's ability to provide valid law and not an argument for free human moral action in any sense other than its determination by that valid law. Once Kant can justify this legislative power of reason, he can defend autonomy of the will and thus the human obligation to will maxims that conform to the categorical imperative, and will have secondarily defended freedom of the will defined as autonomous volition. He will have defended the obligation human beings have to try to make their actions conform to the rational dictates of morality, and to that extent will have shown that it is the responsibility of human beings to attempt to make their actual world conform as closely as possible to a perfectly rational world.

3 BEGINNING AT THE END OF KANT'S ARGUMENT

Groundwork III is divided into five sections of diverse length plus a one paragraph concluding remark. It is worth looking at his final claims to best understand the final conclusion he claims to have reached before turning to the various steps he takes to reach it. This is particularly important because in these last paragraphs, Kant stresses what he *cannot* prove. The final paragraph raises the characteristic of reason that it always pushes its cognition until it finds necessity (*G* IV 463). That is, as explained in the Dialectic of the *Critique of Pure Reason* (*CrV* A 305–9 / B 362–6), reason always seeks a condition as a basis for something it is trying to explain. In each case, the purported condition becomes subject to the same demand for a condition, and that for a further condition, and so on. Reason is never satisfied with

these relative conditions and insists upon claiming that there is an unconditioned condition. In the final paragraph of *Groundwork* III he applies this
to the practical use of reason, which demands an unconditionality, or
necessity, of the moral law for rational beings. The third section of the
Groundwork as a whole has been a search for this absolute necessity of the
moral law; not merely the conditional claim that if there is a moral law
binding on human beings, it is the categorical imperative, but the unconditional claim that in fact there is such a binding moral law. Kant claims here
that this search has failed to provide a comprehensible answer, for the only
explanation of necessity can be one that invokes some 'condition' under
which the necessity is explained. Every explanation of a condition, however,
raises the problem of the search for a further condition to explain it, and so
'reason restlessly seeks the unconditionally necessary and sees itself constrained to assume it without any means of making it comprehensible to
itself'. The necessity of the moral law is thus not proved in *Groundwork* III;
it is merely assumed but is still 'incomprehensible'.[7]

Stepping backward to the previous section, 'On the Extreme Boundary
of All Practical Philosophy', we can find a more specific explanation of the
'incomprehensibility' of the necessity of the moral law (*G* IV 461):

Thus the question, how a categorical imperative is possible, can indeed be answered
to the extent that one can furnish the sole presupposition on which alone it is
possible, namely the idea of freedom, and that one can also see the necessity of this
presupposition, which is sufficient for the practical use of reason, that is for the
conviction of the validity of this imperative as so also of the moral law; but how this
presupposition itself is possible can never be seen by any human reason.

The validity of the categorical imperative depends upon the possibility of
freedom. The kind of freedom that concerns Kant must be one that could
provide validity to the categorical imperative, yet one that remains
incomprehensible.

The standard approaches to *Groundwork* III tend to identify this freedom
as the freedom of the will as a power of choice in determining action

---

[7] Contrast this analysis with that of Dieter Schönecker, who sees the main question of *Groundwork* III
'How is a categorical imperative possible?' as constituted by three subquestions: (a) Why is the
categorical imperative valid? (b) How can freedom be understood, and why may we consider ourselves
to be free?, and (c) How can pure practical reason bring about an interest in the moral law? Schönecker
takes Kant to answer the first two of these three subquestions in the course of *Groundwork* III. None of
his three subquestions concern the comprehensibility (or 'how') of the necessity of the categorical
imperative. (Schönecker, 'How is a Categorical Imperative Possible?', p. 307; and his *Kant:
Grundlegung III*, p. 131).

independent of sensible causation.[8] A person as a thing-in-herself would have to be the cause of actions in appearance by a free choice made as a thing-in-herself. For this standard approach, then, the mystery left unsolved is how freedom of choice of a being in herself can determine effects in the sensible world.

A look at Kant's previous paragraph, however, shows that the standard approach's understanding of freedom is misplaced. In that paragraph Kant notes that the incomprehensible causal relation of freedom is not one of a choice by the will of a person in herself to sensible effects but of 'a causality of reason to determine sensibility in conformity with its principles' (*G* IV 460). Reason's causal power, not the will or choice, must be the inexplicable freedom at issue. The incomprehensible causal relation is not between the will as a cause, through its decision, and the sensible action in nature as effect: this relation in fact can be understood purely in accordance with natural causation as a relation of sensible feeling to will. Both the decision in the will and the resulting action are in time and subject to deterministic causal relations. The inexplicable causal relation is between reason as a cause, through its principles, and the decision of the will as effect.[9] The latter takes place in time in conformity with natural laws, as Kant specifies here, in particular as determined by feelings of pleasure or displeasure. The former, timeless principles of reason, are not occurrences at any precise moment of time. Pure reason provides ideas that are themselves not objects of experience. Pure practical reason provides the idea of the moral law, that is of the 'universality of a maxim as law', a purely formal consideration abstracting from all content. Kant's question is: How can a causal relation be understood between such an abstract formal idea that cannot be made into an object of experience – reason as a cause – and a particular determination of the sensible power of choice (the will) – a feeling of pleasure or displeasure that would determine the will as 'an effect that admittedly lies in experience'. Only the latter is capable of being understood as an object of experience. For the will to be determined freely, it must be determined by the moral law alone; but this free determination of the will need not mean that the will as power of decision must be conceived independent of sensible

[8] For example, Allison understands Kant's autonomy of the will in the *Groundwork* to refer to a 'capacity for self-legislation or self-determination' that represents 'a morally neutral conception of autonomy' (Allison, *Kant's Theory of Freedom*, pp. 95–6).

[9] Strictly speaking, the inexplicable causal relation is between reason as a cause and the feeling of respect as an effect. The feeling of respect can then be understood as a purely natural cause of a decision of the will (*G* IV 460). The inexplicable relation between a timeless idea and a sensible feeling operating at a particular time in the human mind remains.

causation but only mean that there must be a way for pure reason, which alone must be considered independent of sensible objects of experience, to determine the sensible will.

This, then, is the requisite freedom toward which Kant's argument aims. Pure reason must be understood as a faculty independent of objects of sense, but its causal effect on the sensible will is incomprehensible. The choice of the will itself lies within sensible causation; only reason as its cause must be understood independent of the sensible world. At the end of *Groundwork* III, Kant has discussed the limitation of the kind of solution he provides. Stepping further back in the text, my next section will see how the discussion of that solution itself lies in his discussion of the relation between reason and the 'intelligible world'.

4 THE SENSIBLE AND INTELLIGIBLE WORLDS

Amid a book of controversial claims, the one that has long struck me as the least plausible occurs when Kant introduces his distinction between appearances and things-in-themselves with the following caveat: 'No subtle reflection is required to make the following remark, and one may assume that the commonest understanding can make it, though in its own way, by an obscure discrimination of judgement which it calls feeling' (*G* IV 450–1). He then proceeds to provide a précis of the arguments from the *Critique of Pure Reason* regarding the transcendental ideality of appearances! If indeed no subtle reflection is required to posit the doctrine of transcendental idealism, then Kant appears to have misspent his silent decade and misled himself and others about the importance of the *Critique of Pure Reason*. What could Kant possibly have in mind in the claim that such a difficult doctrine is in fact obvious to everyone?

The answer must be that Kant's application of transcendental idealism in this context is not meant to invoke more than the bare minimum distinction between the world as human beings sense it and the world as it is in itself. The commonest understanding can make the claim that sensory experience of the world might not be accurate, that nature operates on its own principles that human beings might not know, that the real nature of things might be different from our thoughts about nature. Kant holds this as 'a distinction, although a crude one, between a world of sense and the world of understanding, the first of which can be very different according to the difference of sensibility in various observers of the world while the second, which is its basis, always remains the same' (*G* IV 451).

The specific meaning of this distinction between the world of sense and the world of understanding should be understood in reference not only to Kant's elaboration in the following few paragraphs but also to relevant passages from the *Critique of Pure Reason*. I believe that looking at the parts of the *Critique of Pure Reason* that discuss moral issues will illuminate the meaning of the term 'intelligible world', namely, the Third Antinomy, which bears a striking resemblance to the solution to the circle in *Groundwork* III, and the Canon of Pure Reason in which Kant discusses a 'moral world'. I believe that there is a fundamental continuity between the first *Critique* and the *Groundwork*, in that Kant anticipated the discussion of practical reason in the first *Critique* when citing the moral law and a moral, or intelligible, world. My next section will look at the corresponding argument that Kant gives in *Groundwork* III. This section will first review the relevant passages from the first *Critique*.

In the solution to the Third Antinomy, Kant invokes the idea of an intelligible character as opposed to the sensible character. The 'character' of a cause is defined as 'a law of its causality without which it would not be a cause at all' (*CrV* A 539/B 567). An agent's actions in appearance are said to have 'an intelligible character, through which it is indeed the cause of those actions as appearances, but which does not stand under any conditions of sensibility and is not itself appearance'. This causal relation does not stand under conditions of time, so no action would arise or perish in it as intelligible. As intelligible, then, it would not change, yet it would have causal effects in the world of sense in time. 'Thus freedom and nature, each in its full significance, would both be found in the same actions, simultaneously and without any contradiction, according to whether one compares them with their intelligible or their sensible cause' (*CrV* A 541/B 569).

One must note, however, that the above part of the solution to the Third Antinomy is his attempt to 'sketch the silhouette of a solution', not to provide the complete solution (*CrV* A 542/B 570). He has only defined the difference between sensible and intelligible and has not claimed that anything is actually known to be intelligible. The mere distinction between sensible and intelligible character does not show that there is in fact an intelligible character for anything. The complete solution invokes this prior outline but applies it to human beings. Specifically, Kant seeks something that can be said to be an intelligible cause of appearances. He looks for 'a faculty that is only intelligible, in that its determination to action never rests on empirical conditions but on mere grounds of the understanding' (*CrV* A 545/B 573). Kant locates this particular faculty not in any free choice of a will but in the capacity of reason itself to provide ideas and laws. The language Kant uses is nearly identical to that in *Groundwork* III (*CrV* A 546–7/B 574–5):

Yet the human being, who is otherwise acquainted with the whole of nature solely through sense, knows himself also through pure apperception, and indeed in actions and inner determinations which cannot be accounted at all among impressions of sense; he obviously is in one part phenomenon, but in another part, namely in regard to certain faculties, he is a merely intelligible object, because the actions of this object cannot at all be ascribed to the receptivity of sensibility. We call these faculties understanding and reason; chiefly the latter is distinguished quite properly and pre-eminently from all empirically conditioned powers, since it considers its objects merely according to ideas and in accordance with them determines the understanding, which then makes an empirical use of its own concepts (even the pure ones).

Human beings count themselves as intelligences because they experience the effects of the understanding and, above all, reason. The understanding with its *a priori* concepts and reason with its ideas appear to exhibit 'spontaneity' because these concepts and ideas cannot be understood as arising from sensible causation. These ideas and concepts cannot be represented as sensible themselves.[10] Hence, individuals must view themselves as intelligences in order to believe that their reason is valid.[11]

The causal power of reason itself – not the agent's causal power as determining individual choices – is repeatedly invoked by Kant in the solution to the Third Antinomy. And it is not theoretical reason but mainly practical reason that Kant has in mind, although he does not use that terminology. The passage just quoted is followed immediately with a new paragraph that invokes moral imperatives as the primary basis for attribution of causal power to reason: 'Now that this reason has causality, or that we can at least represent something of the sort in it, is clear from the imperatives that we propose as rules to our powers of execution in everything practical' (*CrV* A 547/B 575). Practical reason is considered as a faculty

---

[10] Kant's claim appears to be twofold. First, he seems to hold that reason and understanding, as faculties, cannot be understood in empirical terms, that is, as sources of thoughts they cannot themselves appear in inner intuition. I discuss this claim in relation to empirical psychology in my 'Reason as a Natural Cause' in Heiner Klemme, Manfred Kuehn and Dieter Schönecker (eds.), *Moralische Motivation: Kant und die Alternativen* (Hamburg: Meiner, 2006), pp. 97–110. Secondly, he seems to hold that the validity of the *a priori* claims of reason (and, to a lesser extent, the understanding) depends upon their not arising from any contingent cause, as empirical causation would be, but only on some necessary basis. I discuss this claim in 'Razão prática pura como uma faculdade natural' ('Pure Practical Reason as a Natural Faculty') (Milene Consenso Tonetto (trans.), *Ethic@* 5 (2006), pp. 173–92 at www.cfh.ufsc.br/ethic@), where I provide considerations similar to those appearing in this chapter, below.

[11] In contrast, Ameriks takes this passage to be evidence that Kant retained 'pre-critical' rationalist views about freedom into the early 1780s. Freedom is taken to be a property of the soul to think and act independently of determination in nature, and the faculties of reason and understanding are evidence that human beings have immaterial souls that can think and act freely (Ameriks, *Kant's Theory of Mind*, p. 190).

that cannot be understood through sensibility but must be seen as having sensible causal effects, particularly effects on our 'powers of execution', that is, on the will. Practical reason, not the will itself, is considered to require this intelligible status.

The causal power of reason on the sensible will is, importantly, a timeless cause (*CrV* A 551–2/B 579–80):

The causality of reason in the intelligible character does not arise or start working at a certain time in producing an effect. For then it would itself be subject to the natural law of appearances, to the extent that this law determines causal series in time, and its causality would then be nature and not freedom. Thus we could say that if reason can have causality in regard to appearances, then it is a faculty through which the sensible condition of an empirical series of effects first begins. For the condition that lies in reason is not sensible and does not itself begin.

The causal condition that lies in pure reason is a timeless, persistent condition that is able to influence the sensible will to action. Kant does not describe it as different for different individuals, as individual free choices certainly would be. This general, time-independent, determinant of human sensible choices must be the moral law itself understood as the pure structure of reason itself applied to the circumstances of possible human free choice. Pure reason can be a cause of actions in the sensible world by dictating that they ought to occur. Reason as a faculty can be understood as providing a structure for experience, specifically, a structure for systematic and consistent actions.

Note that the Third Antinomy does not purport to explain *how* this freedom is possible. Kant even claims that it does not purport to explain *that* freedom is possible, only that it is not inconsistent with causal necessity in accordance with laws of nature (*CrV* A 557–8/ B 585–6). By this, Kant cannot mean that freedom is impossible per se, only that it is not possible as possibility is understood in the 'Postulates of Empirical Thought', that is, possibility considered as something that conforms to the formal conditions of experience in accordance with laws of nature (*CrV* A 220/B 267). Freedom in the Third Antinomy is certainly not possible in this sense, but it is consistent with all of experience in accordance with the laws of nature. In broader terms, it is consistent with human experience to consider human beings as governed by laws of reason that themselves form a different causal relation than that of laws of nature.

The consequence of this is that human beings not only see themselves as intelligences, they see the world as 'intelligible', that is, as one comprehended accurately by reason. The invocation of reason as an intelligibly free cause of some events in the sensible world provides not only an alternative causal story but an alternative point of view for the entirety of human life. He notes that 'we find a rule and order that is entirely other than the natural order. For perhaps everything that has happened in the course of nature, and on empirical grounds inevitably had to happen, nevertheless ought not to have happened' (*CrV* A 550/B 578). This different order in nature is *in addition to*, not *in replacement of*, the natural order in accordance with the laws of nature.

This order is what Kant will refer to as the 'world of understanding' in *Groundwork* III. In the 'Canon' of the *Critique of Pure Reason*, Kant provides the conception of this intelligible world as a moral order imposed by reason on the sensible world (*CrV* A 808/B 836):

I call the world as it would be if it were in conformity with all moral laws (as it can be in accordance with the freedom of rational beings and should be in accordance with the necessary laws of morality) a moral world. This is conceived thus far merely as an intelligible world, since abstraction is made therein from all conditions (ends) and even from all hindrances to morality in it (weakness or impurity of human nature). Thus far it is therefore a mere, yet practical, idea, which really can and should have its influence on the sensible world, in order to make it agree as far as possible with this idea. The idea of a moral world thus has objective reality, not as if it pertained to an object of an intelligible intuition (for we cannot even think of such a thing), but as pertaining to the sensible world, although as an object of pure reason in its practical use and a corpus mysticum of the rational beings in it, insofar as their free choice under moral laws has thoroughgoing systematic unity in itself as well as with the freedom of everyone else.

There is no sense in which human beings here see themselves as somehow distinct from nature. Rather, they see themselves in nature but subject to intelligible, that is moral, demands. This moral order is, of course, provided by pure reason. Just as in the solution to the Third Antinomy, human beings use their reason to place themselves in a rational order that ought to determine the sensible world. To the extent that human actions exhibit this rationality, they are helping to make the sensible world into a rational world, although their actions will never completely succeed in matching the imagined 'moral world'.

5 THE INTELLIGIBLE WORLD IN *GROUNDWORK* III

The above review of relevant passages from the *Critique of Pure Reason* has shown that Kant's invocation of the world of the understanding in *Groundwork* III is tied to a claim that the world can be understood as governed by reason and human beings can conceive of themselves as governed by reason. The supremacy of the intelligible world is not that it is an ontologically distinct realm in which individuals in their entirety as thinking and acting beings really do their thinking and acting. The supremacy of the intelligible world is that human beings view themselves as rational, justify that reason as having a validity independent of the causal order of the sensible world, and comprehend the sensible world as capable of being governed by reason operating through human actions along with, rather than instead of, the laws of nature. Human beings recognize, however, that the only justification they have for viewing nature as an intelligible world is that they seem to possess this faculty of reason. They cannot independently verify, or even comprehend in detail, how they can possess reason or how it can operate through them.

All of the above characterizations of the intelligible world are also found in *Groundwork* III. Prior to my last section's look back at the first *Critique*, I had identified the crucial distinction in *Groundwork* III between the sensible and intelligible worlds as the point at which Kant invokes the incomprehensibility of their relation, in particular the claim that the intelligible is governed by pure reason, and the manner in which pure reason can have any causal effect in the sensible world, especially on the sensibly determined will. This section will now show that the characterization Kant gives of the intelligible world in *Groundwork* III matches the characterization given in the first *Critique* and conforms to precisely the incomprehensibility that Kant cites in the solution to the Third Antinomy.

The main characterizations of the intelligible world in this section of the *Groundwork* concern 'pure activity' in the human mind as revealing something about how humans are in themselves. The standard view tends to equate this idea of pure activity with a human being as a thing-in-herself and claim that we can have a direct awareness of this activity.[12] But Kant's language is less direct: he claims that our experience of what appears to be pure activity (which he defines as 'what reaches consciousness immediately and not through affection of the senses' (*G* IV 451)) allows us to regard ourselves as not completely defined by our sensible nature. But it does not furnish us with any positive characterization of what a human being would be in herself. The nature of what the self might be independent of sensible

---

[12] Henrich emphasizes that Kant's argument for the consciousness of our freedom depends on his crucial 'two-world doctrine' so that the consciousness of our freedom depends upon the claim that our will belongs to a world other than the sensible world. See Henrich, 'Die Deduktion des Sit-tengesetzes', p. 98 (this section is not included in the translation cited above).

intuitions is still incomprehensible: a human being must 'count himself as belonging to the intellectual world, *of which however he has no further cognizance*' (G IV 451, emphasis added). He warns in the next paragraph against those who want to give content to this 'invisible and active' self because they can succeed only in 'making it an object of intuition' and hence of sensation. All that can be concluded is that there might be more to the self – and to any external objects of experience – than meets the eye, that is, meets the senses in general. This is the kind of distinction between appearance and thing-in-itself that requires 'no subtle reflection' and can be made by the 'commonest understanding'. It is important not to read too much into Kant's claims at this point. In particular, it is important to focus on precisely the extent to which human beings must consider themselves as 'intelligible' rather than sensible.

The particular nature of the non-sensible, apparently active self is not any active awareness of free choice but the more limited awareness of a use of the faculties of understanding and reason. In language nearly identical to that quoted in my previous section from the Third Antinomy, Kant cites the understanding and especially reason as the faculties a human being appears to possess (G IV 452)[13]:

Now a human being really finds in himself a faculty by which he distinguishes himself from all other things, even from himself insofar as he is affected by objects, and that is reason. This, as pure self-activity, is raised even above the understanding by this: that though the latter is also self-activity and does not, like sense, contain merely representations that arise when we are affected by things (and are thus passive), yet it can produce from its activity no other concepts than those which serve merely to bring sensible representations under rules and thereby to unite them in one consciousness, without which use of sensibility it would think nothing at all; but reason, on the contrary, shows in what we call 'ideas' a spontaneity so pure that it thereby goes far beyond anything that sensibility can ever afford it, and proves its highest occupation in distinguishing the world of sense and the world of understanding from each other and thereby marking out limits for the under-standing itself.

Human beings' experience of the uses of their faculties of understanding and, especially, reason causes them to attribute self-activity to themselves. This self-activity is not an act of will but an act of reason as generating ideas and laws. Only to that extent can a human being attribute 'membership in

---

[13] I have altered the translation of '*Vermögen*' from 'capacity' to 'faculty' so that the identical German term will have identical English translations in the *Critique* and the *Groundwork*.

the intelligible world' to herself, that is, only as a being that apparently possesses the faculties of understanding and reason that themselves are not comprehensible through sensation.[14] Epistemic spontaneity of judgement, that is applying rules and making truth claims on their basis as invoked in some versions of the standard approach, is not ascribed to the intelligible world. Only reason as the basis of the ideas and principles is ascribed to the intelligible world.

As in the Third Antinomy, Kant stresses reason as the source of laws for human behaviour. Given the attribution of reason to the self alongside the already accepted sensibility, a human being can view herself as 'belonging' to two 'worlds': in one sense, he recognizes that he is a sensible being and is thus subject to the laws of nature. In another sense he believes himself to be a rational being and thus subject to the constraints of rational moral law on his behaviour. The intelligible world is understood in terms of the possibility that reason itself determines the actions of a being in the sensible world; here, echoes of the intelligible 'moral world' from the 'Canon' can be heard (*G* IV 458):

The concept of a world of understanding is thus only a standpoint that reason sees itself constrained to take outside appearances in order to think of itself as practical ... This thought admittedly brings with it the idea of another order and another law-giving than that of the mechanism of nature, which has to do with the sensible world; and it makes necessary the concept of an intelligible world (i.e. the whole of rational beings as things in themselves), but without the least pretence to think of it further than in terms merely of its formal condition, that is, of the universality of maxims of the will as law and so of the autonomy of the will, which alone is compatible with its freedom.

Human beings consider themselves, *qua* rational beings, as subject to another kind of law-giving applicable to those same beings in the sensible world.

This description of the intelligible world and the faculty of reason allows Kant to partially answer the question he posed for *Groundwork* III, 'How is a categorical imperative possible?', which I have interpreted in relation to

---

[14] Schönecker takes Kant to reach a much stronger conclusion: that the intelligible world is the ontological ground of the sensible world, and in particular that the laws of the intelligible world are the ground of the laws of the sensible world, so that since my will (as power of decision) belongs to the intelligible world, it is subject to the law of reason as a ground for its activity in the world of sense (Schönecker, 'How is a Categorical Imperative Possible?', p. 312; and his *Kant: Grundlegung III*, p. 371 ff.). In my reading, human beings attribute membership in the intelligible world to themselves only insofar as they possess reason, and no ontological claim regarding the actual basis or ground of nature is made.

the faculty of reason. We have to step further back, however, to ask the question why reason cannot itself be sensible and why, in particular, the freedom of reason cannot be understood sensibly.

6 THE PRESUPPOSITION OF FREEDOM

The introduction of the intelligible world/sensible world distinction is intended by Kant to justify the attribution of freedom to human beings and thus to break out of a 'kind of circle' that seemed to doom his entire argument in *Groundwork* III. His statement of this solution uses the intelligible world as the means to escape the alleged circle: 'We now see that when we think of ourselves as free we transfer ourselves into the world of understanding as members of it and cognize autonomy of the will along with its consequence, morality; but if we think of ourselves as put under obligation we regard ourselves as belonging to the world of sense and yet at the same time to the world of understanding' (*G* IV 453). This section will explain what the alleged circle is by stepping even further back to Kant's invocation of the 'idea of freedom'.

The crucial preparatory paragraph, which Kant titles 'Freedom Must be Presupposed as a Property of the Will of All Rational Beings' (*G* IV 447–8), sets out Kant's minimal explanation of freedom of the will. By 'minimal', I do not mean that in this section Kant does not prove freedom but merely claims that human beings presuppose – or act 'under the idea' of – freedom (although, of course, this is part of Kant's argument); rather, I mean that the freedom Kant claims all humans must presuppose is not freedom of particular judgements themselves but merely freedom of reason to determine its own principles which are then used in judgements. The key argument of the passage is as follows (*G* IV 447–8):

Now I assert that to every rational being having a will we must necessarily lend the idea of freedom also, under which alone he acts. For in such a being we think of a reason that is practical, that is, has causality with respect to its objects. Now, one cannot possibly think of a reason that would consciously receive direction from any other quarter with respect to its judgements, since the subject would then attribute the determination of his judgement not to his reason but to an impulse. Reason must regard itself as the author of its principles independently of alien influences; consequently, as practical reason or as the will of a rational being it must be regarded of itself as free.

Part of the standard approach to *Groundwork* III is the claim that Kant is discussing freedom of judgement here, that is, a transcendentally free particular act of the power of judgement independent of any causal determination according to laws of nature.[15] It is thought that if my judge-ment is determined in accordance with laws of nature, then it is determined only by 'an impulse' or some previous efficient cause in accordance with laws of nature. A psychological example of an impulse would be a desire or a passion. Were my judgements or choices determined by an impulse, I would have no reason to ascribe validity to them. Mere impulses are not truth conferring. I must assume, then, that the particular judgement I make is not determined by impulses. The standard approach concludes that every rational being must assume she is free in making particular judgements.

But in focusing on particular judgements as acts, the standard approach makes too broad a jump.[16] The passage does not require that Kant's focus is on particular acts of judgement; it can instead be seen as discussing the principles of the faculty of reason as the basis for judgements. There is no gap for Kant to fill if his argument about freedom concerns not a tran-scendentally free power of choice or decision but only a transcendentally free power of reason to produce the moral law. Kant does not attribute freedom to the particular act of judgement but only to reason itself. An act of judgement can be validated only if the grounds for that judgement are not merely grounds of sensible causality. Judgements using reason can cite the rational basis for those judgements. That rational basis itself must be free, i.e. reason itself must be transcendentally free. If I apply *modus ponens* in a particular case, I do not need to be independent of causal determinism in nature. I must, however, be able to invoke *modus ponens* as a principle of logical reasoning in order to claim that my particular judgement invoking *modus ponens* is valid. The judgement itself might nonetheless be part of a causal chain in nature involving, say, electro-chemical processes among neurons. But if I cannot invoke the independently justified principle of logical reasoning, I am left merely with the causal chain, and I cannot then claim that my judgement possesses validity. All that Kant is claiming is that when rational beings are making judgements, they must 'attribute

---

[15] Henrich stresses the importance of freedom of judgement in reasoning (Henrich, 'Die Deduktion des Sittengesetzes', p. 65; English translation, pp. 311–12). Allison discusses 'epistemic spontaneity' as part of Kant's argument for the freedom of decision for the will ('practical spontaneity') (Allison, *Kant's Theory of Freedom*, p. 36ff., and applied to the *Groundwork* III at pp. 222–3).

[16] Mieth and Rosenthal provide an excellent critique of the standard approach to this question. They note that there are five different ways that one can discuss freedom, the first of which is freedom as rationality. Freedom as rationality entails that one's deliberations and judgements are in accord with reason. Mieth and Rosenthal note that this allows these deliberations and judgements to be simul-taneously caused by impulses in accordance with laws of nature, a point I invoke above. But they do not attribute this dual-causality to Kant as I do (Mieth and Rosenthal, 'Freedom Must be Presupposed as a Property of All Rational Beings' in Horn and Schönecker, *Groundwork for the Metaphysics of Morals*, pp. 272–3).

[*zuschreiben*] the determination of judgement' to reason and not to an impulse. Attribution of the determination need not exclude other causes. If I attribute a particular move to a chess-playing computer, I can claim that it chooses its moves because of the causal network of electronic impulses but I attribute these moves to the rational principles of chess strategy and tactics. There is no contradiction in allowing both a role in the resulting move. When I then make a move (in my futile attempt to avoid checkmate) I similarly attribute my move to those same principles of chess strategy and tactics, but I can also, without contradiction, assume that my judgement is the causal product of chemical and electrical events in my brain.[17]

Note that in this passage Kant also claims that we think that 'reason ... has causality with respect to its objects'. The objects in question are the judgements made in accordance with principles of reason. To attribute a judgement to reason is to attribute a causal role to reason itself as the basis for the judgement. A judgement can be caused by reason or caused by an impulse (or, since the 'or' is inclusive rather than exclusive in the manner explained above, caused by both): 'the subject would then attribute the determination of his judgement not to reason but to an impulse'. Particular judgements are causally determined, not transcendentally free in the way the standard reading assumes. Instead of the power of judgement, 'reason must regard itself as the author of its principles independently of alien causes ... it must be regarded of itself as free'. This is to say that, in making a judgement, I used valid principles of reason. Reason must regard its basic principles – not particular judgements based on them – as independent of alien causes. In moral cases, the categorical imperative would be the basic principle, and claims of the form 'X is wrong' where X is a particular act would be examples of particular judgements that invoke the principle. The question left at the end of this argument is simply whether the attribution of freedom to reason as the author of laws and principles is merely an

---

[17] This might seem similar to the 'anomalous monism' interpretation of Kant's theory of freedom offered by Ralf Meerbote, drawing on the work of Donald Davidson, which treats reasons for actions as different explanatory devices than appeal to causes. Explanations of human actions in this view can be made in two ways: first, using scientific laws that describe causal processes, and secondly, using descriptively different explanations offering reasons. The second kind of description of actions is understood independent of the first, although both are taken to refer to the same objects and events. See Ralf Meerbote, 'Kant on the Nondeterminate Character of Human Actions' in William L. Harper and Ralf Meerbote (eds.), *Kant on Causality, Freedom, and Objectivity* (University of Minnesota Press, 1984) pp. 138–63. The explanation I am giving here differs from Meerbote's in that I take 'reasons' to be part of empirical psychology, and hence part of the explanation of human actions in accordance with natural laws. The part of the judgement that I claim must be understood as independent of causal determinism in nature is the faculty of reason itself, which is invoked in particular judgements but which is identical in each of those judgements.

inescapable but unwarranted assumption of rational beings, or whether it can be independently justified. This is another way of stating the question that Kant posed at the end of *Groundwork* II, namely, whether the moral law is itself possible.

At this point in *Groundwork* III, Kant could simply present a further argument for the possibility of a free reason in order to resolve the issue. But before attempting to do that, he stresses the importance of the upcoming argument. The first four paragraphs of the section entitled 'Of the Interest Attaching to the Ideas of Morality' (*G* IV 448–50) focus on the question of obligation. Having shown that rational beings unavoidably attribute an as-yet-unproven freedom to themselves (and hence attribute the moral law to themselves), he recognizes that mere self-attribution is not enough to provide obligation. 'But why, then, ought I to subject myself to this principle and do so simply as a rational being?' he asks. Perfectly rational beings act rationally without any interference from impulses. But human beings are not perfectly rational beings, and instead find our actions determined by sensibility. Why should human beings not simply allow their actions to be determined by sensibility? Why take any interest in the moral law? If the moral law is merely something human beings assume for themselves, there appears to be no reason to take it as binding. Put another way, if human beings merely assume that they are free, that is, possess a reason that can produce independently valid principles, then what guarantee is there that these alleged principles of reason really are valid? 'It seems, then, that in the idea of freedom we have actually only presupposed the moral law, namely the principle of autonomy of the will itself, and could not prove by itself its reality and objective necessity', Kant notes. On what grounds, he asks, is the moral law binding?

This consideration leads Kant to admit to 'a kind of circle' in his argument. The way that he describes this circle is telling: he notes that he has shifted from talk of 'efficient causes' to talk of 'the order of ends' (*G* IV 450):

It must be freely admitted that a kind of circle comes to light here from which, as it seems, there is no way to escape. We take ourselves as free in the order of efficient causes in order to think ourselves under moral laws in the order of ends; and we afterwards think ourselves as subject to these laws because we have ascribed to ourselves freedom of will: for, freedom and the will's own law-giving are both autonomy and hence reciprocal concepts, and for this very reason one cannot be used to explain the other or to furnish a ground for it but can at most be used only for the logical purpose of reducing apparently different representations of the same object to one single concept (as different fractions of equal value are reduced to their lowest expression).

When he says 'take ourselves to be free in the order of efficient causes' Kant is referring to the claim we make that our reason is independent of the impulses. When he then says we 'think ourselves under moral laws in the order of ends' he implies that from the lack of efficient impulsive cause, we assume that we are free in the use of our reason to legislate the moral law for ourselves. But why is this categorical imperative really valid? Merely our assumption that we are governed by reason is insufficient. Hence, the problem that 'we afterwards think ourselves as subject to these laws because we have *ascribed* to ourselves freedom of will'. Our mere assumption that we are subject to the moral law is not enough to show that we are actually subject to the moral law. There would have to be some additional basis for the claim that we are rational beings and can then assume that reason freely provides its own principles.

The circle can be escaped only if there is an independent way to affirm that we can legitimately take ourselves to be rational. This will affirm the validity of the moral law, and thus affirm the reality of autonomy or freedom of the will, its ability to act on the basis of the moral law. It will confirm that the order of efficient causes in nature is not the source of the categorical imperative, but that a different source of the categorical imperative is available. This is the path Kant takes to escape the circle by invoking the intelligible world as the view that human beings take of themselves as rational and therefore as subject to the moral law provided by reason.

The circle problem is resolved by *G* IV 453, after the discussion of the intelligible world, when Kant declares:

The suspicion that we raised above is now removed, the suspicion that a hidden circle was contained in our inference from freedom to autonomy and from the latter to the moral law — namely that perhaps we took as a ground the idea of freedom only for the sake of the moral law, so that we could afterwards infer the latter in turn from freedom, and that we were thus unable to furnish any ground at all for the moral law but could put it forward only as a petitio principii disposed souls would gladly grant us, but never as a demonstrable proposition. For we now see that when we think of ourselves as free we transfer ourselves into the world of understanding as members of it and cognize autonomy of the will along with its consequence, morality; but if we think of ourselves as put under obligation we regard ourselves as belonging to the world of sense and yet at the same time to the world of understanding.

At this point the circle is avoided because Kant has a reason for individuals to attribute reason to themselves. The awareness of ideas and principles of reason provides a basis for the attribution of reason to ourselves, since there is no other explanation of how these ideas and principles can be valid.

Hence, we are beings who may believe that they possess reason, and indeed believe that the world itself is governed by reason. But we cannot understand how such governance by reason – in particular with regard to our own decisions in the will – is possible. We cannot even confirm independently of the apparent use of reason that we are rational beings. Nonetheless, we now have a reason to assume that the moral law is valid, and that it can govern our actions. We affirm autonomy of the will – its capacity to be governed by the rules of reason – and equally affirm the validity of the moral law based in reason.

7 CONCLUDING REMARKS

I have provided a reading of *Groundwork* III that stresses the validation of reason rather than choice in the will. My aim has been to show that Kant's invocation of the intelligible world is not intended to be a merely theoretical, and certainly not an ontological, claim. Rather, he is identifying a practical self-conception of human beings as rational agents. Our experience of the ideas and principles of reason, in particular of the categorical imperative, cannot be readily explained using the sensible world alone. We invoke a distinct order of reason, yet cannot explain how this order of reason can be the cause of any effects in the world. In particular, we cannot explain how the timeless law of reason can be represented as a temporally located cause, such as a feeling, that can determine our will to act. Yet we are constrained to believe that it can because of the undeniable experience we have of the effects of ideas and principles of reason. Kant's question, 'How is a categorical imperative possible?', remains only partly answered in *Groundwork* III: we cannot explain how it is possible, but our experience of our reason grounds our belief that it is possible and that we are subject to its demands to make it the ruling principle for our behaviour as sensible beings.

Bibliography

Adams, Robert Merrihew, *Finite and Infinite Goods* (Oxford University Press, 1999)

Allison, Henry E., 'Morality and Freedom: Kant's Reciprocity Thesis', *The Philosophical Review* 95 (1986), 393–425

Kant's Theory of Freedom (Cambridge University Press, 1990)

'On a Presumed Gap in the Derivation of the Categorical Imperative', *Philosophical Topics* 19 (1991), 1–15

Almeida, Guido Antonio de, 'Critique, Deduction, and Fact of Reason', in *Brazilian Work on Kant*, Frederick Rauscher and Daniel Omar Perez (eds.), (Rochester University Press, in preparation)

Ameriks, Karl, 'Kant's Deduction of Freedom and Morality', *Journal of the History of Philosophy* 19 (1981), 53–79

Kant's Theory of Mind: an Analysis of the Paralogisms of Pure Reason (Oxford: Clarendon Press, 2000)

'Kant's *Groundwork* III Argument Reconsidered' in his *Interpreting Kant's Critiques* (Oxford: Clarendon Press, 2003), pp. 226–48. Previously published as 'Zu Argumentation am Anfang des Dritten Abschnitts der *Grundlegung*' in Hans-Ulrich Baumgarten and Carsten Held (eds.), *Systematische Ethik mit Kant* (Freiburg: Alber, 2001), pp. 24–54

Aristotle, *Nicomachean Ethics* (T. Irwin (ed. and trans.), Indianapolis/ Cambridge: Hackett, 1999)

Aune, Bruce, *Kant's Theory of Morals* (Princeton University Press, 1979)

Baron, Marcia, *Kantian Ethics Almost Without Apology* (Ithaca, NY/London: Cornell University Press, 1995)

'Acting from Duty' in Immanuel Kant, *Groundwork for the Metaphysics of Morals* (Allen Wood (trans.), Yale University Press, 2003)

Beck, Lewis White, *Commentary on Kant's Critique of Practical Reason* (University of Chicago Press, 1960)

Early German Philosophy: Kant and his Predecessors (Harvard University Press, 1969)

Beck, Lewis White (ed.), *Hoke Robinson Selected Essays on Kant*, North American Kant Society Studies in Philosophy 6 (University of Rochester Press, 2002)

Bittner, Rüdiger and Cramer, Konrad (eds.), *Materialen zu Kants 'Kritik der praktischen Vernunft'* (Frankfurt am Main: Suhrkamp, 1975)

Bojanowski, Jochen, *Kants Theorie der Freiheit: Rekonstruktion und Rehabilitierung* (Berlin/New York: de Gruyter, 2006)

Brink, David O., *Perfectionism and the Common Good: Themes in the Philosophy of T. H. Green* (Oxford University Press, 2003)

Butler, Joseph, *Sermons* (J. H. Bernard (ed.), London, 1900)

Christman, John and Anderson, Joel (eds.), *Autonomy and the Challenges to Liberalism* (Cambridge University Press, 2005)

Cicero, Marcus Tullius, *De Officiis* (Walter Miller (trans.), Harvard University Press, 1947)

Dancy, Jonathan, *Moral Reasons* (Cambridge: Blackwell, 1993)

Ethics Without Principles (Oxford: Clarendon Press, 2004)

Dean, Richard, 'Cummiskey's Kantian Consequentialism', *Utilitas* 12 (2000), 25–40

The Value of Humanity in Kant's Moral Theory (Clarendon Press, 2006)

Düsing, Klaus, 'Das Problem des höchsten Gutes in Kants praktischer Philosophie', *Kant-Studien* 62 (1971), 5–42

Ebbinghaus, Julius, 'Die Formeln des Kategorischen Imperativs und die Ableitung inhaltlich bestimmter Pflichten' in his *Gesammelte Schriften* (Bouvier, 1988), vol. II, pp. 209–29

Esteves, Julio, 'The Non-Circular Deduction of the Categorical Imperative in Groundwork III' in Frederick Rauscher and Daniel Omar Perez (eds.), *Brazilian Work on Kant* (Rochester University Press, in preparation)

Flikschuh, Katrin, 'Kant's Indemonstrable Postulate of Right: a Response to Paul Guyer', *Kantian Review* 12 (2007), 1–39

'Nature, Duty, Right: Kant's Answer to Mendelssohn in "Theory and Practice III"', *Journal of Moral Philosophy* 4 (2007), 223–41

Garve, Christian, 'Review of *Critik der reinen Vernunft*, by Immanuel Kant', *Zugabe zu den Göttingischen Anzeigen von gelehrten Sachen* 1 (1782), 40–8

Über die Verbindung der Moral mit der Politik (Korn, 1788)

Über verschiedene Gegenstände aus der Moral, Literatur und dem gesellschaftlichen Leben (Korn, 1792)

Über Gesellschaft und Einsamkeit (Korn, 1797–1800)

Übersicht der vornehmsten Principien der Sittenlehre, von dem Zeitalter des Aristoteles an bis auf unsre Zeiten (Korn, 1798)

Einige Betrachtungen über die allgemeinen Grundsätze der Sittenlehre (Korn, 1798)

Gellert, Christian Fürchtegott, *Sämmtliche Schriften. Neue verbesserte Auflage* (Leipzig: M. G. Weidmanns Erben und Reich und Caspar Fritsch, 1775)

Geuss, Raymond, 'Morality and Identity' in C. M. Korsgaard, *The Sources of Normativity* (Cambridge University Press, 1996), pp. 189–99

Gibbard, Allan, *Wise Choices, Apt Feelings* (Harvard University Press, 1990)

'Morality as Consistency in Living: Korsgaard's Kantian Lectures', *Ethics* 110 (1999), 140–64

Grenberg, Jeanine, *Kant and the Ethics of Humility: a Story of Dependence, Corruption, and Virtue* (Cambridge University Press, 2005)

Guyer, Paul, *Kant on Freedom, Law and Happiness* (Cambridge University Press, 2000)
  Kant (Routledge, 2006)
  'The Crooked Timber of Humankind' in Amelie Rorty and James Schmidt (eds.), *Philosophy as History: Essays on Kant's Idea for a Universal History* (Cambridge University Press, 2009)
Hamann, Johann Georg, *Briefwechsel* (Arthur Henkel (ed.), Frankfurt: Insel, 1965)
Hare, R. M., *Freedom and Reason* (Oxford University Press, 1963)
  The Language of Morals (New York: Oxford University Press, 1991)
Henrich, Dieter, 'Hutcheson und Kant', *Kant-Studien* 49 (1957/8)
  'Über Kants früheste Ethik', *Kant-Studien* 54 (1963) 404–31
  'Der Begriff der sittlichen Einsicht und Kants Lehre vom Faktum der Vernunft' in Gerold Prauss (ed.), *Kant: Zur Deutung seiner Theorie von Erkennen u. Handeln*, Neue Wissenschaftenliche Bibliothek, 63: Philosophie (Kiepenheuer und Witsch, 1973), pp. 223–54. Translated as 'The Concept of Moral Insight and Kant's Doctrine of the Fact of Reason' in Richard Velkley (ed.), *The Unity of Reason: Essays on Kant's Philosophy* (Harvard University Press, 1994)
  'Die Deduktion des Sittengesetzes: Über die Gründe der Dunkelheit des letzten Abschnittes von Kants "Grundlegung zur Metaphysik Der Sitten"' in Alexander Schwan (ed.), *Denken im Schatten des Nihilismus* (Darmstadt: Wissenschaftliche Buchgesellschaft, 1975), pp. 55–112. Translated as 'The Deduction of the Moral Law: the Reasons for the Obscurity of the Final Section of Kant's *Groundwork of the Metaphysics of Morals*' in Paul Guyer (ed.), *Kant's Groundwork of the Metaphysics of Morals: Critical Essays* (Lanham, Rowman & Littlefield, 1998)
Henson, Richard, 'What Kant Might Have Said: Moral Worth and the Overdetermination of Dutiful Action', *Philosophical Review* 88 (1979), 39–54
Herman, Barbara, 'On the Value of Acting from the Motive of Duty' in *The Practice of Moral Judgment* (Harvard University Press, 1993)
  The Practice of Moral Judgment (Harvard University Press, 1993)
  'Making Room for Character' in Stephen Engstrom and Jennifer Whiting (eds.), *Aristotle, Kant and the Stoics: Rethinking Happiness and Duty* (Cambridge University Press, 1996), pp. 36–62
  'A Cosmopolitan Kingdom of Ends' in Barbara Herman, Christine Korsgaard and Andrews Reath (eds.), *Reclaiming the History of Ethics: Essays in Honour of John Rawls* (Cambridge University Press, 1997), pp. 187–214
Hill, Thomas E., Jr, 'Kant's Argument for the Rationality of Moral Conduct', *Pacific Philosophical Quarterly* 66 (1985), 3–23
  Autonomy and Self-Respect (Cambridge University Press, 1991)
  Dignity and Practical Reason in Kant's Moral Theory (Ithaca, NY: Cornell University Press, 1992)
  'Treating Criminals as Ends in Themselves', *Annual Review of Law and Ethics* 11 (2003), 17–36
Hills, A. E., 'Kant on Happiness and Reason', *History of Philosophy Quarterly* (2006), 234–62

Höffe, Otfried, 'Universalistische Ethik und Urteilskraft: ein aristotelischer Blick auf Kant', *Zeitschrift für philosophische Forschung* (1990), 537–63

'Aristoteles' universalistische Tugendethik' in Klaus Peter Rippe and Peter Schaber (eds.), *Tugendethik* (Stuttgart: Reclam, 1998), pp. 42–68

Hooker, Brad and Little, Margaret Olivia (eds.), *Moral Particularism* (Oxford: Clarendon Press, 2000)

Hurka, Thomas, *Perfectionism* (Oxford University Press, 1993)

Johnson, R., 'Happiness as a Natural End' in M. Timmons (ed.), *Kant's Metaphysics of Morals: Interpretative Essays* (Oxford University Press, 2002)

Kaulbach, Friedrich, *Immanuel Kants 'Grundlegung zur Metaphysic der Sitten'* (Wissenschaftliche Buchgesellschaft, 1988)

Kerstein, Samuel, *Kant's Search for the Supreme Principle of Morality* (Cambridge University Press, 2002)

'Deriving the Formula of Humanity' in C. Horn and D. Schönecker (eds.), *Kant's Groundwork of the Metaphysics of Morals: New Interpretations* (de Gruyter, 2006), pp. 200–21

Kors, Alan Charles (ed.), *Encyclopedia of Enlightenment* (New York: Oxford University Press, 2003)

Korsgaard, Christine M., 'Morality as Freedom' in Yirmiahu Yovel (ed.), *Kant's Practical Philosophy Reconsidered* (Dordrecht: Kluwer, 1989), pp. 23–48

Creating the Kingdom of Ends (Cambridge University Press, 1996)

'Kant's Formula of Humanity' in her *Creating the Kingdom of Ends* (Cambridge University Press, 1996), pp. 106–32

The Sources of Normativity (Cambridge University Press, 1996)

'The Normativity of Instrumental Reason' in Garrett Cullity and Berys Gaut (eds.), *Ethics and Practical Reason* (Oxford University Press, 1997), pp. 215–54

'Reply to Ginsborg, Schneewind and Guyer', *Ethics* 109 (1998), 49–66

The Myth of Egoism, The Lindley Lectures (University of Kansas, 1999)

Kuehn, Manfred, 'The Moral Dimension of Kant's Inaugural Dissertation: a New Perspective on the "Great Light of 1769?"' in *Proceedings of the 8th International Kant Congress in Memphis* (Milwaukee: Marquette University Press, 1995), vol. 1.2, pp. 373–92

Kant: a Biography (Cambridge University Press, 2001)

'Kant and Cicero' in Volker Gerhardt, Rolf-Peter Horstmann and Ralph Schumacher (eds.), *Proceedings of the 9th International Kant Congress in Berlin, April 2000* (Berlin/New York: de Gruyter, 2001), pp. 270–8

'Einleitung' in Werner Stark (ed.), *Immanuel Kant, Vorlesungen zur Moralphilosophie* (Berlin: de Gruyter, 2004), pp. vii–xxxv

'Introduction' in Immanuel Kant, *Anthropology from a Pragmatic Point of View* (Robert Louden (ed.), Cambridge University Press, 2006), pp. vii–xxxiii

Löhrer, Guido, *Menschliche Würde* (Alber, 1995)

Louden, Robert B., 'Go-Carts of Judgment: Exemplars in Kantian Moral Education, *Archiv für Geschichte der Philosophie* 74 (1992), 303–22

Morality and Moral Theory: a Reappraisal and Reaffirmation (New York: Oxford University Press, 1992)

'Examples in Ethics' in Edward Craig (ed.), *Routledge Encyclopedia of Philosophy* (New York: Routledge, 1998), vol. III, pp. 487–90

Kant's Impure Ethics: From Rational Beings to Human Beings (New York: Oxford University Press, 2000)

'The Second Part of Morals' in Brian Jacobs and Patrick Kain (eds.), *Essays on Kant's Anthropology* (Cambridge University Press, 2003), pp. 60–84

The World We Want: How and Why the Ideals of the Enlightenment Still Elude Us (New York: Oxford University Press, 2007)

'Kantian Moral Humility: Between Aristotle and Paul', *Philosophy and Phenomenological Research* 75 (2007), 632–9

Ludwig, Bernd, 'Whence Public Right? The Role of Theoretical and Practical Reasoning in Kant's *Doctrine of Right*' in Mark Timmons (ed.), *Kant's Metaphysics of Morals. Interpretative Essays* (Oxford University Press, 2002), pp. 159–85

McDowell, John, 'Virtue and Reason', *The Monist* 62 (1979), 331–50

Meerbote, Ralf, 'Kant on the Nondeterminate Character of Human Actions' in William L. Harper and Ralf Meerbote (eds.), *Kant on Causality, Freedom, and Objectivity* (University of Minnesota Press, 1984), pp. 138–63

Melnick, Arthur, 'Kant's Formulations of the Categorical Imperative', *Kant-Studien* 93 (2002), 291–308

Mieth, Corinna and Rosenthal, Jacob, '"Freedom Must be Presupposed as a Property of All Rational Beings"' in Christoph, Horn and Dieter Schönecker (eds.), *Groundwork for the Metaphysics of Morals* (de Gruyter, 2006)

Mill, J. S., *Utilitarianism* (Hackett, 1979). Originally published in *Fraser's Magazine* (1861)

Examination of Sir William Hamilton's Philosophy (Longman, 1866)

Morgan, Seiriol, 'The Missing Formal Proof of Humanity's Radical Evil in Kant's *Religion*', *Philosophical Review* 114 (2005), 63–114

Nagel, Thomas, *The Possibility of Altruism* (Princeton University Press, 1978)

Nussbaum, Martha, 'Non-Relative Virtues: an Aristotelian Approach' in Martha C. Nussbaum and Amartya Sen (eds.), *The Quality of Life* (Oxford University Press, 1993), pp. 242–69

O'Neill, Onora, *Acting on Principle* (Columbia University Press, 1975)

Constructions of Reason (Cambridge University Press, 1989)

'Universal Law and Ends-in-Themselves' in her *Constructions of Reason* (Cambridge University Press, 1989), pp. 126–44

'Consistency in Action' in Paul Guyer (ed.), *Kant's Groundwork of the Metaphysics of Morals: Critical Essays* (Rowman & Littlefield, 1998), pp. 103–31

'Kant on Duties Regarding Nonrational Nature II', *Aristotelian Society Supplement* 72 (1998), 211–28

Paton, H. J., *The Categorical Imperative: a Study in Kant's Moral Philosophy* (London: Hutchinson's University Library, 1947)

Pippin, Robert, 'Kant on the Spontaneity of Mind', *Canadian Journal of Philosophy* 17 (1987), 449–75

Pogge, Thomas, 'The Categorical Imperative' in Otfried Höffe (ed.), *Grundlegung zur Metaphysik der Sitten. Ein kooperativer Kommentar* (1989), pp. 172–93

Pöschl, Viktor, 'Der Begriff der Würde im antiken Rom und später' in *Sitzungsberichte der Heidelberger Akademie der Wissenschaften. Philosophisch-historische Klasse* (Carl Winter, 1969), vol. III, pp. 7–67

Prauss, Gerald, *Kant über Freiheit als Autonomie* (Klostermann, 1983)

Pufendorf, Samuel, *The Whole Duty of Man* (Ian Hunter and David Saunders (eds.), Liberty Fund, 2003)

Quarfood, Marcel, 'The Circle and the Two Standpoints' in Christoph Horn and Dieter Schönecker (eds.), *Groundwork for the Metaphysics of Morals* (Berlin/New York: de Gruyter, 2006), pp. 285–300

Quinn, Philip L. and Miller, Christian B. (eds.), *Essays in the Philosophy of Religion* (Oxford University Press, 2006)

Rauscher, Frederick, 'Razão prática pura como uma faculdade natural' ['Pure Practical Reason as a Natural Faculty'], Milene Consenso Tonetto (trans.), in *Ethic@* 5 (2006), 173–92 at www.cfh.ufsc.br/ethic@

'Reason as a Natural Cause' in Heiner Klemme, Manfred Kuehn and Dieter Schönecker (eds.), *Moralische Motivation: Kant und die Alternativen* (Hamburg: Meiner, 2006)

Rawls, John, *Lectures on the History of Moral Philosophy* (Barbara Herman (ed.), Harvard University Press, 2000)

Reath, Andrews, 'Legislating for a Realm of Ends: the Social Dimension of Autonomy' in his *Agency and Autonomy* (Oxford University Press, 2006), pp. 173–96

Reich, Klaus, 'Kant and Greek Ethics II', *Mind* 48 (1939), 446–63

Ricken, Friedo, 'Homo noumenon und homo phaenomenon' in Otfried Höffe (ed.), *Grundlegung zur Metaphysik der Sitten. Ein kooperativer Kommentar* (Klostermann, 1989), pp. 234–52

Ross, David, *Kant's Ethical Theory* (Oxford: Clarendon Press, 1954)

Rousseau, Jean-Jacques, *Émile* (Barbara Foxley (trans.), London: Dent, 1911)

Sassen, Birgitte (ed.), *Kant's Early Critics: the Empiricist Critique of the Theoretical Philosophy* (Cambridge University Press, 2000)

Schneewind, J. B., *The Invention of Autonomy* (Cambridge University Press, 1998)

'Hume and the Religious Significance of Moral Rationalism', *Hume Studies* 26 (2000), 211–23

Schönecker, Dieter, *Kant: Grundlegung III: Die Deduktion des kategorischen Imperativs* (Freiburg: Alber, 1999)

'How is a Categorical Imperative Possible? Kant's Deduction of the Categorical Imperative' in C. Horn and D. Schönecker, *Groundwork for the Metaphysics of Morals* (de Gruyter, 2006), pp. 301–24

Schönecker, Dieter and Wood, Allen W., *Kants 'Grundlegung zur Metaphysik der Sitten': Ein einführender Kommentar* (Paderborn: Schöningh, 2002)

Sensen, Oliver, 'Kants Begriff der Menschenwürde' in Franz-Josef Bormann and Christian Schröer (eds.), *Abwägende Vernunft* (de Gruyter, 2004), pp. 220–36

'Kant's Treatment of Human Dignity in the *Groundwork*' in Valerio Rohden, Ricardo R. Terra and Guido A. de Almeida (eds.), *Recht und Frieden in der Philosophie Kants. Akten des X. Internationalen Kant-Kongresses* (de Gruyter, 2008), vol. III, pp. 391–401

'Kant's Conception of Human Dignity', in *Kant-Studien* (forthcoming)

Sherman, Nancy, *Making a Necessity of Virtue: Aristotle and Kant on Virtue* (Cambridge University Press, 1997)

Sidgwick, Henry, *The Methods of Ethics* (London: Macmillan, 1907)

Siep, Ludwig, 'Wozu eine Metaphysik der Sitten?' in Otfried Höffe (ed.), *Grundlegung zur Metaphysik der Sitten. Ein kooperativer Kommentar* (Klostermann, 1989)

Skorupski, John, 'Internal Reasons and the Scope of Blame' in Alan Thomas (ed.), *Bernard Williams* (Cambridge University Press, 2007), pp. 73–103

Sobel, David, 'Do the Desires of Rational Agents Converge?', *Analysis* 59 (1999), 137–42

Stocker, Michael, 'The Schizophrenia of Modern Ethical Theories', *Journal of Philosophy* 73 (1976), 453–66

Stratton-Lake, Philip, *Kant, Duty and Moral Worth* (Routledge, 2000)

Ethical Intuitionism: Re-evaluations (Oxford University Press, 2002)

Sullivan, Roger J., *Immanuel Kant's Moral Theory* (Cambridge University Press, 1989)

Introduction to Kant's Ethics (Cambridge University Press, 1994)

Sussman, David, 'Perversity of the Heart', *Philosophical Review* 114 (2005), 153–78

Taylor, James Stacy (ed.), *Personal Autonomy: New Essays on Personal Autonomy and its Role in Contemporary Moral Philosophy* (Cambridge University Press, 2005)

Timmermann, Jens, *Sittengesetz und Freiheit: Untersuchungen zu Immanuel Kants Theorie des Freien Willens, Quellen und Studien zur Philosophie, Bd. 60* (Berlin/ New York: de Gruyter, 2003)

'Sollen und Können: "Du kannst, denn du sollst" und "Sollen impliziert Können" im Vergleich', *Philosophiegeschichte und logische Analyse* (*Logical Analysis and History of Philosophy*) 6 (2003), 113–22

'Value Without Regress: Kant's "Formula of Humanity" Revisited', *European Journal of Philosophy* 14 (2006), 69–83

Kant's 'Groundwork of the Metaphysics of Morals': a Commentary (Cambridge University Press, 2007)

Timmermann, Jens (ed.), *Immanuel Kant: Grundlegung zur Metaphysik der Sitten*, (Vandenhoek & Ruprecht, 2004)

von Schönborn, Alexander, 'Kant and the Absolute', *Southwestern Journal of Philosophy* 7 (1976), 145–52

White, Nicholas, *Individual and Conflict in Greek Ethics* (Oxford University Press, 2002)

Wilde, Oscar, *The Portable Oscar Wilde* (Richard Arlington (ed.), New York: Viking, 1965)

Willaschek, Marcus, *Praktische Vernunft: Handlungstheorie und Moralbegründung bei Kant* (Stuttgart: Metzler, 1992)

Williams, Bernard, *Ethics and the Limits of Philosophy* (Cambridge University Press, 1985)

Wolff, Robert Paul, *The Autonomy of Reason* (New York: Harper and Row, 1973)

Wood, Allen, 'Kant on Duties Regarding Nonrational Nature I', *Aristotelian Society Supplement* 72 (1998), 189–210

Kant's Ethical Thought (Cambridge University Press, 1999)

'The Moral Law as a System of Formulas' in Hans Friedrich Fulda and Jürgen Stolzenberg (eds.), *Architektonik und System in der Philosophie Kants* (Hamburg: Meiner, 2001), pp. 287–306

'The Final Form of Kant's Practical Philosophy' in Mark Timmons (ed.), *Kant's Metaphysics of Morals: Interpretative Essays* (Oxford University Press, 2002), pp. 1–22

'The Supreme Principle of Morality' in Paul Guyer (ed.), *The Cambridge Companion to Kant and Modern Philosophy* (Cambridge University Press, 2006), pp. 342–80

Index

Abbt, Thomas 23
Adams, Robert 157
Allison, Henry 84, 88, 168, 189, 205
Ameriks, Karl 204
anthropology 7–28, 61, 68, 74, 120
Aristotle 9, 17, 94
autonomy 52, 61, 65, 68, 79, 83, 89, 101, 113, 116,
    118, 119, 140–58, 159–75, 177, 178, 181, 182,
    184, 187, 207, 217, 218, 221–3
    See also 'categorical imperative'

Barbeyrac, Jean 157
Baumgarten, Alexander Gottlieb 12, 146
beneficence 48, 49, 50, 56
Bentham, Jeremy 149
Butler, Joseph 156

Calvin, John 157
categorical imperative 21–5, 42, 43, 45, 72, 73,
    82–101, 103, 112, 113, 120, 140, 144, 159–62,
    168, 169, 174, 207, 208, 220, 222
    concept of 127
    law of nature formula 57, 98, 108, 111, 124, 127
    formula of autonomy 131–2, 135
    formula of humanity as an end-in-itself 102–18,
        124, 129, 130–1, 160, 166
    kingdom of ends formula 119–39
    possibility of 187, 208, 223
causal determination 203, 205, 209, 218
causality, causation 88–101, 109, 125, 128, 163, 165,
    186, 194, 195, 204, 209, 211, 212–23
cause, concept of 96
character 9, 15–21, 57, 76, 77, 211
    good character as the ultimate moral
        achievement 15
    noumenal character as the sole ground of
        phenomenal character 178, 195–6
Cicero 115, 116
circle 180–9, 193, 211, 218–23
Clarke, Samuel 157
common moral consciousness 50, 176

common sense 14, 153, 176
conscience 13, 57, 139
consequentialism 55, 57
Crusius, Christian August 5, 12, 147, 153, 158

desire 11, 29–44, 149, 219
    capacity for 126
    desire-satisfaction theories of happiness 30, 43
dignity 24, 61, 62, 65, 102–18
    as distinguished from price 117, 135
disposition 14, 15, 18, 26, 174–5, 198
duty 14, 15, 56, 79, 104, 108–9, 120, 125, 143, 161,
    176, 179, 201
    acting from duty 45–62, 156
    acting in mere conformity with duty 45–62, 74
    action from duty always preferable to action
        from inclination 56, 60
    as a 'backup motive' 51–3, 56
    duties of virtue 26–7

Eberhard, Johann August 146
egoism 149, 154–6, 171, 173
    egoistic hedonism – see 'happiness, principle of'
    rational egoism 167–8, 169, 173
ends 35, 36–44, 102–18
    final end 110–11
Enlightenment 23, 64–5, 78
Epicurus 146
examples,
    emulation as opposed to imitation of 75–7
    their role in Kant's ethical theory 63–81
experience, 71, 96, 178, 191, 192, 202, 209–10,
    213, 215
    as a ground for ethical theories 66
    categories of 194

fact of reason 97, 190, 191, 193, 203, 204
freedom 49, 89–90, 96, 97, 102, 108, 109, 110–18,
    128, 134, 138, 159–75, 176–202, 203–23
    negative freedom 49, 181–202
    positive freedom 49, 180, 181–202

theory of freedom reconciled with
deterministic theory of experience 195–6
transcendental freedom 204, 206, 218, 219

Gellert, Johann Fürchtegott 2, 11–18
Goethe, Johann Wolfgang von 12
good will 19–25, 29, 47, 50, 71, 91, 102, 103, 106–8,
176, 177, 182
relation to the Highest Good 137

happiness 13, 19, 29–44, 59, 79, 104, 111, 121, 135, 145
principle of 147, 148–50, 151, 154–6, 158
Hare, Richard Mervyn 86–7, 88
hedonism 149
egoistic hedonism – see 'happiness, principle of'
paradox of 31
Hegel, Georg Wilhelm Friedrich 140
Henrich, Dieter 204
Herman, Barbara 9
heteronomy 59, 65, 79, 140–58, 168, 181, 183, 187
Hobbes, Thomas 146
Höffe, Otfried 5, 9
holy or perfect will 36, 54, 134–6, 221
hope 72–5
human reason,
limitations of 70–5
Hume, David 5, 9, 96, 146, 153–4, 158
Hutcheson, Francis 10, 12, 18, 146
hypothetical imperatives 34–5, 42–3, 44, 85, 95,
104, 129, 168
compared to categorical imperatives 126–7

idealism, transcendental 96, 165, 180, 181, 184, 191,
195–7, 200, 203, 210
immoral action, the possibility of 178, 189, 195,
197–202
impartiality 159–75
incentives 36, 50, 52, 53, 58, 60, 69, 72, 73, 177, 185,
198, 199
inclination 45–62, 176, 178, 198
consequentialist nature of inclination 55
higher order inclination 45, 47–8
direct inclination 46, 48
interest 54, 132, 133–9, 150, 171–5
difference between moral and non-moral 53–6
in the moral law 59, 106, 221
intuitionism 157–8, 160, 172, 173–5

justice 119, 139, 154

Korsgaard, Christine 120, 133

laws
govern all human action 46
logical 86, 192

of nature 92, 93, 94–5, 98, 125, 163, 194, 213, 217
of reason 14, 163, 213, 217
Leibniz, Gottfried Wilhelm 157
Lessing, Gotthold Ephraim 23
liberalism 155
Luther, Martin 147, 153, 157

Mandeville, Bernard 146
maxims
as character-building 16–17, 23–8
as subjective principles of volition 23, 36–43,
47–62, 69, 82, 84–5, 95, 112, 126, 134, 179,
198–202
Mendelssohn, Moses 23
metaphysics, meaning of 109
Mill, John Stuart 3, 29–44, 155, 157
Montaigne, Michel de 146
moral categories 47
moral education 12, 61–2, 68–70, 72, 77, 79
moral feeling/sense 10–18, 22, 107, 145, 146,
150–1, 156
moral judgement 69, 80–1, 144
moral law as causal law 82–101, 177–202
moral psychology 16
moral value or worth 14, 15–16, 19, 22, 24, 45–62,
71, 104–18
its *ratio cognoscendi* 61
its *ratio essendi* 61
morality
empirical concepts of 8
pervasiveness of 60–1
Mosheim, Johann Lorenz von 12
motivating ground 21–2, 26, 50, 91, 117, 143, 153, 196
argument that motive to virtue is the same as
motive to vice 149
heterogeneity of inclination and duty as types
of motivation 57, 59–60

Nagel, Thomas 3, 36, 38–43
necessitation 192
necessity 68, 79, 109, 112, 152, 192, 193, 195, 208
Nietzsche, Friedrich 158
noumena 96, 97, 165, 177–202
knowledge of noumenal self 193–7

O'Neill, Onora 82

perfectionism 146–7, 151–2, 156–7, 158
pleasure 10–11, 29, 146, 209
Price, Richard 157
principles 54–62, 100, 143
objective 15, 19, 21–8, 36, 45, 50, 63, 64, 65,
68–81, 82, 83, 90, 93, 104, 105, 112, 119–39,
159–60, 163, 169, 171, 172, 176–7, 180, 182,
186, 189, 190–202, 220–3

principles (cont.)
    'spurious principles of morality' 140–58
    subjective – see 'maxims'
prudence 38–43, 47–8, 60
Pufendorf, Samuel 153, 157

Quinn, Philip 157

Rawls, John 119, 128
Reath, Andrews 120
Reinhold, Karl Leonhard 197
respect for others 102–18
    impartial respect 166
    respect for non-rational beings 114
respect or reverence for the law 52, 53, 58, 60, 91,
    107, 127
rigorism, motivational 45–7, 51, 58
Rousseau, Jean-Jacques 80

schematism 71–2
Schmid, Carl Christian Erhard 197
Schönecker, Dieter 205
self-love 148, 179, 198–9
Shaftesbury, Earl of 146
Sidgwick, Henry 143, 144, 167
Spalding, Johann Joachim 23
Spinoza, Baruch 140
standpoints 165, 184, 187, 214, 217
Stocker, Michael 51
Stoics 155

supervenience 86–7
sympathy 48–50, 52, 57, 146, 151

teleology 31–3, 147, 148–50
Timmermann, Jens 130
Tittel, Gottlob August 143

universality 65, 74, 79, 82–101, 128, 148, 167–9,
    209, 217
utilitarianism 149, 155, 166, 167

virtue 14, 15, 18, 20, 24–5, 26–8, 31, 61, 69, 138
    as distinguished from right 139
    ethics 25
voluntarism 157

Weyman, Daniel 18
will
    as a causal faculty 46, 93, 125–6, 128, 136,
        163, 181
    concept of the 109, 125–39
Williams, Bernard 8, 28, 158
Wolff, Christian 5, 146, 147, 155, 157
Wood, Allen 35
world of sense and world of understanding 21, 94,
    129, 186, 210–14
    humans as members of both worlds 123, 178,
        185, 186, 187, 188, 196, 203, 205, 212, 216–18
    intelligible world 101, 186–9, 204–10,
        214–18, 223

Lightning Source UK Ltd.
Milton Keynes UK
UKOW030914230613

212687UK00003B/109/P